True Knights

CHRISTIAN HUSBANDS, FATHERS AND SONS

COMBAT TRAINING
DAILY PRAYERS FOR PURITY
WWW.TRUEKNIGHTS.ORG

Compiled & Edited by
Kenneth Henderson and Jesse Romero

"Blessed are the clean of heart, for they shall see God."
(St. Matthew 5:8)

TRUE KNIGHTS PUBLISHING

"*True Knights: Combat Training Daily Prayers for Purity* is an excellent tool to assist one in fortifying his armor (of God). Marriage is under attack on all fronts but pornography is one of the primary ways Satan utilizes to destroy this sacrament. Pornography is a direct attack on the dignity of man and woman; it takes us away from the ideal of being a gift of self to our spouse physically; which in turn transforms the marital embrace into a simple act of selfish gratification and is conducive to the sin of masturbation. Ken has done an outstanding job in laying out a "daily" practical plan to fight against this evil."

> ~ **Gregory Alexander**, Co-founder and Director of the Alexander House and co-host of the EWTN program "Marriage Works in Christ." (www.theAlexanderHouse.org)

"Life on the highest plane is impossible without God's help. And the beautiful virtue of chastity belongs to life on the highest plane. King Solomon, whom God made wise beyond measure, said, "As I knew that I could not otherwise be continent except God gave it…I went to the Lord and besought Him." With the wisdom of Solomon, Ken Henderson has written an excellent and timely book, *True Knights: Combat Training Daily Prayers For Purity*. At the same moment Satan grips so many children of God in his clutches through the evil scourge of pornography, Ken provides the safety net to catch and convert those souls struggling in the moral freefall.

Christian husbands, fathers and sons learn the necessary tools to become the True Knights God intended them to be. Their combat training includes: 7 Steps to Freedom and Purity, the True Knights Code of Chivalry and the Ten Promises of True Knights and much more. Ken knows that an impure person becomes spiritually dead. Without God's grace, it is impossible to be pure, to be happy, to be holy. Grace is Power. COMBAT TRAINING, DAILY PRAYERS FOR PURITY provides the power, the stern stuff that transforms true men into True Knights!"

> ~ **Barbara McGuigan**, Prolife Speaker
> Voice of Virtue International and Host of *"Voices of Virtue"* on EWTN

"It is a privilege to recommend *True Knights: Combat Training Daily Prayers For Purity* to help our brothers in Christ become men of honor, virtue and purity. In a culture that far too often glorifies sin; many men are duped into spiritual darkness, slavery and oppression thus resulting in an epidemic of spiritual weaklings. The world needs courageous Christian witnesses, as powerfully modeled in the lives of the Saints, to inspire others to become the saints we were all created by God to be. May all who read this mighty prayer book be graced with the strength of Heaven!"

> ~ **Eddie Cotter, Jr.**, Co-Founder and Executive Director
> Dead Theologians Society (www.DeadTheologiansSociety.com)

True Knights

CHRISTIAN HUSBANDS, FATHERS AND SONS

COMBAT TRAINING
DAILY PRAYERS FOR PURITY

Oath of Fidelity

to his Holiness, Pope Benedict XVI   in union with the Magesterium

and the Teachings of the One, Holy, Catholic and Apostolic Church

Founded by Jesus Christ 2000 years ago!

DEDICATED TO

The most incredible woman in the world,
my wonderful wife Michelle, who has been
with me to Hell and back. I give thanks to God
for giving her the grace to stay by my side through it all.
I'm sorry for all the pain I have ever caused you.
I love you!

- Kenneth Henderson

BISHOP'S BLESSING AND APPROVAL*

On June 21st, 2006, Kenneth Henderson and his ministry, True Knights received the Blessing and enthusitic Approval* from the Most Reverend Edward J. Slattery, Bishop of the Diocese of Tulsa. As a result Kenneth has been given official permission to go ahead with plans to establish a public Confraternity for men who wish to grow closer in their walk with Christ and achieve holy purity, to be known as:

The Brotherhood of True Knights
under the Patronage of
Our Lady of the Immaculate Heart.

*This statement does not constitue as an Imprimter or endorsement for this book.

St. Michael's fight against the dragon

And there was war in heaven: Michael and his angels fought against the dragon; and the dragon fought and his angels, and prevailed not; neither was their place found any more in heaven. - *Revelation xii.7*

by Albrecht Dürer, 1498

Table of Contents

ABOUT PRAYER...

"For me, prayer is a surge of the heart; it is a simple look turned toward heaven, it is a cry of recognition and of love, embracing both trial and joy"
~ *St. Therese of Lisieux – CCC 2558.*

"Prayer is conversation with God"
~ *Clement of Alexandria*

"Let my prayer be counted as incense before you"
~ *Psalm 141*

An easy to remember the different kinds of prayer is captured in the acrostic ACTS:

    A = Adoration (Worship)
    C = Contrition (Confession of specific sins)
    T = Thanksgiving (Gratitude)
    S = Supplication – (Specific request & petitions)

Each letter stands for a specific aspect of prayer, arranged in a very natural order.

WHAT TO PRAY FOR!

In St. John's Gospel our Lord Jesus Christ commands us to "ask" in prayer nine times. Supplication and petitionary prayer is God's idea, not just a result of our personal needs. The Lord wants us to ask him for certain things. But what should we pray for? In Sacred Scripture, the Lord shows us what he wishes us to pray for:

SELF: Pray for personal growth to become Christlike (Col 1:9-10;) and for personal holiness (1 Thess 4:3).

FAMILY: Pray for your spouse, children, and grandchildren; that your progeny may become an unbroken heritage of God fearing God loving people.

COMMUNITY: Pray for the conversion and welfare of your city (Jer 29:7). Pray for a visible witness and unity among God's people in our communities (Philippians 4:2-3).

CHURCH: Pray for the unity of purpose, vision and heart. Pray for the desire to please God rather than people (Philippians 2:1-4).

CHURCH LEADERS: Pray for the humility to surrender to the will of God, fidelity to Christ and the Magisterium (Heb 13:17; 1 Tim 5:17). Pray for a deep conviction to evangelize one on one (2 Tim 2:2).

THE NATION: Pray for national repentance (2 Chron 7:14), also pray for the moral consciousness of our nation to know who God is (Psalm 33:12; Prov 14:34).

LEADERS IN GOVERNMENT: Pray for their wisdom and integrity so that they may be aware of their accountability before the Lord (1 Tim 2:1-2; Rom 13:1).

NONBELIEVERS: Pray for their openness to the Holy Spirit's promptings and for their conversion to Christ. Pray that believers will be patient and sensitive with nonbelievers (1 Tim 2:1-6).

THE SICK: Pray for the Lord's healing power of mind, body and soul for someone who is ill (James 5:14-16).

THOSE IN PRISON: Pray so that prisoners may come to an understanding of Christ's forgiveness. Pray that the Lord strengthens their resolve against sin and that HE comforts them in their loneliness (Heb 13:3; Colossians 4:18).

CHILDREN: Pray for the unborn who have been aborted and for those who face abortion today. Pray for those lives that have been devastated by divorce (Malachi 4:6; Matthew 19:14).

A WEEKLY PRAYER STRATEGY

Sunday: Spiritual Growth
Pray for the Gifts of the Holy Spirit and for the strengthening of your soul against sin. Holy Spirit, sanctifier of souls, grace our souls with the holiness of God.

Monday: Family
Pray for immediate family members. Pray for extended family members and friends of your family (you may want to get requests from them individually). Heavenly Father, help us to make our home a place of nurturing and love.

Tuesday: Church & Vocations
Pray for the Pope, your Bishop, Pastor and your Parish clergy. Pray for the marriages and families of those lay people in your Parish involved in leadership (they are key targets of Satan). Pray for specific ministries and apostolates in the Church. Pray for our seminaries that are training and preparing our future Priests.

Wednesday: Community
Pray for Political Leaders in your Community. Pray for other Churches in your community. Pray for your local Pro-Life efforts, Catholic Charities, Conferences, Retreats and other Evangelistic outreach efforts in your diocese.

Thursday: Nation
Pray for the President. Pray for our elected officials from your state.

Friday: World
Pray for world peace. Pray for our Catholic Missionaries around the world. Pray for those nations that are closed to the Gospel.

Saturday: Afflicted
Pray for those ministering in difficult situations in 3rd world countries. Pray for those in prison. Pray for those from your Parish who are sick or hospitalized. Pray for the children impacted negatively by divorce. Pray for women and children who have been or are in abusive situations. Pray for the homeless and poor. Pray for aborted children and their mothers and fathers.

Daily: Those Affected by the sin of Lust
Pray for all of the women, men and children around the world who are affected in some way because of the sin of lust; men and women involved in the pornography industry; all people who are or have been sexually abused; all people who are addicted to lust and are in denile of the damage the sin of lust causes to the soul and all those trying to break free of addictions to lust, especially all True Knights and their families.

The Fall of Adam and Eve

...the serpent said to the woman: "You certainly will not die! No, God knows well that the moment you eat of it your eyes will be opened and you will be like gods who know what is good and what is bad." - *Genesis iii.4-5*

by Albrecht Dürer, 1504

Introduction

What's Wrong with a "Little" um...*Lust?*
by Kenneth Henderson
Originally Published June 7, 2005 on CatholicExchange.com

In the world we live in today, we are bombarded by many strange notions of sexuality — whether it's pornography on the Internet or TV adds selling shampoo with sex. Lust is so common in our modern world that you are seen as strange or prude if you don't embrace the *laissez faire* attitude about this free-love notion of sexuality.

It's Only Natural

Jesus Christ teaches us in Matthew 5:27-28, "You have heard that it was said, 'You shall not commit adultery.' But I say to you that every one who looks at a woman lustfully has already committed adultery with her in his heart." Still, many people, even many "good" Christians, reject this teaching. Some say it's only natural for people to act on their sexual impulses — whatever they are. Others say that the sensual temptations around us are too much to resist.

But human beings are not animals controlled by instinct or by passions. If a man is angered by the actions of another, he is not free to act on that "natural" anger and injure the other. Unless a person is mentally ill, his reason must control his understanding of his external surroundings and his internal passions. Christians must ignore all these bizarre secular notions of sexuality and follow the teachings of Christ. The Catholic Church and God clearly condemn pornography. As we saw above, Jesus Christ condemned looking at any woman with lust and called it adultery.

Any Catholic who says it's okay — even if he is a priest, even if it's within the bounds of marriage — is very mistaken. Am I just speaking about hardcore pornography? No. As our Lord said: "every one who looks at a woman lustfully has already committed adultery with her in his heart" and that includes *any* pictorial representation, whether it is intended to be "pornography" or not.

Sadly, I hear comments like these all the time: "I'm not into that hard stuff that you were into. I'm not obsessed with it. I just like to look at the *Sports Illustrated Swimsuit Edition*"; or "It's only natural. Men are attracted to beautiful women. There is nothing wrong with looking at some harmless pictures of attractive women once and a while"; and "I just use it to enhance my marriage.

I'm a very sexual person and I need it to help fulfill my needs." In addition to these arguments, I have also often heard the argument that "If you are married then it's 'anything goes' as long as both the husband and wife agree."

If you agree with any of the above statements, I urge you to read on and then ask yourself if it's all right to entertain your fantasies with pictures of scantily clad women as long as it's not the "hard stuff"!

The Slow Poison of Selfishness

Before my own conversion to the Catholic faith, I too used the above arguments to "justify" my own indulgence in pornography. However, in my heart I knew it was destroying me, and it was certainly destroying my marriage. The attitudes that are so prevalent in our modern age are disordered. The majority of people form their opinions and attitudes based on popular media — and that is the problem. The popular media is saturated with selling the human body as a product. We are told that sex is the primary goal of all humans. However, contrary to popular belief, it is one of the primary causes of the destruction of marriages and yes, even Catholic marriages.

It's bad enough that adultery afflicts some Catholic marriages, and that artificial birth control is welcomed into far too many sacramental covenants, but I see that the deceptions of our sex-saturated society slowly poisons many marriages little by little with the ultimate goal of destroying families and more importantly, leaving men impotent to defend them.

In many ways, the sex-hungry pagan attitudes of our Western media resemble the debauchery of the waning days of the ancient Roman Empire. Though many people are either blind to or choose to remain silent about its real harm to our society, pornography is very destructive to our morals. It is a major contributor to the problems that we face in the world today. Pornography is just one of the aspects of the "culture of death" that seeks to destroy the family, devalue the dignity of human beings and disdain any references to God. Pornography is a symptom of a disordered view of the human person and the purpose of sexual behavior.

Pornography is based on selfishness no less than the "choice" to kill children in the womb and so-called "freedom" to entertain any sexual perversion at any cost. It reduces human beings to valueless commodities to be ogled and disposed of like used tissue. Sadly, many of the individuals whom pornographers target and then dispose of are vulnerable young men and women. Their vulnerability to exploitation by pornographers often is a result of their introduction to homosexual behavior. They have been told that this type of behavior is normal and desirable, but it warps their sense of themselves and makes them easy prey.

The root cause is the intrinsic evil of obstinate selfishness flaunted by the media. Virtually all advocates of a purely secular sexual code of behavior center on an "It's all about me" philosophy. Selfishness is at the core, rather than mutual love and care for one's partner. Abortion is tragically too often the result of sex being separated from a committed marital relationship that is both open to life and centered on uplifting one another. The unborn child does not fit into the selfish program of using another person for self-gratification. This too is the supreme motivation behind pornography. It promotes intrinsic selfishness and says that sexual pleasure is more important than quality, life-giving relationships. The false message of pornography is that sexual pleasure equals happiness. But as I have experienced and I'm sure others have too, it actually causes much unhappiness and leaves a wake of destruction in our lives. It leaves a person feeling empty and used up and more and more selfish. Ultimately it may succeed in destroying a person's soul and leaving him mentally afflicted, even spiritually dead.

The sexual union within marriage, between one man and one woman, is meant by the Creator to be an act of supreme love, giving and unity. It's a picture, if you will, of the supreme selflessness. Sadly, when pornography is allowed to be included in a conjugal relationship between a husband and wife, it brings a destructive force into many areas of the relationship. I'm personally aware of several marriages which have ended, in large part, because of pornography. I know of others which are currently suffering because of the husband's addiction to pornography. In fact, my own marriage was nearly destroyed because of my own problems with pornography.

Polluting What Should Be Holy

The *Catechism of the Catholic Church* (2354) condemns pornography as "a grave offense...because it perverts the conjugal act, the intimate giving of spouses to each other. It does grave injury to the dignity of its participants." The consequences of pornography are, in fact, contrary to the many blessings that God wills for us through His gift of the sacrament of matrimony. "Marriage," declares the *Catechism* (1609) "helps to overcome self-absorption, egoism, pursuit of one's own pleasure, and to open oneself to the other, to mutual aid and to self-giving." Nothing can more clearly exemplify self-absorption, egoism, and self-pleasure than one's willingness to make one's marriage vulnerable to the evils of pornography.

So why is pornography allowed to intrude into so many marriages? The main reason is that we have been duped by society and the Great Deceiver. We have been lied to and told that we need this "toxic waste" in our lives or we are not normal. I'd liken it to serving a wonderful meal for dinner each evening, but adding a small amount of rat poison to it. Even a little is deadly over time.

Conversely, while one spouse might initiate the inclusion of pornography in the relationship as a so-called "enhancement" to a couple's sex life, both spouses are culpable. One spouse cannot initiate that to which the other does not agree. Sadly, many women will accept their husband's perverse habits for fear they would only do it behind their backs anyway — or even worse have an affair. I have often heard wives rationalize this behavior by saying, "I would rather have him looking at pictures of women than sleeping around." They are using the so-called "lesser of two evils" argument.

For the truly serious couple who are devoted to each other, to their vows, and to the higher level of holiness into which they entered with Christ at the altar, God provides everything necessary for a blessed, happy and satisfying conjugal life: "God who created man out of love," states the *Catechism* (1604-1605), "also calls him to love — the fundamental and innate vocation of every human being. Since God created him man and woman, their mutual love becomes an image of the absolute and unfailing love with which God loves man. Man and woman were created for each other: it is not good that the man should be alone."

Thus, we have been given everything that is necessary to live a holy and happy marriage as bestowed by Christ through His Holy Spirit in the graces received on our wedding day. When pornography is allowed to intrude into a marriage it only serves to adulterate and pollute what should be a pure reflection of Christ's love for His bride the Church. What should be "of God" should be zealously defended against influences of this world, lest they become worldly and pass away with this world in its time rather than last forever, as do all things that are of God.

Therefore, it is not "anything goes" between husband and wife. God wants us to live a holy and pure life — *especially* as husband and wife. Pornography *is* adultery — plain and simple. Jesus Christ said so Himself in Matthew 5:27-28 quoted above. That includes looking at any woman for the sake of lust, including *Sports Illustrated* swimsuit models, Victoria's Secret catalogs and even including your own wife! If a man that looks at the *Sports Illustrated Swimsuit Edition* were honest with himself, he would have to say he is looking at the models in lust, not because he wants to give glory to God and praise Him for His great work in creating these beautiful women. If he says he is not lusting, he is lying to himself and to God and he's certainly not honoring his wife by looking at them.

Entrapped in a Web of Sin

Lust is *not* Love! Lust is disordered and harmful to our ability to see women and men for who they truly are — God's greatest gifts to each other. Seriously! For it was not good for man to be alone. Lust is a result of the fall of our original parents in the beginning, and the Enemy is constantly attacking us with it to try to bring us down into Hell.

Our Lady at Fatima also said to the three child seers *"More souls are falling into Hell because of sins of the flesh than any other sin."*

By looking at pornography or even "soft" porn, you participate in a whole series of sins. You sin by looking at it, which is lust and adultery. You contribute to others' sin by creating a demand for the industry — thus the industry seeks women and men who are willing to participate in the industry because of the money, which is greed. The fact is many of these people who participate in pornography are usually from homes where the fathers either indulged in pornography themselves or the father was totally absent from the scene while they were growing up — the sins of the father are thereby inherited by his children. There are many more sins that are committed and encouraged because of pornography. In fact, just about every mortal sin is committed in some way because of pornography, and it is spreading like the plague. Everyday the industry seeks to push the envelope of what is acceptable. It is constantly attempting to infiltrate mainstream society with more and more perversity.

When we indulge in pornography, we separate the body of the person in the pictures or movies from the whole person — the unity of body, soul and mind as God created him to be. We "use" their bodies for our own selfish pleasure, and many today, especially young women, are convinced by the messages they receive from society that should allow themselves to be "used" in this way. The lines have been blurred between lust and love. Lust is selfishness and selfishness is the opposite of love.

The God Who Sees Is the God Who Frees

Saint Francis de Sales said the best definition of love is "to will the greater good for another." This is exactly what Jesus did for us when He took upon Himself the penalty of our sins and died upon the Cross. He willed our greater good. Christ commanded us to love our neighbor as ourselves. That does not just mean the person that lives next door, but all people, male and female, all around the world, whether you know them or not. Men should respect all women who are older than themselves as they would their own mothers, and all women who are younger than themselves as they would their own sisters, except in the case of their wives.

A man should show an even greater respect for his wife than he would for any other woman. The relationship between a man and his wife is the most special and sacred union ever created by God and as such should be the greatest expression of love, as defined by Saint Francis de Sales. Using anyone, including your own spouse, for your own sexual and selfish pleasure is not love; neither is allowing yourself to be used for that purpose. It is a sin and a mortal sin at that.

I ask you to reflect on this passage from Sirach 23:18-21, 27:

> *And the man who dishonors his marriage bed and says to himself "Who can see me? Darkness surrounds me, walls hide me; no one sees me; why should I fear to sin?" Of the Most High he is not mindful, fearing only the eyes of men; he does not understand that the eyes of the LORD, ten thousand times brighter than the sun, observe every step a man takes and peer into hidden corners. He who knows all things before they exist still knows them all after they are made. Such a man will be punished in the streets of the city; when he least expects it, he will be apprehended.... Thus all who dwell on the earth shall know, and all who inhabit the world shall understand, that nothing is better than the fear of the LORD, nothing more salutary than to obey His commandments.*

Addiction to pornography will not go away on its own, and I feel it is the greatest problem among Catholic men. You can never be free by your own power, no human being is strong enough to do so. It is only possible with the help of our Lord and Savior Jesus Christ. Only He can set you free. Humility is the key. Satan holds us prisoner when we allow our sin to dwell in the dark, but when we bring it the light of Christ, Satan and his demons flee. Admit your problem and bring it out into the light of Truth.

COMBAT TRAINING
DAILY PRAYERS FOR PURITY

"Each day draw your strength from the Lord and from his mighty power. Put on the full armor of God so that you may be able to stand firm against the tactics of the devil. For our battle is not with forces of flesh and blood but against the principalities and powers, with the rulers of this present world of darkness, the evil spirits in the regions above. You must put on the armor of God, if you are to resist on the evil day; do all that your duty requires and hold your ground. Stand fast, with Truth as a belt around your waist, justice as your breastplate, and zeal to propagate the Gospel of peace as your footgear. In all circumstances, hold faith up before you as your shield; it will help you extinguish the fiery darts of the evil one. Take the helmet of salvation and the sword of the Spirit, the Word of God. At every opportunity, pray in the Spirit, using prayers and petitions of every sort. Pray constantly and attentively for all in the holy company."
Ephesians 6:10-18

The Knight, Death and The Devil

Put on the armor of God so that you may be able to stand firm against the tactics of the devil.
- *Ephesians vi.11*

by Albrecht Dürer, 1514

True Knights Daily Combat Prayer

Lord Jesus, I am thankful that You love me with a love that rights the greatest wrongs and heals the most hurtful wounds. Cleanse my heart of any darkness or evil that prevents me from knowing and enjoying the gift of pure love. Lord, I give You my memory, my mind, my soul, my body, my sexuality; I promise not to engage in sexually impure acts, either physically or mentally. From this day on, I will not read, buy, or watch pornographic materials. I solemnly promise to pray every day, to read the Holy Bible, to go to Confession regularly, to receive your Real and True Presence in Holy Communion as often as possible, and to live my life according to the **True Knights 7 Principles of Freedom and Purity**[1], the **True Knights Code of Chivalry**[2] and the **Ten Promises of a True Knight**[3] in my call to be a holy, sanctified man. Lord Jesus, be the one master of my life. Teach me to control my sexual desires and emotions and heal my mind and spirit of any harm I may have caused myself from any past sinful behavior. Help me avoid everything that weakens and enslaves the will: cigarettes, alcohol, and drugs. Teach me to be a sacrificing servant for my family, a spiritual leader for my domestic church and vigilant protector of all whom You have given to my charge. Make love the most important part of my life.

O Blessed Virgin, my Mother and Queen, lead me along the paths of faith, to the very source of Love, to Jesus, that I may trust in Him only, and believe in Him alone.

Dear Saint Joseph, most chaste spouse of the Blessed Virgin, pray that I may imitate you as an example of a true man as you were a true husband and father for the Holy Family.

O holy Saint Michael the Archangel defend us against the deception and attacks of the enemy as we traverse the battle field in the valley of tears.

Lord Jesus, True King of all creation, I give my life to You totally as a True Knight in the service of my king.
Amen!

---

1) 7 Principles of Freedom and Purity - page 54
2) True Knights Code of Chivalry - page 54
3) Ten Promises of a True Knight - page 57

𝕸𝖔𝖗𝖓𝖎𝖓𝖌 𝕻𝖗𝖆𝖞𝖊𝖗𝖘

† = *Make the Sign of the Cross (See page 99 about the Sign of the Cross)*

Prayer to be Said Before Praying

† "Almighty Father, I place the Precious Blood of Jesus before my lips before I pray, that my prayers may be purified before they ascend to Your divine altar. Amen.

St. Mary Magdalen de Pazzi

Be Humble before the Lord

Lord Jesus, by Your loving grace, please make the imperfect prayers of me, a sinner, pleasing, wholesome and acceptable to you. Amen

Liturgy of the Hours - *Morning Prayer or Office of the Hours*

Lord God Almighty (Domine, Deus omnipotens)

Lord, God Almighty, you have brought us safely to the beginning of this day. Defend us today by your mighty power, that we may not fall into any sin, but that all our words may so proceed and all our thoughts and actions be so directed, as to be always just in your sight. Through Christ our Lord. Amen.

Breathe in me O Holy Spirit

Breathe in me O Holy Spirit, that my thoughts may all be holy; Act in me O Holy Spirit, that my work, too, may be holy; Draw my heart O Holy Spirit, that I love but what is holy; Strengthen me O Holy Spirit, to defend all that is holy; Guard me, then, O Holy Spirit, that I always may be holy.

St. Augustine

Secret of Sanctity

O Holy Spirit, Soul of my soul, I adore You. Enlighten me, guide me, strengthen me, console me. Show me what I ought to do and command me to do it. I promise to be submissive to You in everything that you permit to happen to me. Merely show me what is Your Will.

A Scriptural Morning Prayer by Patty Harrison, April 1995 (Catholic Charismatic Center)

Praise and honor to You, O' Blessed Trinity: Father, Jesus, Holy Spirit! Praise, Honor, and Adoration! Be exalted, O' God of Gods! O' King of Kings! O' Holy One! O' Mighty One! O' God of all Mercies and of Love beyond comprehension! I entrust to you my life.

This day I lay before you all my circumstances and all that I encounter. "A man's heart plans out his way, but it is the Lord who makes his steps secure." *(Prov. 16:9)* Lord, order this day so it will give you glory and be in keeping with your holy will for me. For Jesus came to do the will of His Father and to give you glory. *(Jn. 6:38)* I pray not only for myself, but also for all whom you have given me to love, especially _____.

(Here take five to ten minutes to hold them in God's Love.)

Pour into our hearts, O' Lord, for the oil of gladness and clothe us in a garment of praise *(Is. 61:3)* that we may rejoice in you all day and give you a sacrifice of praise *(Jer. 17:26)* in all the circumstances. I thank you and praise you, my Lord, for the truth that sets us free. *(Jn. 8:32)* Do not let me/us be conformed to this age, but be transformed by the renewing of our minds. *(Rom. 12:1,2 Eph. 4:23,24)* Ground me/us in your truth and establish me/us on the Gospel of Jesus

Christ. Reveal to me the hidden stones and idols of my heart *(Ez. 36:25-27)* that I may repent and return to you with all of my heart. *(Ps. 51)* I pray for humility to believe as Mary did that the promises spoken to her would be fulfilled; *(Lk. 1:45)* and the interior gifts to ponder as she did the action of God in all circumstances. *(Lk. 2:19)* I pray also for the readiness to respond quickly as Joseph and Mary did to the lead and promptings of the Holy Spirit. *(Mt. 1:24; 2:14)*

Thank you, Father God, for the love of the Holy Spirit that is poured into our hearts in Christ Jesus. A love that builds us up in hope, a hope that does not disappoint. *(Rm. 5:5)* I pray for that peace that surpasses all understanding; your peace that binds us together in love and preserves the unity of the Spirit. *(Eph. 4:3)* Cause me to walk in that peace each day. "You will keep him in perfect peace whose mind is stayed on Thee..." *(Is. 26:3)*

Each morning awaken me to listen as a disciple. Grant me an attentive ear to listen in sincerity and integrity of heart, to follow you faithfully. Lead me into deep worship and daily study of your Word.

I pray for a disciple's tongue. Cause me to know how to reply to the wearied. Put a guard at my mouth to speak as a godly woman/man, to speak that which will edify and encourage, to speak the truth in love. *(Js. 1:26, Prov. 10:11+;13:3, Si. 28:14)*

Thank you Jesus, that I may come before you, united in intercession to and with Mary, Joseph, and all the heavenly community, particularly St. _____. I present to you, my God, all my needs and those of my family, friends, all You have given me to love. Wash us in the precious tide of your mercy, the blood and life giving waters that flow from the pierced side of Jesus. *(Zc. 13:1)* Cause us to rely on your armor *(Eph. 6:10-18)* that we may be able to stand firm, united in faith *(Phil. 1:27,28; Heb. 4:14)* and not falter in times of hardship. For in due season we will see the victory of our God and will have a testimony of praise, to give Him glory and to defeat the works of the enemy. *(Rev. 12:11)* Encircle us, O' God, with your protection. *(Ps. 3:3)* St. Michael the archangel, defend us in the day of battle.

I present to You, O' Lord, the needs of the whole Church; the Holy Father, Pope Benedict XVI; my diocese, parish, and all pastors and laborers in your kingdom. I further entrust to you the needs of my neighborhood, city, and nation; as well as the nations of the world. Cause those in leadership to exercise it in a godly manner. *(1 Tim. 2:1)* I pray especially for _____.

In the name of Jesus Christ, I pray for a renewal of the Holy Spirit--His fountain of life giving water, to spring up within, and a release of His fire, His gifts, and the evidence of His fruits within me and the lives of all for whom I pray.

Praise, Glory, and Adoration be unto You, O' Lord of Lords! Amen! Amen! Amen!

Morning Offering to the Sacred Heart

† My dear Father, I offer you this day all my prayers, works, joys and sufferings in union with Jesus in the Holy Sacrifice of the Mass throughout the world, in the Holy Spirit.

I unite with our Mother Mary, all the angels and saints, and souls in purgatory, to pray to the Father for myself, for each member of my family, for my friends, for all people throughout the world, for all the souls in purgatory, and for all other intentions of the Sacred Heart.

I love You, Jesus, and I give You my heart. I love you, Mary, and I give you my heart. Amen.

For Purity: Saluting the Blessed Virgin with Three Aves
Adding after each one the aspiration that St. Alphonsus himself recommended:

"By thy holy and Immaculate Conception, O Mary, purify my body and sanctify my soul."

O Domina Mea (Fr. Zucchi) *To entrust yourself to Mary:*
My Queen, my Mother, I give myself entirely to you, and to show my devotion to you I consecrate to you this day/night my eyes †, my ears †, my mouth †, my heart †, my whole body † without reserve. Wherefore, good Mother, as I am your own, keep me and guard me as your property and possession. Amen.

† O Heart most pure of the Blessed Virgin Mary, obtain for me from Jesus a pure and humble heart. Amen.

Morning Offering to the Immaculate Heart of Mary
It is recommended that all True Knights wear and are enrolled in the Brown Scapular of Our Lady of Mt. Carmel. (See Appendix VIII, Page 84)

O my God, in union with the Immaculate Heart of Mary *(here kiss your Brown Scapular as a sign of your consecration, partial indulgence also)*, I offer Thee the Precious Blood of Jesus from all the altars throughout the world, joining with it the offering of my every thought, word and action of this day.

O my Jesus, I desire today to gain every indulgence and merit I can, and I offer them, together with myself, to Mary Immaculate — that She may best apply them to the interests of Thy most Sacred Heart.

Precious Blood of Jesus, save us!
Immaculate Heart of Mary, pray for us!
Sacred Heart of Jesus, have mercy on us!

Daily Miraculous Medal Prayer
It is recommended that all True Knights wear the Miraculous Medal and Consecrate themselves to Our Lady. (See Appendix VIII, Page 81)

O Virgin Mother of God, Mary Immaculate, We dedicate and consecrate ourselves to you under the title of Our Lady of the Miraculous Medal. May this Medal be for each one of us a sure sign of your affection for us and a constant reminder of our duties toward you. Ever while wearing it, may we be blessed by your loving protection and preserved in the grace of your Son. O Most Powerful Virgin, Mother of Our Savior, keep us close to you every moment of our lives. Obtain for us, your children, the grace of a happy death; so that in union with you, we may enjoy the bliss of Heaven forever.

O Mary, conceived without sin. Pray for us who have recourse to you, and for all those who do not have recourse to you, especially the enemies of the Holy church and all those recommended to you. Amen.

Consecration to God the Father
Almighty and Eternal Father, I admit that I have sinned against You in the past by _____ (list your sins). In the most Holy Name of Our Lord Jesus Christ, I reject all these sins and any sinful use I have ever made of my body. If I have not yet confessed any of them in the Sacrament of Penance, I resolve now to do so as soon as possible.

I renounce Satan, all his works and pomps; may the Lord Jesus rebuke him, I humbly pray. May the Immaculate Queen of Angels and Terror of demons crush him underfoot; may Holy Michael the Archangel cast him into Hell, along with any evil spirits who seek to ruin my soul.

By Your grace, I refuse to be mastered by sin from now on. I offer You my body as a living sacrifice, and present my members to You as instruments for righteousness, and not for sin. I beg you to create in me a clean heart and a right spirit; may I live and die for You alone, my God and my All! I ask all this in the Name of Our Lord Jesus Christ, Your Son, Who lives and reigns with you and the Holy Spirit, One God forever and ever. Amen.

Prayer of Abandonment
Father, I abandon myself into Your hands; Do with me whatever You will. Whatever You may do, I thank You. I am ready for all, I accept all. Let only Your will be done in me, And in all Your creatures. I wish no more than this, O lord. Into Your hands I commend my spirit; I offer it to You, Lord, and so need to give myself, to surrender myself into Your hands, Without reserve and with boundless confidence, For You are my Father. Amen.

Jean-Pierre de Caussade

Prayer to "Be" Christ
O my Divine Savior, transform me into yourself.
May my hands be the hands of Jesus.
May my tongue be the tongue of Jesus,
Grant that every faculty of my body may serve only to glorify you.
Above all, transform my soul and all its powers,
that my memory, my will and my affections
may be the memory, the will and the affections of Jesus.
I pray you to destroy in me all that is not you.
Grant that I may live but in you and for you,
and that I may truly say with St. Paul:
"I live, now not I, but Christ lives in me" *(Gal 2:20).*

Prayers in Honor of the Seven Sorrow and Joy of St. Joseph
Composed by Ven. Januarius Sarnelli, C.SS.R. (d. 1744)
It is recommended that all True Knights wear the Cord of St. Joseph for his intercession for purity. (See Appendix VIII, Page 89)

1st Sorrow: The doubt of St. Joseph. (Matt. 1:19).
But Joseph her husband, being a just man, and not wishing to expose her to reproach, was minded to put her away privately.

1st Joy: The message of the Angel. (Matt. 1:20).
But while he thought on these things, behold, an angel of the Lord appeared to him in a dream, saying, "Do not be afraid, Joseph, son of David, to take to you Mary your wife, for that which is begotten in her is of the Holy Spirit.

O chaste Spouse of Mary most holy, glorious St. Joseph, great was the trouble and anguish of your heart when you wert minded to put away privately your inviolate Spouse, yet your joy was unspeakable when the surpassing mystery of the Incarnation was made known to you by the Angel!

By this sorrow and this joy, we beseech you to comfort our souls, both now and in the sorrows of our final hour, with the joy of a good life and a holy death after the pattern of your own, in the arms of Jesus and Mary.

Our Father . . . Hail Mary . . . Glory be . . .

2nd Sorrow: The poverty of Jesus' birth. (Luke 2:7).
And she brought forth her first born son, and wrapped him in swaddling clothes, and laid him in a manger, because there was no room for them in the inn.

2nd Joy: The birth of the Savior. (Luke 2:10-11).
And the angel said to them, "Do not be afraid, for behold, I bring you good news of great joy which shall be to all people; for today in the town of David, a Savior has been born to you, who is Christ the Lord."

O most blessed Patriarch, glorious St. Joseph, who was chosen to be the foster father of the Word made flesh, your sorrow at seeing the Child Jesus born in such poverty was suddenly changed into heavenly exultation when you did hear the angelic hymn and beheld the glories of that resplendent night.

By this sorrow and this joy, we implore you to obtain for us the grace to pass over from life's pathway to hear the angelic songs of praise, and to rejoice in the shining splendour of celestial glory.

Our Father . . . Hail Mary . . . Glory be . . .

3rd Sorrow: The Circumcision. (Luke 2:21).
And when eight days were fulfilled for his circumcision, his name was called Jesus, the name given to him by the angel before he was conceived in the womb.

3rd Joy: The Holy Name of Jesus. (Matt. 1:25).
And he did not know her until she brought forth her first born son. And he called his name Jesus.

O glorious St. Joseph you faithfully obeyed the law of God, and your heart was pierced at the sight of the Precious Blood that was shed by the Infant Savior during His Circumcision, but the Name of Jesus gave you new life and filled you with quiet joy.

By this sorrow and this joy, obtain for us the grace to be freed from all sin during life, and to die rejoicing, with the holy Name of Jesus in our hearts and on our lips.

Our Father . . . Hail Mary . . . Glory be . . .

4th Sorrow: The prophecy of Simeon. (Luke 2:34).
And Simeon blessed them, and said to Mary his mother, "Behold this child is destined for the fall and the rise of many in Israel, and for a sign that shall be contradicted. And your own soul a sword shall pierce."

4th Joy: The effects of the Redemption. (Luke 2:38).
And coming up at that very hour, she began to give praise to the Lord, and spoke of him to all who were awaiting the redemption of Jerusalem.

O most faithful Saint who shared the mysteries of our Redemption, glorious St. Joseph, the prophecy of Simeon regarding the sufferings of Jesus and Mary caused you to shudder with mortal dread, but at the same time filled you with a blessed joy for the salvation and glorious resurrection which, he foretold, would be attained by countless souls.

By this sorrow and this joy, obtain for us that we may be among the number of those who, through the merits of Jesus and the intercession of Mary the Virgin Mother, are predestined to a glorious resurrection.

Our Father . . . Hail Mary . . . Glory be . . .

5th Sorrow: The flight into Egypt. (Matt. 2:14).
So he arose, and took the child and his mother by night, and withdrew into Egypt.
5th Joy: The overthrow of the idols of Egypt. (Is. 19:1).
The burden of Egypt. Behold the Lord will ascend upon a swift cloud and will enter into Egypt, and the idols of Egypt will be moved at his presence, and the heart of Egypt shall melt in the midst thereof.

O most watchful Guardian of the Incarnate Son of God, glorious St. Joseph, what toil was your in supporting and waiting upon the Son of the most high God, especially in the flight into Egypt! Yet at the same time, how you did rejoice to have always near you God Himself, and to see the idols of the Egyptians fall prostrate to the ground before Him.

By this sorrow and this joy, obtain for us the grace of keeping ourselves in safety from the infernal tyrant, especially by flight from dangerous occasions; may every idol of earthly affection fall from our hearts; may we be wholly employed in serving Jesus and Mary, and for them alone may we live and happily die.

Our Father . . . Hail Mary . . . Glory be . . .

6th Sorrow: The return from Egypt. (Matt. 2:22).
But hearing that Archelaus was reigning in Judea in place of his father Herod, he was afraid to go there; and being warned in a dream, he withdrew into the region of Galilee.

6th Joy: Life with Jesus and Mary at Nazareth. (Luke 2:39).
And when they had fulfilled all things prescribed in the Law of the Lord, they returned into Galilee, into their own town of Nazareth.

O glorious St. Joseph, an angel on earth, you did marvel to see the King of Heaven obedient to your commands, but your consolation in bringing Jesus out of the land of Egypt was troubled by your fear of Archelaus; nevertheless, being assured by the Angel, you dwelt in gladness at Nazareth with Jesus and Mary.

By this sorrow and this joy, obtain for us that our hearts may be delivered from harmful fears, so that we may rejoice in peace of conscience and may live in safety with Jesus and Mary and may, like you, die in their company.

Our Father . . . Hail Mary . . . Glory be . . .

7th Sorrow: The loss of the Child Jesus. (Luke 2:45).
And not finding him, they returned to Jerusalem in search of him

7th Joy: The finding of the Child Jesus in the Temple. (Luke 2:46).
And it came to pass after three days, that they found him in the Temple, sitting in the midst of the teachers, listening to them and asking them questions.

O glorious St. Joseph, pattern of all holiness, when you did lose, through no fault of your own, the Child Jesus, you sought Him sorrowing for the space of three days, until with great joy you did find Him again in the Temple, sitting in the midst of the doctors.

By this sorrow and this joy, we supplicate you, with our hearts upon our lips, to keep us from ever having the misfortune to lose Jesus through mortal sin; but if this supreme misfortune should befall us, grant that we may seek Him with unceasing sorrow until we find Him again, ready to show us His great mercy, especially at the hour of death; so that we may pass over to enjoy His presence in Heaven; and there, in company with you, may we sing the praises of His Divine mercy forever.

Our Father . . . Hail Mary . . . Glory be . . .

Antiphon And Jesus Himself was beginning about the age of thirty years, being (as it was supposed) the Son of Joseph.

V. Pray for us, O holy Joseph.
R. That we may be made worthy of the promises of Christ.

Let Us Pray
O God, Who in Your ineffable Providence did vouchsafe to choose Blessed Joseph to be the spouse of Your most holy Mother, grant, we beseech You, that he whom we venerate as our protector on earth may be our intercessor in Heaven. Who lives and reigns forever and ever. Amen.

St. Joseph Prayer for Purity
O Guardian of Virgins and holy Father St. Joseph, into whose faithful keeping were entrusted Christ Jesus, Innocence itself, and Mary, Virgin of virgins, I pray and beseech thee by these dear pledges, Jesus and Mary, that, being preserved from all uncleanness, I may with spotless mind, pure heart and chaste body ever serve Jesus and Mary most chastely all the days of my life. Amen.

A Prayer to St. Joseph
St. Joseph, head of the Holy Family and earthly guardian of our Lord Jesus Christ, I pray, through the power of your special intercession, for God to grant me the strength, guidance, insight and discernment to always be

> The best husband/wife that I can be,
> The best father/mother that I can be,
> The best son/daughter that I can be,
> The best worker that I can be,
> The purest soul that I can be,

So that all of my labors, all of my thoughts, words and deeds may ceaselessly give glory to the Father, Son and Holy Spirit. This we ask in Jesus' name. Amen.

The Angelus
The Angelus is traditionally recited morning (6:00 a.m.), noon and evening (6:00 p.m.) throughout the year except during Paschal time, when the Regina Coeli is recited instead.
V. The Angel of the Lord declared unto Mary.
R. And she conceived of the Holy Spirit.
Hail Mary, etc.

V. Behold the handmaid of the Lord.
R. Be it done unto me according to thy word.
Hail Mary, etc.

8

V. And the Word was made Flesh.
R. And dwelt among us.
Hail Mary, etc.

V. Pray for us, O holy Mother of God.
R. That we may be made worthy of the promises of Christ.

Let us pray: Pour forth, we beseech Thee, O Lord, Thy grace into our hearts, that we to whom the Incarnation of Christ Thy Son was made known by the message of an angel, may by His Passion and Cross be brought to the glory of His Resurrection. Through the same Christ Our Lord. Amen.

Regina Coeli
This prayer, which dates from the twelfth century, is substituted for the Angelus during Easter Season.
Queen of Heaven rejoice, alleluia: For He whom you merited to bear, alleluia, Has risen as He said, alleluia. Pray for us to God, alleluia.

V. Rejoice and be glad, O Virgin Mary, alleluia.
R. Because the Lord is truly risen, alleluia.

Let us pray: O God, who by the Resurrection of Thy Son, our Lord Jesus Christ, granted joy to the whole world: grant we beseech Thee, that through the intercession of the Virgin Mary, His Mother, we may lay hold of the joys of eternal life. Through the same Christ our Lord. R. Amen.

Prayer for Sanctity
O Model of humility, divest me of all pride and arrogance. Let me acknowledge my weakness and sinfulness, contempt for your sake and esteem myself as lowly in your site.

Prayer Before Reading of Sacred Scripture *(Sacrae Scripturae lectio)*
Holy Spirit of God and inspirer of the Word, may this reading of the Bible draw me more deeply into the mystery of your love. Help me to understand what I read and respond to it with my life. It was the Divine Word that brought creation out of chaos. Let it bring a new creation into the chaos of my life.

It was your Word that the prophets spoke to arouse people from their lukewarmness. Let it bring fire of your love into my life. Make me hunger for your Word, for it speaks to me of Jesus Christ, who alone can satisfy. Amen.

Any amount of reading. *(Partial Indulgence)*
30 minutes of reading. *(Plenary Indulgence)*
15 Minutes of Mental Prayer *(Oratio mentalis) (partial Indulgence) Spending time in*
Contreplative Prayer everyday is vitally important. *- See page 108 for more information on Contemplative Prayer.*

Pray the following Recommended Daily Scripture Readings, Mass Readings or other scripture reading then go to page 13 to continue daily prayers.

Recommended Daily Scripture Readings
Sirach 23:18-21, 27
[18] ...the man who dishonors his marriage bed and says to himself "Who can see me? Darkness surrounds me, walls hide me; no one sees me; why should I fear to sin?" Of the Most High he is not mindful, [19] fearing only the eyes of men; He does not understand that the eyes of the LORD, ten thousand times brighter than the sun, Observe every step a man takes and peer into hidden

corners. [20] He who knows all things before they exist still knows them all after they are made. [21] Such a man will be punished in the streets of the city; when he least expects it, he will be apprehended... [27] Thus all who dwell on the earth shall know, and all who inhabit the world shall understand, That nothing is better than the fear of the LORD, nothing more salutary than to obey his commandments.

1 Corinthians 6:15-20

[15]Do you not know that your bodies are members of Christ? Shall I therefore take the members of Christ and make them members of a prostitute? Never! [16]Do you not know that he who joins himself to a prostitute becomes one body with her? For, as it is written, "The two shall become one flesh." [17]But he who is united to the Lord becomes one spirit with him. [18]Shun immorality. Every other sin which a man commits is outside the body; but the immoral man sins against his own body. [19]Do you not know that your body is a temple of the Holy Spirit within you, which you have from God? You are not your own; [20]you were bought with a price. So glorify God in your body.

Romans 13:11-14

[11]Besides this you know what hour it is, how it is full time now for you to wake from sleep. For salvation is nearer to us now than when we first believed; [12]the night is far gone, the day is at hand. Let us then cast off the works of darkness and put on the armor of light; [13]let us conduct ourselves becomingly as in the day, not in reveling and drunkenness, not in debauchery and licentiousness, not in quarreling and jealousy. [14]But put on the Lord Jesus Christ, and make no provision for the flesh, to gratify its desires.

Sirach 2:1-7

"When you come to serve the Lord, prepare yourself for trials. Be sincere of heart and steadfast, undisturbed in times of adversity. Cling to Him, forsake Him not; thus, will your future be great. Accept what befalls you; in crushing misfortune be patient. For, in fire gold is tested and worthy men in the crucible of humiliation. Trust God and He will help you. Make straight your ways and hope in Him. You who fear the Lord, wait for His mercy. Turn not away, lest you fall."

Ephesians 6:10-20

[10]...be strong in the Lord and in the strength of his might. [11]Put on the whole armor of God, that you may be able to stand against the wiles of the devil. [12]For we are not contending against flesh and blood, but against the principalities, against the powers, against the world rulers of this present darkness, against the spiritual hosts of wickedness in the heavenly places. [13]Therefore take the whole armor of God, that you may be able to withstand in the evil day, and having done all, to stand. [14]Stand therefore, having girded your loins with truth, and having put on the breastplate of righteousness, [15]and having shod your feet with the equipment of the gospel of peace; [16]besides all these, taking the shield of faith, with which you can quench all the flaming darts of the evil one. [17]And take the helmet of salvation, and the sword of the Spirit, which is the word of God. [18]Pray at all times in the Spirit, with all prayer and supplication. To that end keep alert with all perseverance, making supplication for all the saints, [19]and also for me, that utterance may be given me in opening my mouth boldly to proclaim the mystery of the gospel, [20]for which I am an ambassador in chains; that I may declare it boldly, as I ought to speak.

Philippians 4:8-9

[8]Finally, brethren, whatever is true, whatever is honorable, whatever is just, whatever is pure, whatever is lovely, whatever is gracious, if there is any excellence, if there is anything worthy of praise, think about these things. [9]What you have learned and received and heard and seen in me, do; and the God of peace will be with you.

Pray the previously Recommended Daily Scripture Readings, Mass Readings or other Scripture reading then go to page 13 to continue daily prayers.

Favorite Scripture Passages

The Four Horsemen of the Apocalypse

For our struggle is not with flesh and blood but with the principalities, with the powers, with the world rulers of this present darkness, with the evil spirits in the heavens. - *Ephesians vi.12*

by Albrecht Dürer, 1498

Spiritual Warfare Prayers

Anytime we are working to break free of slavery to addictions we are also fighting against the principalities and powers of the spirits of darkness. These prayers are very important In arming yourself daily to defending yourself and fighting temptations. *(See page 68 concerning important information about Spiritual Warfare, how to prepare for Spiritual Warfare and the tools of Spiritual Warfare.)*

Afraid of the Devil? by Saint Teresa of Jesus- *See page 66*

Spiritual Armor Prayer

† Heavenly Father, I(we) ask You today for Your Truth as a belt tight around my/our loins. † I(We) put on the zeal to announce your good news of peace as shoes for my (our) feet. † I(We) put on Your righteousness, O Christ, as my(our) breastplate, and the hope of salvation as a helmet for our head. † Father, I(we) take up faith as a shield which is able to put out all the fiery darts of the enemy, and the sword of the Spirit, which is Your Word, O Lord. † Father, may the love with which you have loved Jesus be in me(us), and may Jesus be in me(us). † I(We) ask You for the grace of a servant heart, a humble heart, a contrite heart. Amen. †

Prayer for Filling of The Spirit

[This prayer should also be said after the Sacrament of Reconciliation. It is wise to say it daily or at least regularly in addition.]

† Lord Jesus Christ, I want to belong to You from now on. I want to be free from the dominion of darkness and the rule of Satan, and I want to enter into Your Kingdom and be part of Your people. I will turn away from all sin, and I will avoid everything that leads me to wrongdoing. I ask You to forgive all the sins I have committed. Come into my heart as my personal Savior and Lord. I offer my life to You, and I promise to obey You as my Lord and Master. I ask You to fill me with Your Holy Spirit. Amen. †

Prayer for a Spiritual Canopy

† Dear Lord Jesus, please forgive me for all the times I have not submitted to you. Forgive me for all sinfulness and for agreeing with the enemy and his lies. † I now submit to you as my Lord, dear Jesus. † Now I break every agreement that I have made with the enemy.

† Lord Jesus, please have your warring angels remove and bind to the abyss all demons and their devices that had access to me because I believed their lies. † I now ask you to establish a hedge of protection around me, over me, and under me, and seal it with your blood, Lord Jesus Christ.

† I now choose to put on the full armor of God and ask that you cleanse me and seal me, body, mind, soul and spirit, with your blood, Lord Jesus Christ. † Please have your warring angels bind up and remove all demons, their devices, and all their power from within this protective hedge and have them sent to the abyss.

† Please have your warriors destroy all demonic, occult, or witchcraft assignments directed against me including all backups and replacements. † Please have your warriors remove all trafficking people and send them back to their own bodies and seal them there with your blood, Lord Jesus Christ. † Please have your angels stand guard over me and protect me from all the attacks of the enemy.

Preparation Protection Prayer

† In the name of the Lord Jesus Christ, and by the power of the Word mad flesh, and the shed blood of Jesus Christ and the Holy Spirit, I ask you Heavenly Father to bind all the powers and forces in the air, in the ground, in the water, in the netherworld, in nature and in fire.

† You are the Lord over all the universe, and I give You the glory for your creation. I ask you Heavenly Father to bind all demonic forces that have come against us and our families, and I ask you Heavenly Father to seal all of us in the protection of the Precious Blood of our Lord Jesus Christ that was shed for us on the cross.

† O Holy Saint Michael the Archangel and all of our guardian angels, come and defend us and our families in battle against all the evil ones that roam the earth.

† I ask you Heavenly Father to bind and command all the powers and forces of evil to depart right now away from us, our homes and our lands. And I thank you, Lord Jesus, for You are a faithful and compassionate God. Amen. †

Binding Evil Spirits for Self

† In the name of the Lord Jesus Christ, and by the power of the word, and the shed blood of Jesus Christ and the Holy Spirit, † I ask you Heavenly Father to bind the evil spirits of pride, ignorance, unforgiveness, gossip, envy, competitiveness, criticism, impatience, resentment, haughtiness, rebellion, stubbornness, deceitfulness, defiance, disobedience, strife, violence, divorce, laziness, accusation, confusion, procrastination, self-hatred, suicide, shame, depression, oppression, rejection, poor self image, anger, schizophrenia, manipulation, anxiety, timidity, jealously, greed, revenge, covetousness, fear, possessiveness, control, division, retaliation, distrust, selfishness, loneliness, isolation, ostracism, lack, paranoia, nervousness, passivity, indecision, doubt, deception, dishonesty, unbelief, withdrawal, betrayal, escape, infirmity, nerve disorder, lung disorder, brain disorder or dysfunction, AIDS, cancer, hypochondria, fatigue, anorexia, bulimia, addictions, gluttony, perfectionism, alcoholism, workaholism, nicotine, self-abuse, sexual addictions, sexual impurities and sexual perversion, seduction, lust, incest, pedophilia, lesbianism, homosexuality, pornography, adultery, masturbation, homophobia, frigidity, impotency, immorality, witchcraft, enticing spirits, deaf, dumb, blind, mute and sleeping spirits, hyperactivity, new-age spirits, occult spirits, religious spirits, anti-Christ spirits, and any other spirits of death and darkness all in the name of the risen Lord Jesus Christ.

† In the name of Jesus Christ, I call forth and ask the Holy Spirit to fill me with the gifts of peace, patience, love, joy, charity, humility, forgiveness, kindness, generosity, faithfulness, gentleness, goodness, discipline, relinquishment, freedom from shame, good self image, prosperity, obedience, a sound mind, order, fulfillment in Christ, truth, acceptance of self, acceptance of others, trust, self control, freedom from addictions, freedom of having-to-control, wholeness, wellness, health, and the light and life of the Lord Jesus Christ. Amen. †

Prayer for Inner Healing

† Lord Jesus, please come and heal my wounded and troubled heart. I beg you to heal the torments that cause anxiety in my heart; I beg you, in a particular way, to heal all who are the causes of my sinfulness. I beg you to come into my life and heal me of the psychological harms that struck me in my childhood and from the injuries that they caused throughout my life.

† Lord Jesus, you know my burdens. I lay them all on your Good Shepherd's Heart. I beseech

you — by the merits of the great open wound in your heart — to heal the small wounds that are in mine. Heal the pain of my memories, so that nothing that has happened to me will cause me to remain in pain and anguish, filled with anxiety.

✝ Heal, O Lord, all those wounds that have been the cause of all the evil that is rooted in my life. I want to forgive all those who have offended me. Look to those inner sores that make me unable to forgive. You who came to forgive the afflicted of heart, please, heal my heart.

✝ Heal, my Lord Jesus, those intimate wounds that cause me physical illness. I offer you my heart. Accept it, Lord, purify it and give me the sentiments of your Divine Heart. Help me to be meek and humble.

✝ Heal me, O Lord, from the pain caused by the death of my loved ones, which is oppressing me. Grant me to regain peace and joy in the knowledge that you are the Resurrection and the Life. Make me an authentic witness to your Resurrection, your victory over sin and death, your living presence among all men. Amen. ✝

Prayer for My Marriage

✝ Loving heavenly Father, I thank You for Your perfect plan for our marriage. I know that a marriage functioning in Your will and blessing is fulfilling and beautiful. In the name of the Lord Jesus Christ, I bring our marriage before You, that You might make it all You desire it to be. Please forgive me for my sins of failure in our marriage.

[Confess specific and particular areas of failure.]

✝ In the name of the Lord Jesus Christ, strengthened by the intercession of the Immaculate Virgin Mary, Mother of God, of Blessed Michael the Archangel, of the Blessed Apostles Peter and Paul, and all the Saints and Angels of Heaven, and powerful in the holy authority of His Name, I ask you, O Lord, to tear down all of Satan's strongholds designed to destroy our marriage. ✝ In the name of the Lord Jesus Christ, I ask Father that You help us to break all relationships between us that have been established by Satan and his wicked spirits. I will accept only the relationships established by You and the blessed Holy Spirit. I invite the Holy Spirit to enable me to relate to *[spouse's name]* in a manner that will meet his/her needs. I will submit our conversation to You, that it may please You. I submit our physical relationship to You that it may enjoy Your blessing. I submit our love to You that You may cause it to grow and mature.

✝ I desire to know and experience in marriage the fullness of Your perfect will. Open my eyes to see all areas where I am deceived. Open *[spouse's name]* eyes to see any of Satan's deception upon him/her. Make our Union to be the Christ-centered and blessed relationship You have designed in Your perfect will. I ask this in the name of the Lord Jesus Christ with thanksgiving. Amen. ✝

Prayer for our Children

✝ I(We) bow humbly before You, heavenly Father, to pray for our children, *[names of children]*, and for my/our whole family. I(We) bring my/our children and my/our family before You in the name of the Lord Jesus Christ.

✝ I(We) thank You, Lord, that You love *[names of children]* and our entire family, with the love of Calvary. I(We) thank You that You have given *[names of children]* to us to love and nurture in Christ.

✝ I(We) ask You to forgive us together as parents, and each of us alone in our roles as father and mother, for all our failures to guide our children in the way they ought to go. Help us Lord to be the parents You want us to be; that we may train *[names of children]* in Your ways, that we may model the Christ-life before them, so that when they grow-up they will love You and live for You.

✝ Heavenly Father, accepting our position through You of having "divine power to demolish strongholds" (2 Cor. 10:4) that come into our family, I(we) ask You Father to bring all the work of the Lord Jesus, strengthened by the intercession of the Immaculate Virgin Mary, Mother of God, of Blessed Michael the Archangel, of the Blessed Apostles Peter and Paul, and all the Saints and Angels of Heaven, and powerful in the holy authority of His Name, to focus directly against the powers of darkness that do now or may later bother, influence, and bind *[names of children]* and our family in any way; and specifically against *(name specific areas of troubles or problems)*.

✝ I(We) pray that You shall bring the victory of our Lord's incarnation, crucifixion, resurrection, Ascension, and glorification directly against all of Satan's power brought against us in our family and specifically in the lives of *[names of children]*. ✝ I(We) ask You heavenly Father to bind up all powers of darkness set to destroy *[names of children]*, or our family, and we ask you Father to loose *[names of children]*, and this family, from the influence and harassment of Satan and his demons, in the name of the Lord Jesus Christ.

✝ I(We) invite the blessed Holy Spirit to move in hearts of *[names of children]* that they may know the truth as they are able at their age. I(We) invite the blessed Holy Spirit to move in our hearts and to convict us of sin, of righteousness, and of our responsibility as parents to raise *[names of children]* in Your name.

✝ I(We) plead the blood of Christ over *[names of children]* and this family. We claim for us a life yielded to serve the true and living God in the name of the Lord Jesus Christ. Amen. ✝

Hedge Prayer for Protection of Household

✝ Trusting in the promise that whatever we ask the Father in Jesus' name He will do, I(we) now approach You Father with confidence in Our Lord's words and in Your infinite power and love for me(us) and for our household and family, and with the intercession of the Blessed Virgin Mary, Mother of God, the Blessed Apostles Peter and Paul, Blessed Archangel Michael, my(our) guardian angel(s) and the guardian angels of our household and family, with all the saints and angels of heaven, and Holy in the power of His blessed Name, as ask you Father to protect our household and its members and keep us from the harassment of the devil and his minions.

✝ Father I(we) ask in desire to serve You and adore You and to live our lives for You that You build a hedge of protection around our household, like that which surrounded Job, and to help us to keep that hedge repaired and the gate locked so that the devil and his minions have no access or means to breach the hedge except by your expressed will.

✝ Father, I(we) am(are) powerless against the spiritual forces of evil and recognize my(our) utter dependence on You and Your power. Look with mercy upon me(us) and upon our household and family. Do not look upon our sins, O Lord; rather, look at the sufferings of your Beloved Son and see the Victim who's bitter passion and death has reconciled us to You. By the victory of the cross, protect us from all evil and rebuke any evil spirits who wish to attack, influence, or breach Your hedge of protection in any way. Send them back to Hell and fortify Your Hedge for our protection by the blood of Your Son, Jesus. Send your Holy Angels to watch over us and protect us.

✝ Father, all of these things I(we) ask in the most holy name of Jesus Christ, Your Son. Thank you, Father, for hearing my(our) prayer. I(we) love You, I(we) worship You, I(we) thank You and I(we) trust in You. Amen. ✝

Prayer for a Friend

✝ Heavenly Father, I bring before You and the Lord Jesus Christ one who is very dear to You and to me, *[person's name(s)]*. ✝ I have come to see that Satan is blinding and binding him/her/them in awful bondage. He/She/They is/are in such a condition that he/she/they cannot or will not come to You for help on his/her/their own. ✝ I stand in for him/her/them in intercessory prayer before Your throne. ✝ I draw upon the Person of the Holy Spirit that He may guide me to pray in wisdom, power, and understanding.

✝ In the name of the Lord Jesus Christ, strengthened by the intercession of the Immaculate Virgin Mary, Mother of God, of Blessed Michael the Archangel, of the Blessed Apostles Peter and Paul, and all the Saints and Angels of Heaven, and powerful in the holy authority of His Name, ✝ I ask You Heavenly Father to loose *[person's name(s)]* from the awful bondage the powers of darkness are putting upon him/her/them; and to bind all powers of darkness set on destroying his/her/their life/lives, binding these powers aside in the name of the Lord Jesus Christ and forbidding them to work. ✝ Father, bind up all powers of depression that are seeking to cut *[person's name(s)]* off and imprison him/her/them in a tomb of despondency;

✝ bind up all powers of delusion that are seeking to blind *[person's name(s)]* and keep him/her/them from knowing the Truth and the will You have for him/her/them. ✝ In the name of the Lord Jesus Christ, and by the power of the word, and the shed blood of Jesus Christ and the Holy Spirit, ✝ I ask you Heavenly Father to bind the evil spirits of pride, ignorance, unforgiveness, gossip, envy, competitiveness, criticism, impatience, resentment, haughtiness, rebellion, stubbornness, deceitfulness, defiance, disobedience, strife, violence, divorce, laziness, accusation, confusion, procrastination, self-hatred, suicide, shame, depression, oppression, rejection, poor self image, anger, schizophrenia, manipulation, anxiety, timidity, jealously, greed, revenge, covetousness, fear, possessiveness, control, division, retaliation, distrust, selfishness, loneliness, isolation, ostracism, lack, paranoia, nervousness, passivity, indecision, doubt, deception, dishonesty, unbelief, withdrawal, betrayal, escape, infirmity, nerve disorder, lung disorder, brain disorder or dysfunction, AIDS, cancer, hypochondria, fatigue, anorexia, bulimia, addictions, gluttony, perfectionism, alcoholism, workaholism, nicotine, self-abuse, sexual addictions, sexual impurities and sexual perversion, seduction, lust, incest, pedophilia, lesbianism, homosexuality, pornography, adultery, masturbation, homophobia, frigidity, impotency, immorality, witchcraft, enticing spirits, deaf, dumb, blind, mute and sleeping spirits, hyperactivity, new-age spirits, occult spirits, religious spirits, anti-Christ spirits, and any other spirits of death and darkness ✝

[List other specific "powers" of darkness that may be at work in the person's life.]

All in the name of the risen Lord Jesus Christ.

✝ I bring in prayer the focus of the Person and work of the Lord Jesus Christ directly upon *[person's name(s)]* to his/her/their strengthening and help. ✝ I bring the mighty power of my Lord's incarnation, crucifixion, resurrection, Ascension, and glorification directly against all forces of darkness seeking to destroy *[person's name(s)]*. ✝ I ask the Holy Spirit to apply all of the mighty work of the Lord Jesus Christ directly against all forces of darkness seeking to destroy *[person's name(s)]*.

✝ I pray, heavenly Father, that You may open *[person's name(s)]* eyes of understanding. ✝ Remove all blindness and spiritual deafness from his/her/their heart(s). ✝ Comfort and still all emotions and thoughts of fear and hesitation.

✝ As a royal priest of God in *[person's name(s)]* life, I plead Your mercy over his/her/their sins of failure and rebellion. ✝ I ask for mercy and forgiveness for the sins of *[person's name(s)]* by which he/she/they has/have grieved You. ✝ I plead the sufficiency of the blood of Christ to meet the full penalty for which his/her/their sins deserve. ✝ I ask you Heavenly Father to claim back the ground of his/her/their life/lives which he/she/they has given to Satan by believing the enemy's deception. ✝ I ask you Heavenly Father to claim all of his/her/their life/lives united together in obedient love and service to the Lord Jesus Christ. ✝ May the Spirit of the living God focus His mighty work upon *[person's name(s)]* to grant him/her/them repentance and to set him/her/them completely free from all that binds him/her/them.

✝ In the name of the Lord Jesus Christ I ask you Heavenly Father to break all of Satan's activity to hold *[person's name(s)]* in blindness and darkness. ✝ I ask you Lord to pull down the strongholds which the kingdom of darkness has formed against *[person's name(s)]* and to smash and break and destroy all those plans formed against *[person's name(s)]* mind, his/her/their will(s), his/her/their emotions, and his/her/their body(s). ✝ Destroy, O Lord, the spiritual blindness and deafness that Satan keeps upon him/her/them. ✝ I invite the Holy Spirit of God to bring the fullness of His power to convict, to bring to repentance, and to lead *[person's name(s)]* into faith in the Lord Jesus Christ, and to bring him/her/them to Your Church, the One, Holy, Catholic and Apostolic Church for the fullness of all Truth. ✝ Father, please break Satan's power to blind *[person's name(s)]* to the truth of God.

✝ In the name of Jesus Christ, I call forth and ask the Holy Spirit to fill *[person's name(s)]* with the gifts of peace, patience, love, joy, charity, humility, forgiveness, kindness, generosity, faithfulness, gentleness, goodness, discipline, relinquishment, freedom from shame, good self image, prosperity, obedience, a sound mind, order, fulfillment in Christ, truth, acceptance of self, acceptance of others, trust, self control, freedom from addictions, freedom of having-to-control, wholeness, wellness, health, and the light and life of the Lord Jesus Christ.

✝ Believing that Your Holy Spirit is leading me, I claim *[person's name(s)]* for You in the name of the Lord Jesus Christ, and I thank You for the answer to my prayer. Grant me the grace to be persistent and faithful in my intercessions for *[person's name(s)]*, that You may be glorified through this deliverance. Amen. ✝

Hedge Prayer for Protection of Others

✝ Trusting in the promise that whatever we ask the Father in Jesus' name He will do, I now approach You Father with confidence in Our Lord's words and in Your infinite power and love for me and for *[person's name(s)]*, and with the intercession of the Blessed Virgin Mary, Mother of God, the Blessed Apostles Peter and Paul, Blessed Archangel Michael, my guardian angel and the guardian angels of *[person's name(s)]*, with all the saints and angels of heaven, and Holy in the power of His blessed Name, as ask you Father to protect *[person's name(s)]* and keep him/her/them from the harassment of the devil and his minions.

✝ Father I ask on behalf of *[person's name(s)]* that You build a hedge of protection around him/her/them, like that which surrounded Job, and to help *[person's name(s)]* to keep that hedge repaired and the gate locked so that the devil and his minions have no access or means to breach the hedge except by your expressed will.

† Father, I know that we are powerless against the spiritual forces of evil and recognize our utter dependence on You and Your power. † Look with mercy upon *[person's name(s)]*. Do not look upon his/her/their sins, O Lord; rather, look at the sufferings of your Beloved Son and see the Victim who's bitter passion and death has reconciled us to You. By the victory of the cross, † protect *[person's name(s)]* from all evil and rebuke any evil spirits who wish to attack, influence, or breach Your hedge of protection in any way. Send them back to Hell and fortify Your Hedge for his protection by the blood of Your Son, Jesus. † Send your Holy Angels to watch over him/her/them and protect him/her/them.

† Father, all of these things I ask in the most holy name of Jesus Christ, Your Son. † Thank you, Father, for hearing my prayer. I love You, I worship You, I thank You and I trust in You. Amen. †

Prayer for a Conversion

† Dear Lord, You took on our human nature, to suffer and die, to win salvation for all of us. Look graciously on those who have drifted away from You and the Faith. Grant them the grace, O Lord, to see how much you love and care for them, so that they may return to Your fold. Grant us the grace, O Lord, to refrain from criticizing them, but by prayer, kindness and example, lead them back to You, and the Church You established for our guidance and care. Amen. †

Prayer to St. Anthony of Padua for a Conversion

† Loving Saint Anthony you always reached out in compassion to those who had lost their faith or never knew it. You were especially concerned because they had no access to the healing words of Jesus found in the Sacrament of Reconciliation and in the nourishing presence of Jesus in the Sacrament of the Eucharist.

(For one who has fallen-away from the Fullness of Truth in the Catholic Church)
† Intercede for (name(s) who has stopped practicing his/her/their faith. Ask Our Lord to reawaken in his/her/their heart(s) a love for our Church and the sacraments, and enkindle in his/her/their heart a sense of forgiveness for the ways he/she/they might have been hurt by members of the Church who fell short of the teaching of Christ.

(For one who has never known the Fullness of Truth in the Catholic Church)
† Intercede for (name(s) who because of the actions of those who came before them know very little if anything of the Truth of our Church. Ask Our Lord to awaken in his/her/their heart(s) a need to search for the complete fullness of Truth that can only be found in the Catholic Church. Pray that he/she/they will develop a hunger and thirst for our Church and the sacraments, and a sense of forgiveness for the ways he/she/they might have been hurt by members of the Church who fell short of the teaching of Christ. Pray that any walls, misconceptions of false teachings that he/she/they may have received are removed and the virtue of humility is fostered to allow for true conversion.

Finally, St. Anthony, help me to respond to my own call to conversion so that I might become an example of someone who has found great peace in the arms of Christ. † May the joy I experience as a Catholic be an invitation to those who are lost to come home again to the Church which we love. Amen. †

Prayer to Defeat the Work of Satan

✝ O Divine Eternal Father, in union with your Divine Son and the Holy Spirit, and through the Immaculate Heart of Mary, I beg You to destroy the Power of your greatest enemy - the evil spirits.

Cast them into the deepest recesses of hell and chain them there forever! Take possession of your Kingdom which You have created and which is rightfully yours.

Heavenly Father, give us the reign of the Sacred Heart of Jesus and the Immaculate Heart of Mary. ✝ I repeat this prayer out of pure love for You with every beat of my heart and with every breath I take. Amen ✝

Prayer to St. Michael

✝ O Holy Michael, the Archangel, defend us in battle; be our safeguard against the wickedness and snares of the devil. May God rebuke him we humbly pray; and do Thou, Prince of the heavenly host, by the power of God cast into hell Satan and all the evil spirits, who wander through the world seeking the ruin of souls. Amen. ✝

St. Gertrude's Guardian Angel Prayer

✝ O most holy angel of God, appointed by God to be my guardian, I give you thanks for all the benefits which you have ever bestowed on me in body and in soul. I praise and glorify you that you condescended to assist me with such patient fidelity, and to defend me against all the assaults of my enemies. Blessed be the hour in which you were assigned me for my guardian, my defender and my patron. In acknowledgement and return for all your loving ministries to me, I offer you the infinitely precious and noble heart of Jesus, and firmly purpose to obey you henceforward, and most faithfully to serve my God. Amen ✝

Offering of the Precious Blood Jesus

✝ "Eternal Father, I offer You the Most Precious Blood of Jesus Christ in atonement for my sins, and in supplication for the holy souls in Purgatory and for the needs of Holy Church."

The Raccolta

Pleading the Blood of Jesus

✝ Father in heaven, may we all be cleansed by the saving Blood of Jesus; may our consciences be purged of dead works. ✝ Scripture says that evil is defeated by the Blood of the Lamb, so we ask that the Blood of Jesus cover all who are in need of protection, all civil, religious and lay leaders, our families, friends, enemies, all those for whom we have promised to pray, and ourselves). (*Name all the people you will be covering in the Blood of Jesus -- then list your intentions in the specific areas below.*)

FOR OUR SALVATION - That none of us would be lost, led astray or deceived. We plead the Precious Blood of Jesus. ✝

FOR OUR SAFETY - That we would all be protected and safe from all harm (*spiritual, mental, physical or violent, satanical harm*). We plead the Precious Blood of Jesus. ✝

FOR OUR MINISTRY - That the areas of ministry God has for us would be fulfilled. We plead the Precious Blood of Jesus. ✝

FOR OUR MARRIAGE - That God would heal the things that are wounded or broken in my marriage and strengthen the good things. We plead the Precious Blood of Jesus. ✝

FOR OUR CHILDREN - That God would protect them from all harm and lead them in His paths. To not stray from the faith and for our sake as parents, to raise them up to know the Lord and to make right our mistakes as parents. We plead the Precious Blood of Jesus. ✝

FOR OUR RELATIONSHIPS - That all of our relationships would be based on good and Godly principles. *(If you need to name anyone, do so.)* We plead the Precious Blood of Jesus. ✝

FOR OUR HEALTH - That we would all be made whole, spiritually, mentally and physically. *(Mention anyone on the list with health problems.)* We plead the Precious Blood of Jesus. ✝

FOR OUR HOMES - That they would be protected from destruction, spiritually, physically, or materially. That they would be havens from the world for us. Places where God's love is shared. *(Also include our churches, schools, places of employment and any public places we may visit.)* We plead the Precious Blood of Jesus. ✝

FOR OUR VEHICLES - That we would be protected in all of our travels *(all modes)*. Safe from accidents or harm that no one may ever be injured through them. We plead the Precious Blood of Jesus. ✝

FOR OUR FINANCES - That God would bless our jobs, businesses, and that our needs would be met *(all bills, financial obligations - state needs)*. We plead the Precious Blood of Jesus. ✝

We mark the borders of our nation and the door posts of our churches, homes, schools and places of employment with the Precious Blood of Jesus. ✝ We thank You, Lord, for shedding Your Blood for us. ✝ May the Water and Blood that came from the side of Jesus create a protecting fountain of grace, one which flows directly from the throne of God to us. Come, Lord, and fill us with Your Holy Spirit. Amen ✝

Prayer of St. Faustina
✝ "O Blood and Water, which gushed forth from the Heart of Jesus as a Fount of Mercy for us, I trust in You."

Closing of Deliverance Prayers
✝ Thank you, Lord Jesus, for awakening my sleeping spirit and bringing me into your light. ✝ Thank you, Lord, for transforming me by the renewing of my mind. ✝ Thank you, Lord, for pouring out your Spirit on me, and revealing your Word to me. ✝ Thank you, Lord, for giving your angels charge over me in all my ways. ✝ Thank you for my faith in you and that from my innermost being shall flow rivers of living water. ✝ Thank you for directing my mind and heart into the love of the Father and the steadfastness of all your ways. ✝ Fill me to overflowing with your life and love, my Lord and King, Jesus Christ. Amen. ✝

Closing of Morning Prayers

Litany of the Saints for Purity

Holy Virgin of Virgins, pray for me.

Saint Joseph most chase, pray for me.

Saint John the Baptist, pray for me.

Saint Peter, pray for me.

Saint John the Evangelist, pray for me.

Saint Paul the Apostle, pray for me.

Pope Saint Gregory the Great, pray for me.

Saint Athanasius of Alexandria pray for me.

Saint John Chrysostom, pray for me.

Saint Dismas, the Good Thief, pray for me.

Saint Mary Magdalen, patroness of penitent sinners, pray for me.

Holy Job, pray for me.

Saint Catherine of Sienna, pray for me.

Saint Alphonsus de Liguori, pray for me.

Saint Francis de Sales, pray for me.

Saint John Baptist Vianney, the Cure d'Ars, pray for me.

Saint Philip of Neri, pray for me.

Saint Ignatius of Loyola, pray for me.

Saint Anthony Mary Claret, pray for me.

Saint Bonaventure, pray for me.

Saint Rose of Lima, pray for me.

Saint Augustine of Hippo, pray for me.

Saint Monica, pray for me.

Saint Patrick, pray for me.

Saint Brighid, pray for me.

Saint Margaret of Cortona, pray for me.

Saint Mary of Egypt, pray for me.

Saint Terese the Little Flower, pray for me.

Saint Padre Pio, pray for me.

Saint Thomas More, pray for me.

Saint Francis de Sales, pray for me.

Saint John Bosco, pray for me.

Saint Faustina Kowalska, Apostle of Divine Mercy, pray for me.

All ye holy virgins, who follow the Divine Lamb withersoever he goeth, be ever watchful over me a sinner, lest I should fail in thought, in word, or in deed, and lest at any time I should depart from the most chaste Heart of Jesus, pray for me.

All you holy angels and saints, pray for me.

Most Holy Trinity, One God in Three Persons, have mercy on me.

Jesus, Mary and Joseph, I offer you my heart and soul.

Prayer of Saint Thomas Aquinas for Angelic Warfare Confraternity
It is recommended that all True Knights enroll in the Angelic Warfare Confraternity and wear the Cord of Saint Thomas Aquinas for Purity. (See Appendix VIII, Page 92)

DEAR JESUS, I know that every perfect gift and especially that of chastity depends on the power of your Providence. Without you, a mere creature can do nothing. Therefore, I beg you to defend by your grace the chastity and purity of my body and soul. And if I have ever sensed anything that can stain my chastity and purity, blot it out, Supreme Lord of my powers, that I may advance with a pure heart in your love and service, offering myself on the most pure altar of your divinity all the days of my life. Amen.

Prayer to Saint Thomas Aquinas for Purity
Chosen Lily of innocence, pure St. Thomas, who kept chaste the robe of baptism, and became an angel, I implore you to commend me to Jesus, the Immaculate Lamb, and to Mary, Queen of Virgins, Gentle protector of my purity, ask them that I who wear the holy sign of your victory of the flesh may also share your purity and that after imitating you on earth, I may at last come to be crowned with you among the angels. Amen.

Prayer to Saint Benedict
Glorious Saint Benedict, sublime model of virtue, pure vessel of God's grace! Behold me humbly kneeling at your feet. I implore you in your loving kindness to pray for me before the throne of God. To you I have recourse in the dangers that daily surround me. Shield me against my selfishness and my indifference to God and to my neighbor. Inspire me to imitate you in all things. May your blessing be with me always, so that I may see and serve Christ in others and work for His kingdom.

Graciously obtain for me from God those favors and graces which I need so much in the trials, miseries and afflictions of life. Your heart was always full of love, compassion and mercy toward those who were afflicted or troubled in any way. You never dismissed without consolation and assistance anyone who had recourse to you. I therefore invoke your powerful intercession, confident in the hope that you will hear my prayers and obtain for me the special grace and favor I earnestly implore. *{mention your petition}*

Help me, great Saint Benedict, to live and die as a faithful child of God, to run in the sweetness of His loving will, and to attain the eternal happiness of heaven. Amen.

Daily St. Philomena Cord Prayer
It is recommended that all True Knights wear the Cord of St. Philomena for her intercession for purity. (See Appendix VIII, Page 95)
O St. Philomena, glorious Martyr of Faith and Purity, grant me the same strength of mind that enabled you to resist the most terrible assaults; grant me your ardent love for Jesus Christ which the most atrocious tortures were not able to extinguish, so that, by wearing your Cord and imitating you on earth, I will be incoronated with you in heaven. Amen.

Prayer to Saint Maria Goretti, Martyr for Purity
O Saint Maria Goretti, who, strengthened by God's grace, did not hesitate, even at the age of eleven, to shed your blood and sacrifice life itself to defend your virginal purity, deign to look graciously on the unhappy human race which has strayed far from the path of eternal salvation. Teach us all, and especially our youth, the courage and promptness to flee for love of Jesus, anything that could offend Him or stain our souls with sin. Obtain for us from Our Lord and Our Lady Immaculate, victory in temptation, comfort in the sorrows of life, and the grace which we earnestly beg of thee, purity in soul and body, so that we may one day enjoy with thee the imperishable glory of heaven. Amen.

Closing of Morning Prayers   *23*

Prayer to Pope John Paul the Great

John Paul, Karol Wojtyla, you were a faithful servant of God on Earth. Risking your life to become a priest, you tirelessly served the Master. Pray that I too may have the courage to do so.

You had great devotion to Our Lady, taking as your motto "Totus Tuus - Totally Yours" and calling her corredemptrix in your audiences. Pray that I may have such devotion to our mother.

When an attempt on your life was made, you forgave the man who tried to take your life. Pray that I may be as forgiving as you.

Your book "Love and Responsibility" is a theological masterpiece unlike any other. Pray that by God's grace I may begin to understand God as you did.

You traveled all over the world, preaching the Gospel to all people. Pray that I may have the courage to speak the Good News to those around me.

As Supreme Pontiff, you raised to the altar more saints than any other pope. Pray that I may learn from these examples of holiness and grow in my own sanctity.

John Paul, we, the people of the Church you sheparded in Christ's name, ask you to pray for us to Him, He who is our savior and brother, that we may...*(name your need)* Amen.

Prayer for Purity

O my God, thou who hast given me a body to keep pure and clean and healthy for thy service and my eternal happiness, forgive me for all my unfaithfulness in this great responsibility. Forgive me for every mean use which I have made of thy gifts in thought, word or deed since my rebirth as thine own adopted child in Baptism and my registration as a soldier of Jesus on the day of my Confirmation.

Create in me a clean heart, O God, and give me a steadfast will that I may be a strength to others around me. Teach me to reverence my body and the bodies of my fellow creatures. Help me to see the glory of perfect manhood in Jesus Christ and of perfect womanhood in Mary Immaculate. Inspire me with such love for the ideals for which our Savior lived and died, that all my passions and energies will be caught up into the enthusiasm of His service and evil things will lose their power. May my body be the servant of my soul, and may both body and soul be Thy servants, through Christ, our Lord. Amen.

We fly to your Patronage (Sub tuum praesidium)

We fly to your patronage, O holy Mother of God; despise not our petitions in our necessities, but deliver us always from all dangers, O glorious and blessed Virgin. *(Partial Indulgence)*

Actiones nostras

Direct, we beg you, O Lord, our actions by your holy inspirations, and carry them on by your gracious assistance, that every prayer and work of ours may begin always with you, and through you be happily ended. Amen.   *(Partial Indulgence)*

May the Lord Bless and Keep us from temptation. Amen.

Mid-Morning Prayers

Liturgy of the Hours - *Mid-Morning Prayer*

Works of Mercy Prayer

Matthew 25:31-46 (The Last Judgement)

[31]"When the son of man comes in his glory, and all the angels with him, then he will sit on his glorious throne. [32]Before him will be gathered all nations, and he will separate them one from another as a shepherd separates his sheep from the goats, [33]and he will place the sheep at his right hand, but the goats at the left. [34]Then the King will say to those at his right hand, 'Come O blessed of my father, inherit the kingdom prepared for you from the foundation of the word; [35]for I was hungry and you gave me food, I was thirsty and you gave me drink, I was a stranger and you welcomed me, [36]I was naked and you clothed me, I was sick and you visited me, I was in prison and you came to me.' [37]Then the righteous will answer him, 'Lord when did we see thee hungry and feed thee, or thirsty and give thee drink? [38]And when did we see thee a stranger and welcome thee, or naked and clothe thee? [39]And when did we see thee sick or in prison and visit thee? [40]And the King will answer them, 'Truly, I say to you, as you did it to one of the least of these my brethren, you did it to me.' [41]Then he will say to those at his left hand, 'Depart from me, you cursed, into the eternal fire prepared for the devil and his angels; [42]for I was hungry and you gave me no food, I was thirsty and you gave me no drink, [43]I was a stranger and you did not welcome me, naked and you did not clothe me, sick and in prison and you did not visit me.' [44]Then they will also answer, 'Lord, when did we see thee hungry or thirsty or a stranger or naked or sick or in prison, and did not minister to thee?' [45]Then he will answer them, 'Truly, I say to you, as you did it not to one of the least of these, you did it not to me.' [46]And they will go away to eternal punishment, but the righteous into eternal life."

Corporal & Spiritual Works of Mercy

Opening Prayer:

Jesus Christ taught that man not only receives and experiences the mercy of God, but that he is also called to practice mercy towards others. *"Blessed are the merciful, for they shall obtain mercy"* (Mt 5:7). The Church sees in these words a call to action and she tries to practice mercy.

Corporal

For the grace to: Feed the hungry, Jesus, I trust in You.
For the grace to: Give drink to the thirsty, Jesus, I trust in You.
For the grace to: Clothe the naked, Jesus, I trust in You.
For the grace to: Shelter the homeless, Jesus, I trust in You.
For the grace to: Comfort the imprisoned, Jesus, I trust in You.
For the grace to: Visit the sick, Jesus, I trust in You.
For the grace to: Bury the dead, Jesus, I trust in You.

Spiritual

For the grace to: Admonish sinners, Jesus, I trust in You.
For the grace to: Instruct the ignorant, Jesus, I trust in You.
For the grace to: Counsel the doubtful, Jesus, I trust in You.
For the grace to: Comfort the sorrowful, Jesus, I trust in You.
For the grace to: Bear wrongs patiently, Jesus, I trust in You.

For the grace to: Forgive all injuries, Jesus, I trust in You.
For the grace to: Pray for the living and the dead, Jesus, I trust in You.
Glory Be to the Father...

Prayer of Saint Francis of Assisi

Lord, Make me an instrument of your peace. Where there is hatred, let me sow love; where there is injury, pardon; where there is doubt, faith; where there is darkness, light; and where there is sadness, joy. O Divine Master, grant that I may not so much seek to be consoled as to console; to be understood as to understand; to be loved as to love; for it is in giving that we receive; it is in pardoning that we are pardoned; and it is in dying that we are born to eternal life.

Litany of Humility

O Jesus, meek and humble of heart,	Hear me.
From the desire of being esteemed,	Deliver me, O Jesus.
From the desire of being loved,	Deliver me, O Jesus.
From the desire of being extolled,	Deliver me, O Jesus.
From the desire of being honored,	Deliver me, O Jesus.
From the desire of being praised,	Deliver me, O Jesus.
From the desire of being preferred to others,	Deliver me, O Jesus.
From the desire of being consulted,	Deliver me, O Jesus.
From the desire of being approved,	Deliver me, O Jesus.
From the fear of being humiliated,	Deliver me, O Jesus.
From the fear of being despised,	Deliver me, O Jesus.
From the fear of suffering rebukes,	Deliver me, O Jesus.
From the fear of being calumniated,	Deliver me, O Jesus.
From the fear of being forgotten,	Deliver me, O Jesus.
From the fear of being ridiculed,	Deliver me, O Jesus.
From the fear of being wronged,	Deliver me, O Jesus.
From the fear of being suspected,	Deliver me, O Jesus.

That others may be loved more than I, Jesus, grant me the grace to desire it.
That others may be esteemed more than I, Jesus, grant me the grace to desire it. That, in the opinion of the world, others may increase and I may decrease,
Jesus, grant me the grace to desire it.

That others may be chosen and I set aside, Jesus, grant me the grace to desire it.
That others may be praised and I go unnoticed, Jesus, grant me the grace to desire it.
That others may be preferred to me in everything, Jesus, grant me the grace to desire it.
That others may become holier than I, provided that I may become as holy as I should, Jesus, grant me the grace to desire it.

Charity

"Charity is patient, is kind; charity does not envy, is not pretentious, is not puffed up, is not ambitious, is not self-seeking, is not provoked; thinks no evil, does not rejoice over wickedness, but rejoices with the truth, bears with all things, believes all things, hopes all things, endures all things. (1 Cor. 13:4-7).

Midday Prayers

Liturgy of the Hours - *Daytime Prayer*

The Angelus
The Angelus is traditionally recited morning (6:00 a.m.), noon and evening (6:00 p.m.) throughout the year except during Paschal time, when the Regina Coeli is recited instead.

V. The Angel of the Lord declared unto Mary.
R. And she conceived of the Holy Spirit.
Hail Mary, etc.

V. Behold the handmaid of the Lord.
R. Be it done unto me according to thy word.
Hail Mary, etc.

V. And the Word was made Flesh.
R. And dwelt among us.
Hail Mary, etc.

V. Pray for us, O holy Mother of God.
R. That we may be made worthy of the promises of Christ.

Let us pray: Pour forth, we beseech Thee, O Lord, Thy grace into our hearts, that we to whom the Incarnation of Christ Thy Son was made known by the message of an angel, may by His Passion and Cross be brought to the glory of His Resurrection. Through the same Christ Our Lord. Amen.

Regina Coeli
This prayer, which dates from the twelfth century, is substituted for the Angelus during Easter Season.

Queen of Heaven rejoice, alleluia: For He whom you merited to bear, alleluia, Has risen as He said, alleluia. Pray for us to God, alleluia.

V. Rejoice and be glad, O Virgin Mary, alleluia.
R. Because the Lord is truly risen, alleluia.

Let us pray: O God, who by the Resurrection of Thy Son, our Lord Jesus Christ, granted joy to the whole world: grant we beseech Thee, that through the intercession of the Virgin Mary, His Mother, we may lay hold of the joys of eternal life. Through the same Christ our Lord. R. Amen.

Prayer for My Heart
Jesus, meek and humble of heart, make my heart like Your heart.
Mary, Mother of God, show yourself a mother to me.
Saint Joseph, protector of the Holy Family, protect me in all dangers.
Jesus, Mary and Joseph, I give you my heart and my soul.

Prayers for Confession

Confession is very important and indispensable in rooting out persistent sins and addictions. If you are faced with exceptionally strong temptations go to confession as often as necessary. At the very least go once a month. It's advisable to go bi-weekly. Be sure to confess even your venial sins.

Guide for Examination of Conscience for Confession of Sins

6 STEPS FOR A GOOD CONFESSION
1. Examine your conscience - what sins have you committed since your last good confession.
2. Be sincerely sorry for your sins.
3. Confess your sins to the priest.
4. Make certain that you confess all your mortal sins and the number of them.
5. After your confession, do the penance the priest gives to you.
6. Pray daily for the strength to avoid the occasion of sin, especially for those sins you were just absolved from.

FIRST COMMANDMENT
"I am the Lord your God. You shall not have strange gods before Me." (Ex 20:2,3)
• Did I doubt or deny that God exists?
• Did I refuse to believe what God as revealed to us?
• Did I believe in fortune telling, horoscopes, dreams, the occult, good-luck charms, tarot cards, palmistry, Ouija boards, seances, reincarnation?
• Did I deny that I was Catholic?
• Did I leave the Catholic Faith?
• Did I give time to God each day in prayer?
• Did I love God with my whole heart?
• Did I despair of or presume on God's mercy?
• Did I have false gods in my life that I gave greater attention to than God, like money, profession, drugs, TV, fame, pleasure, property, etc.?

SECOND COMMANDMENT
"You shall not take the Name of the Lord your God in vain." (Ex 20:7)
• Did I blaspheme or insult God?
• Did I take God's name carelessly or uselessly?
• Did I curse, or break an oath or vow?
• Did I get angry with God?

THIRD COMMANDMENT
"Remember that you keep holy the Sabbath Day." (Ex 20:8)
• Did I miss Mass Sunday or a Holy Day of Obligation through my own fault?
• Did I come to Mass on time? Leave early?
• Did I do work on Sunday that was not necessary?
• Did I set aside Sunday as a day of rest and a family day?
• Did I show reverence in the presence of Jesus in the Most Blessed Sacrament?

FOURTH COMMANDMENT
"Honor your father and your mother." (Ex 20:12)
• Did I disobey or disrespect my parents or legitimate superiors?
• Did I neglect my duties to my husband, wife, children or parents?
• Did I neglect to give good religious example to my family?
• Did I fail to actively take an interest in the religious education and formation of my children?
• Did I fail to educate myself on the true teachings of the Church?
• Did I give scandal by what I said or did, especially to the young?
• Did I cause anyone to leave the faith?
• Did I cause tension and fights in my family?
• Did I care for my aged and infirm relatives?
• Did I give a full day's work for a full day's pay?
• Did I give a fair wage to my employees?

FIFTH COMMANDMENT
"You shall not kill." (Ex 20:13)
• Did I kill or physically injure anyone?

- Did I have an abortion, or advise someone else to have an abortion? (One who procures and abortion is automatically excommunicated, as is anyone who is involved in an abortion, Canon 1398. The excommunication will be lifted in the Sacrament of Reconciliation.)
- Did I use or cause my spouse to use birth control pills (whether or not realizing that birth control pills do abort the fetus if and when conceived)?
- Did I attempt suicide?
- Did I take part in or approve of "mercy killing" (euthanasia)?
- Did I get angry, impatient, envious, unkind, proud, revengeful, jealous, hateful toward another, lazy?
- Did I give bad example by drug abuse, drinking alcohol to excess, fighting, quarreling?
- Did I abuse my children?

SIXTH COMMANDMENT

"You shall not commit adultery." (Ex 20:14) *"You shall not covet your neighbor's wife."* (Ex 20:17)
Note: In the area of deliberate sexual sins listed below, all are mortal sins if there is sufficient reflection and full consent of the will. *"No fornicators, idolaters, or adulterers, no sodomites,... will inherit the kingdom of God."* (1 Cor 6:9-10) *"Anyone who looks lustfully at a woman has already committed adultery with her in his thoughts."* (Mt 5:28)
- Did I willfully entertain impure thoughts or desires?
- Did I use impure or suggestive words? Tell impure stories? Listen to them?
- Did I deliberately look at impure TV, videos, plays, pictures or movies? Or deliberately read impure materials?
- Did I commit impure acts by myself (masturbation)?
- Did I commit impure acts with another - fornication (premarital sex), adultery (sex with a married person)?
- Did I practice artificial birth control (by pills, device, withdrawal)?
- Did I marry or advise anyone to marry outside the Church?
- Did I avoid the occasions of impurity?
- Did I try to control my thoughts?
- Did I engage in homosexual activity?
- Did I respect all members of the opposite sex, or have I thought of other people as objects?
- Did I or my spouse have sterilization done?
- Did I abuse my marriage rights?

SEVENTH & TENTH COMMANDMENTS

"You shall not steal." (Ex 20:15) *"You shall not covet your neighbor's goods."* (Ex 20:17)
- Did I steal, cheat, help or encourage others to steal or keep stolen goods? Have I made restitution for stolen goods?
- Did I fulfill my contracts; give or accept bribes; pay my bills; rashly gamble or speculate; deprive my family of the necessities of life?
- Did I waste time at work, school or at home?
- Did I envy other people's families or possessions?
- Did I make material possessions the purpose of my life?

EIGHTH COMMANDMENT

"You shall not bear false witness against your neighbor." (Ex 20:16)
- Did I lie?
- Did I deliberately deceive others, or injure others by lies?
- Did I commit perjury?
- Did I gossip or reveal others' faults or sins?
- Did I fail to keep secret what should be confidential?

OTHER SINS

- Did I fast on Ash Wednesday and Good Friday?
- Did I eat meat on the Fridays of Lent or Ash Wednesday?
- Did I fail to receive Holy Communion during Eastertime?
- Did I go to Holy Communion in a state of mortal sin? Without fasting (water and medicine permitted) for one hour from food and drink?
- Did I make a bad confession?
- Did I fail to contribute to the support of the Church?

"Whoever eats the bread and drinks the cup of the Lord unworthily sins against the Body and Blood of the Lord. ... He who eats and drinks without recognizing the Body eats and drinks judgement on himself." (1 Cor 11:27-29)

So, to receive Holy Communion while in the state of mortal sin (having committed a mortal sin which has not been confessed and forgiven in the Sacrament of Confession) is itself a mortal sin - **a mortal sin of sacrilege.**

God is Merciful!

"O God, be merciful to me, a sinner." (Lk 18:13)

"Whose sins you shall forgive, they are forgiven..." (Jn 20:23)

"Though your sins be like scarlet, they shall become white as snow. Though they be red like crimson, they shall become white as wool." (Is 1:18)

"If we confess our sins, He who is upright can be depended upon to forgive sins, and to cleanse us from every wrong." (1 Jn 1:9)

"Father, forgive them; they do not know what they are doing." (Lk 23:24)

"Forgive us our sins, for we too forgive all who do us wrong." (Lk 11:4)

Prayer Asking God To Reveal Forgotten Sins

Dear Heavenly Father. I ask You to reveal to my mind all unconfessed sins in my life so that I may bring these sins to You to be wash clean from my soul so that Satan may not have an opportunity to attack me through these sins. Amen.

Prayer Of Confession And Taking Back Ground From Satan

[This prayer may be used to confess venial sins, or for mortal sins until such time as confession is made in the Sacrament of Reconciliation. Catholic must bring all mortal sins to the Sacrament of Confession.]

Lord, I confess that I have sinned by _____. I ask Your forgiveness, and I renounce _____ and take back the ground in my life gained by Satan through his sin. I reclaim this ground and my life for Christ. Amen.

Act of Contrition
O my God, I am heartily sorry for having offended Thee,
and I detest all of my sins because of Your just punishment,
but most of all, because they offend Thee, my God,
who are all good and deserving of all my love.
I firmly resolve, with the help of Thy grace,
to sin no more and to avoid the near occasion of sin.
Amen.

Prayer After Confession To Re-Claim Ground Taken By Satan

[This prayer, however, may be substituted as the regular prayer of "reclaiming Ground" after Confession]

Dear Heavenly Father, strengthened by the intercession of the Immaculate Virgin Mary, Mother of God, of Blessed Michael the Archangel, of the Blessed Apostles Peter and Paul, and all the Saints and Angels in Heaven, and powerful in the holy authority if His Name, I cancel all ground that evil spirits have gained through my willful involvement in sin. I reclaim that ground and my life for Christ. Amen.

𝔓𝔯𝔞𝔶𝔢𝔯𝔰 𝔣𝔬𝔯 𝔗𝔥𝔢 𝔥𝔬𝔩𝔶 𝔐𝔞𝔰𝔰

The Holy Sacrifice of the Mass, the Holy Eucharist, the Body, Blood, Soul and Divinity is the most powerful weapon we have against addictions. If possible, participate daily.

Chaplet of St. Michael - *Before Mass*

O God, come to my assistance. O Lord, make haste to help me. Glory be to the Father, etc.

1. By the intercession of St. Michael and the celestial Choir of Seraphim may the Lord make us worthy to burn with the fire of perfect charity. Amen.
One Our Father and three Hail Marys

2. By the intercession of St. Michael and the celestial Choir of Cherubim may the Lord grant us the grace to leave the ways of sin and run in the paths of Christian perfection. Amen.
One Our Father and three Hail Marys

3. By the intercession of St. Michael and the celestial Choir of Thrones may the Lord infuse into our hearts a true and sincere spirit of humility. Amen.
One Our Father and three Hail Marys

4. By the intercession of St. Michael and the celestial Choir of Dominions may the Lord give us grace to govern our senses and overcome any unruly passions. Amen.
One Our Father and three Hail Marys

5. By the intercession of St. Michael and the celestial Choir of Powers may the Lord protect our souls against the snares and temptations of the devil. Amen.
One Our Father and three Hail Marys

6. By the intercession of St. Michael and the celestial Choir of Virtues may the Lord preserve us from evil and falling into temptation. Amen.
One Our Father and three Hail Marys

7. By the intercession of St. Michael and the celestial Choir of Principalities may God fill our souls with a true spirit of obedience. Amen.
One Our Father and three Hail Marys

8. By the intercession of St. Michael and the celestial Choir of Archangels may the Lord give us perseverance in faith and in all good works in order that we may attain the glory of Heaven. Amen.
One Our Father and three Hail Marys

9. By the intercession of St. Michael and the celestial Choir of Angels may the Lord grant us to be protected by them in this mortal life and conducted in the life to come to Heaven. Amen.
One Our Father and three Hail Marys

Say one Our Father in honor of each of the following leading Angels:
St. Michael, St. Gabriel, St. Raphael and our Guardian Angel.

Concluding prayers:
O glorious prince St. Michael, chief and commander of the heavenly hosts, guardian of souls, vanquisher of rebel spirits, servant in the house of the Divine King and our admirable conductor, you who shine with excellence and superhuman virtue deliver us from all evil, who turn to you with confidence and enable us by your gracious protection to serve God more and more faithfully every day.

Pray for us, O glorious St. Michael, Prince of the Church of Jesus Christ, that we may be made worthy of His promises.

Almighty and Everlasting God, Who, by a prodigy of goodness and a merciful desire for the salvation of all men, has appointed the most glorious Archangel St. Michael Prince of Your Church, make us worthy, we ask You, to be delivered from all our enemies, that none of them may harass us at the hour of death, but that we may be conducted by him into Your Presence. This we ask through the merits of Jesus Christ Our Lord. Amen.

Short prayer of Consecration before the Mass

Jesus and Mary, I love You. I give myself to You. I consecrate my heart to Your Hearts. Dear Holy Spirit, enlighten and strengthen me. I give You myself.

Prayer Before the Holy Sacrifice of the Mass

Let me be a holy sacrifice and unite with God in the sacrament of His greatest love. I want to be one in Him in this act of love, where He gives Himself to me and I give myself as a sacrifice to Him. Let me be a holy sacrifice as I become one with Him in this my act of greatest love to Him.

Let me unite with Him more, that I may more deeply love Him. May I help make reparation to His adorable Heart and the heart of His Mother, Mary. With greatest love, I offer myself to You and pray that You will accept my sacrifice of greatest love. I give myself to You and unite in Your gift of Yourself to me. Come and possess my soul.

Cleanse me, strengthen me, heal me. Dear Holy Spirit act in the heart of Mary to make me more and more like Jesus.

Father, I offer this my sacrifice, myself united to Jesus in the Holy Spirit to You. Help me to love God more deeply in this act of my greatest love.

Give me the grace to grow in my knowledge, love and service of You and for this to be my greatest participation in the Mass. Give me the greatest graces to love You so deeply in this Mass, You who are so worthy of my love.

The Chaplet of the Divine Mercy - After Receiving Eucharist

To be recited on the beads of the Rosary.
In the name of the Father, and of the Son, and of the Holy Spirit. Amen.

Our Father, Hail Mary, Apostles' Creed.

On the Our Father beads, say the following:

Eternal Father, I offer You the Body and Blood, Soul and Divinity of Your dearly beloved Son, Our Lord Jesus Christ, in atonement for our sins and those of the whole world.

On the Hail Mary beads, say the following:

For the sake of His sorrowful Passion, have mercy on us and on the whole world.

In conclusion, say three times:

Holy God, Holy Mighty One, Holy Immortal One, have mercy on us and on the whole world.

In the name of the Father, and of the Son, and of the Holy Spirit. Amen.

Anima Christi
[Pray this after receiving the Holy Eucharist]
Soul of Christ, sanctify me.
Body of Christ, save me.
Blood of Christ, inebriate me.
Water from the side of Christ, wash me.
Passion of Christ, strengthen me.
O good Jesus, hear me.
Within Thy wounds hide me.
Suffer me not to be separated from Thee.
From the malignant enemy, defend me.
In the hour of my death, call me.
And bid me come to Thee.
That with Thy saints I may praise Thee.
Forever and ever. Amen
An indulgence of 300 days. An indulgence of 7 years, if recited after Holy Communion.
-St. Ignatius Loyola

The Spiritual Communion

If you cannot participate in The Holy Sacrifice of the Mass, then make a Spiritual Communion daily as a very powerful substitute. However, this is not a replacement for Mass.

"O Jesus I turn toward the holy tabernacle where You live hidden for love of me. I love you, O my God. I cannot receive you in Holy Communion. Come nevertheless and visit me with Your grace. Come spiritually into my heart. Purify it. Sanctify it. Render it like unto Your own. Amen."

Lord, I am not worthy that thou shouldst enter under my roof, but only say the word and my soul shall be healed.

Prayer to One's Guardian Angel When Unable to Assist at Mass for Spiritual Communion

Go, my Angel Guardian dear, To Church for me, the Mass to hear. Go, kneel devoutly at my place And treasure for me every grace. At the Offertory time Please offer me to God Divine. All I have and all I am, Present it with the Precious Lamb. Adore for me the great Oblation. Pray for all I hold most dear Be they far or be they near. Remember too, my own dear dead For whom Christ's Precious Blood was shed. And at Communion bring to me Christ's flesh and blood, my food to be. To give me strength and holy grace, a pledge to see Him face to face and when the Holy Mass is done, then with His blessing, come back home.

PRAYER OF SAINT THOMAS AQUINAS
THANKSGIVING AFTER MASS

Lord, Father all-powerful and ever-living God, I thank You, for even though I am a sinner, your unprofitable servant, not because of my worth but in the kindness of your mercy, You have fed me with the Precious Body & Blood of Your Son, our Lord Jesus Christ. I pray that this Holy Communion may not bring me condemnation and punishment but forgiveness and salvation. May it be a helmet of faith and a shield of good will. May it purify me from evil ways and put an end to my evil passions. May it bring me charity and patience, humility and obedience, and growth in the power to do good. May it be my strong defense against all my enemies, visible and invisible, and the perfect calming of all me evil impulses, bodily and spiritual. May it unite me more closely to you, the One true God, and lead me safely through death to everlasting happiness with You. And I pray that You will lead me, a sinner, to the banquet where you, with Your Son and holy Spirit, are true and perfect light, total fulfillment, everlasting joy, gladness without end, and perfect happiness to your saints, grant this through Christ our Lord, AMEN.

Prayer of Adoration for the Year of the Eucharist

Almighty God, We pray especially in this time that human weakness may come to pose less of an obstacle to the action of the Most Holy Sacrament of the Eucharist, and that with all distortion set aside and every reprobated practice removed, through the intercession of the Blessed Virgin Mary, the "Woman of the Eucharist", the saving presence of Christ in the Sacrament of his Body and Blood may shine brightly upon all people. Let all Christ's faithful participate in the Most Holy Eucharist as fully, consciously and actively as they can, honouring it lovingly by their devotion and the manner of their life. Inspire all Bishops, Priests and Deacons, in the exercise of the sacred ministry, to examine their consciences as regards the authenticity and fidelity of the actions they have performed in the name of Christ and the Church in the celebration of the Sacred Liturgy. We ask this through Christ our Lord. Amen.

Mid-Afternoon Prayers

Liturgy of the Hours - *Mid-Afternoon Prayer*

Most Sweet Jesus -- Act of Reparation

Most sweet Jesus, whose overflowing charity for men is requited by so much forgetfulness, negligence and contempt, behold us prostrate before you, eager to repair by a special act of homage the cruel indifference and injuries to which your loving Heart is everywhere subject.

Mindful, alas! that we ourselves have had a share in such great indignities, which we now deplore from the depths of our hearts, we humbly ask your pardon and declare our readiness to atone by voluntary expiation, not only for our own personal offenses, but also for the sins of those, who, straying far from the path of salvation, refuse in their obstinate infidelity to follow you, their Shepherd and Leader, or, renouncing the promises of their baptism, have cast off the sweet yoke of your law.

We are now resolved to expiate each and every deplorable outrage committed against you; we are now determined to make amends for the manifold offenses against Christian modesty in unbecoming dress and behavior, for all the foul seductions laid to ensnare the feet of the innocent, for the frequent violations of Sundays and holy-days, and the shocking blasphemies uttered against you and your Saints. We wish also to make amends for the insults to which your Vicar on earth and your priests are subjected, for the profanation, by conscious neglect or terrible acts of sacrilege, of the very Sacrament of your divine love, and lastly for the public crimes of nations who resist the rights and teaching authority of the Church which you have founded.

Would that we were able to wash away such abominations with our blood. We now offer, in reparation for these violations of your divine honor, the satisfaction you once made to your Eternal Father on the cross and which you continue to renew daily on our altars; we offer it in union with the acts of atonement of your Virgin Mother and all the Saints and of the pious faithful on earth; and we sincerely promise to make recompense, as far as we can with the help of your grace, for all neglect of your great love and for the sins we and others have committed in the past. Henceforth, we will live a life of unswerving faith, of purity of conduct, of perfect observance of the precepts of the Gospel and especially that of charity. We promise to the best of our power to prevent others from offending you and to bring as many as possible to follow you.

O loving Jesus, through the intercession of the Blessed Virgin Mother, our model in reparation, deign to receive the voluntary offering we make of this act of expiation; and by the crowning gift of perseverance keep us faithful unto death in our duty and the allegiance we owe to you, so that we may all one day come to that happy home, where with the Father and the Holy Spirit you live and reign, God, forever and ever. Amen.

𝕰𝖛𝖊𝖓𝖎𝖓𝖌 𝕻𝖗𝖆𝖞𝖊𝖗𝖘

Liturgy of the Hours - *Evening Prayer*

Pray the Family Rosary

Dear Mother, we give you all our worries, fears, frustrations, anxieties, hopes and joys and in exchange please give us yours. It is with great joy that we offer this rosary up for your intentions, we ask it for the greater Glory of God, for your own honor and for the good of souls, my own and especially for those most in need. We pray that you add our rosary to all rosaries being said thus forming one great prayer. Amen.

The Angelus

The Angelus is traditionally recited morning (6:00 a.m.), noon and evening (6:00 p.m.) throughout the year except during Paschal time, when the Regina Coeli is recited instead.

V. The Angel of the Lord declared unto Mary.
R. And she conceived of the Holy Spirit.
Hail Mary, etc.

V. Behold the handmaid of the Lord.
R. Be it done unto me according to thy word.
Hail Mary, etc.

V. And the Word was made Flesh.
R. And dwelt among us.
Hail Mary, etc.

V. Pray for us, O holy Mother of God.
R. That we may be made worthy of the promises of Christ.

Let us pray: Pour forth, we beseech Thee, O Lord, Thy grace into our hearts, that we to whom the Incarnation of Christ Thy Son was made known by the message of an angel, may by His Passion and Cross be brought to the glory of His Resurrection. Through the same Christ Our Lord. Amen.

Regina Coeli

This prayer, which dates from the twelfth century, is substituted for the Angelus during Easter Season.

Queen of Heaven rejoice, alleluia: For He whom you merited to bear, alleluia, Has risen as He said, alleluia. Pray for us to God, alleluia.

V. Rejoice and be glad, O Virgin Mary, alleluia.
R. Because the Lord is truly risen, alleluia.

Let us pray: O God, who by the Resurrection of Thy Son, our Lord Jesus Christ, granted joy to the whole world: grant we beseech Thee, that through the intercession of the Virgin Mary, His Mother, we may lay hold of the joys of eternal life. Through the same Christ our Lord. R. Amen.

Night Prayers

Liturgy of the Hours - *Night Prayer*

Nightly Examination of Conscience

Before applying the particular examen to my own spiritual life, it is well to first ask myself, "What are the virtues that I know from experience I most need to develop?"

We can fail in the practice of these virtues either by commission, omission, or by tepidity, in not acting as generously as we might in responding to the grace we have received from God.

Progress or Failures in FAITH

1. Do I make an honest effort to grow in the virtue of faith by daily mental prayer on the mysteries of the faith as revealed in the life of Jesus Christ?
2. Do I make at least a short act of faith every day?
3. Do I pray daily for an increase of faith?
4. Do I ever tempt God by relying on my own strength to cope with the trials in my life?
5. Do I unnecessarily read or listen to those who oppose or belittle what I know are truths of my Catholic faith?
6. What have I done today to externally profess my faith?
7. Have I allowed human respect to keep me from giving expression to my faith?
8. Do I make a serious effort to resolve difficulties that may arise about my faith?
9. Do I ever defend my faith, prudently and charitably, when someone says something contrary to what I know is to be believed?
10. Have I helped someone overcome a difficulty against the faith?

Progress or Failures in HOPE

1. Do I immediately say a short prayer when I find myself getting discouraged?
2. Do I daily say a short act of hope?
3. Do I dwell on my worries instead of dismissing them from my mind?
4. Do I fail in the virtue of hope by my attachment to the things of this world?
5. Do I try to see God's providence in everything that "happens" in my life?
6. Do I try to see everything from the viewpoint of eternity?
7. Am I confident that, with God's grace, I will be saved?
8. Do I allow myself to worry about my past life and thus weaken my hope in God's mercy?
9. Do I try to combine every fully deliberate action with at least a momentary prayer for divine help?
10. How often today have I complained, even internally?

Progress or Failures in CHARITY

1. Have I told God today that I love Him?
2. Do I tell Jesus that I love Him with my whole heart?
3. Do I take the occasion to tell God that I love Him whenever I experience something I naturally dislike?
4. Have I capitalized on the difficulties today to tell God that I love Him just because He sent me the trial or misunderstanding?
5. Do I see God's love for me in allowing me to prove my love for Him in the crosses He sent me today?
6. Have I seen God's grace to prove my love for Him in every person whom I met today?
7. Have I failed in charity by speaking unkindly about others? ..
8. Have I dwelt on what I considered someone's unkindness toward me today?
9. Is there someone that I consciously avoid because I dislike the person?
10. Did I try to carry on a conversation today with someone who is difficult to talk to?
11. Have I been stubborn in asserting my own will?
12. How thoughtful have I been today in doing some small favor for someone?
13. Have I allowed my mood to prevent me from being thoughtful of others today?

14. Am I given to dwelling on other people's weaknesses or faults?
15. Have I been cheerful today in my dealings with others?
16. Do I control my uncharitable thoughts as soon as they arise in my mind?
17. Did I pray for others today?
18. Have I written any letters today?
19. Have I controlled my emotions when someone irritated me?
20. Have I performed any sacrifice today for someone?

Act of Perfect Contrition

O my God, I am heartily sorry and beg pardon for all my sins, not so much because these sins bring suffering and Hell to me, but because they have crucified my loving Savior Jesus Christ and offended Thy infinite Goodness. I firmly resolve, with the help of Thy grace to confess my sins, to do penance and to amend my life.

Prayer for Daily Neglects

Eternal Father, I offer Thee the Sacred Heart of Jesus with all Its Love, all Its sufferings and all Its merits:

First - To expiate all the sins I have committed this day and during all my life. Glory be to the Father...etc.

Second - To purify the good I have done badly this day and during all my life. Glory be...

Third - To supply the good I ought to have done, and all that I have neglected this day and during all my life. Glory be...

Nightly Consecration of the Family to the Sacred Heart

(To be said at night prayers in union with all families in which the Sacred Heart has been enthroned.)

Most sweet Jesus, humbly kneeling at Thy feet, we renew the Consecration of our family to Thy Divine Heart. Be Thou our King forever! In Thee we have full and entire confidence. May Thy spirit penetrate our thoughts, our desires, our words and our works. Bless our undertakings, share in our joys, in our trials and in our labors. Grant us to know Thee better, to love Thee more, to serve Thee without faltering.

By the Immaculate Heart of Mary, Queen of Peace, set up Thy kingdom in our country. Enter closely into the midst of our families and make them Thine own through the Solemn Enthronement of Thy Sacred Heart, so that soon one cry may resound from home to home: "May the triumphant Heart of Jesus be everywhere loved, blessed and glorified forever!" Honor and glory to the Sacred Hearts of Jesus and Mary! "Sacred Heart of Jesus, protect our families."

Efficacious Novena to the Sacred Heart of Jesus

O my Jesus, you have said: "Truly I say to you, ask and you will receive, seek and you will find, knock and it will be opened to you." Behold I knock, I seek and ask for the grace of ... (here name request and for all those on prayer list).

Our Father, Hail Mary, Glory Be to the Father, Sacred Heart of Jesus, I place all my trust in you.

O my Jesus, you have said: "Truly I say to you, if you ask anything of the Father in my name, he will give it to you." Behold, in your name, I ask the Father for the grace of... *(here name request and for all those on prayer list).*

Our Father, Hail Mary, Glory Be to the Father, Sacred Heart of Jesus, I place all my trust in you.

O my Jesus, you have said: "Truly I say to you, heaven and earth will pass away but my words will not pass away." Encouraged by your infallible words I now ask for the grace Of … (here name request and for all those on prayer list).

Our Father, Hail Mary, Glory Be to the Father, Sacred Heart of Jesus, I place all my trust in you.

Sacred Heart of Jesus, for whom it is impossible not to have compassion on the afflicted, have pity on us miserable sinners and grant us the grace which we ask of you, through the Sorrowful and Immaculate Heart of Mary, your tender Mother and ours.

Prayer for our Family

Father, Son and Holy Spirit, sharing life and love, bless this family. Strengthen us in love as you are a God who is love. Help us to abide in love so that we may ever abide in you.

Withdraw from each of us whatever is of ego and selfishness. Implant in us a spirit of affirmation and trust. Live with us so that in the experience of life with you, we will realize what it truly means to be a family patterned on the Divine sharing!

Awaken in us the realization of the gift that you have made us to be for each other. Stir us up lest we neglect your gifts and take each other for granted.

Bless us that we may be a blessing upon all who see our love for each other. Grace us that we may be instruments of your transforming power in this world that you made to be the home for the whole human family.

Lead and guide us that one day we may dwell with you in our heavenly home, forever and ever. Amen.

For Families in Pain (To Venerable Fr. Solanus Casey)

Father Solanus Casey, We pray, through the help of your intercession, for the healing of all suffering children and families in the world, especially those victims of illness, tragedy, violence, family strife, neglect and abuse, as well as all who are suffering from layoffs and financial woes. We pray most fervently for the instigators and innocent victims of war and, in particular, for those young women contemplating or succumbing to abortion, including the many doctors, nurses and politicians who use their skills and talents, not to heal, but to kill.

Please bring God's graces of conversion, reconciliation and salvation to the perpetrators of these unconscionable acts of evil. And, to the victims, please bestow all the peace, mercy, comfort, compassion, consolation and tender loving kindness of our Lord Jesus and His Holy Family, which these people so desperately need in their hour of pain, grief and confusion. This we ask in Jesus' name. Amen

Healing Prayer at Bedtime

Lord Jesus, through the power of the Holy Spirt, go back into my memory as I sleep. Every hurt that has ever been done to me, heal that hurt. Every hurt that I have ever caused another person, heal that hurt. All relationships that have been damaged in my whole life that I am not aware of, heal those relationships. But, Lord, if there is anything that I need to do. If I need to go to a person because he or she is still suffering from my hand, bring to my awareness that person, I choose to forgive, and I ask to be forgiven. Remove whatever bitterness may be in my heart, O Lord, and fill the empty spaces with Your love. Amen

For Purity: Saluting the Blessed Virgin with Three Aves

Adding after each one the aspiration that St. Alphonsus himself recommended:

"By thy holy and Immaculate Conception, O Mary, purify my body and sanctify my soul."

O Domina Mea (Fr. Zucchi) *To entrust yourself to Mary:*

My Queen, my Mother, I give myself entirely to you, and to show my devotion to you I consecrate to you this day/night my eyes, my ears, my mouth, my heart, my whole body without reserve. Wherefore, good Mother, as I am your own, keep me and guard me as your property and possession. Amen.

+ O Heart most pure of the Blessed Virgin Mary, obtain for me from Jesus a pure and humble heart.

St. Gertrude's Guardian Angel Prayer

O most holy angel of God, appointed by God to be my guardian, I give you thanks for all the benefits which you have ever bestowed on me in body and in soul. I praise and glorify you that you condescended to assist me with such patient fidelity, and to defend me against all the assaults of my enemies. Blessed be the hour in which you were assigned me for my guardian, my defender and my patron. In acknowledgement and return for all your loving ministries to me, I offer you the infinitely precious and noble heart of Jesus, and firmly purpose to obey you henceforward, and most faithfully to serve my God. Amen

Prayer to all Guardian Angels

O pure and happy spirits whom the Almighty selected to become the Angels and Guardians of men, I most humbly prostrate myself before thee to thank thee for the charity and zeal with which thou dost execute this commission. Alas, how many pass a long life without ever thanking their invisible friends, to whom they owe a thousand times their preservation!

O charitable Guardians of those souls for whom Christ died, O flaming spirits who cannot avoid loving those whom Jesus eternally loves, permit me to address thee on behalf of all those committed to thy care, to implore for each of them a grateful sense of thy many favors and also the grace to profit by thy charitable assistance.

O Angels of those happy infants who as yet are "without spot before God," I earnestly beseech thee to preserve their innocence.

O Angels of youth, conduct them, exposed to so many dangers, safely to the bosom of God, as Tobias was conducted back to his father.

O Angels of those who employ themselves in the instruction of youth, animate them with thy zeal and love, teach them to emulate thy purity and continual view of God, that they may worthily and successfully cooperate with the invisible Guardians of their young charges.

O Angels of the clergy, of those "who have the eternal Gospel to preach to them that sit upon the earth," present their words, their actions and their intentions to God and purify them in that fire of love which consumes thee.

O Angels of the missionaries who have left their native land and all who were dear to them in order to preach the Gospel in foreign fields, protect them from the dangers which threaten them, console in their hours of discouragement and solitude, and lead them to those souls who are in danger of dying without Baptism.

O Angels of infidels and pagans, whom the True Faith has never enlightened, intercede for them, that they may open their hearts to the rays of grace, respond to the message delivered by God's missioners and acknowledge and adore the one true God.

O Angels of all who travel by air, land or water, be their guides and companions, protect them from all dangers of collision, fire, and explosion and lead them safely to their destination.

O Guardian Angels of sinners, charitable guides of those unhappy mortals whose perseverance in sin would embitter even thine unutterable joys, wert thou not established in the peace of God! Oh join me, I ardently beseech thee, in imploring their conversion!

And thou, O Guardian Angels of the sick, I entreat thee especially to help, console and implore the spirits of joy for all those who are deprived of health, which is among God's most precious gifts to man. Intercede for them, that they may not succumb to despondency or lose by impatience the merits they can gain in carrying with resignation and joy the cross which Christ has laid upon them as a special token of His love.

O Angels of those are at this moment in the agonies of death, strengthen, encourage and defend them against the attacks of their infernal enemy.

O faithful Guides, holy spirits, adorers of the Divinity, Guardian Angels of all creatures, protect us all; teach us to love, to pray, to wage combat on earth, so that one day we may reach Heaven and there be happy for all eternity! Amen.

O Angels of those who are lingering in Purgatory, intercede for them that God may permit thee to bring them some balm; console them that they may know that we are praying for them and that we ask thee to join in our entreaties.

Prayer of St. Gertrude for the Souls in Purgatory
Eternal Father, I offer You the most Precious Blood of Your Divine Son, Jesus, in union with the Masses said throughout the world today, for all the Holy Souls in Purgatory, for sinners everywhere, for sinners in the Universal Church, those in my own home and within my family. Amen.

For the Holy Souls
O God, Creator and Redeemer of all the faithful, grant to the souls of your servants departed full remission of all their sins, that, through the help of devout supplications, they may obtain the pardon of which they have always been desirous. Who lives and reigns, world with out end. Amen

Eternal rest grant unto them, O Lord, and let perpetual light shine upon them. May they rest in peace. Amen.

For The Gift of Holy Fear
Come, O blessed Spirit of Holy Fear, penetrate my inmost heart, that I may set Thee, my Lord and God, before my face forever; help me to shun all things that can offend Thee, and make me worthy to appear before the pure eyes of Thy Divine Majesty in heaven.

O Divine Spirit! penetrate my soul with true horror and loathing of sin. Grant that I may be more exact in the fulfillment of my duties, and strengthen my by Thy grace, that I may not again yield to temptation.

Thank you O God, for you alone are the source of my strength, you alone give me life, you alone protect me! Amen.

Bedtime Protection Prayer

In the name of the Lord Jesus Christ, strengthened by the intercession of the Immaculate Virgin Mary, Mother of God, of Blessed Michael the Archangel, of the Blessed Apostles Peter and Paul, and all the Saints and Angels of Heaven, and powerful in the holy authority of the name His Name, I subject my mind and my dreams only to the work of the Holy Spirit. I ask you Lord to bind up all powers of darkness and forbid them to work in my dreams or any part of my subconscious while I sleep. Amen.

Prayer at Day's End

Lord, as darkness begins to fall, and the busy day draws to a close, quiet our hearts and minds, and draw them close to You. We thank You for the graces of this day, and we repent of the ways we have fallen short. Be with us in our sleep, we pray, and grant us the strength to greet the morning renewed. Amen.

Hail, Holy Queen

Hail Holy Queen, Mother of mercy, our life, our sweetness, and our hope. To thee do we cry, poor banished children of Eve, to thee do we send up our sighs, mourning and weeping in this valley of tears. Turn then, most gracious advocate, thine eyes of mercy toward us; and after this our exile show unto us the blessed fruit of thy womb, Jesus. O clement, O loving, O sweet Virgin Mary. Pray for us, O Holy Mother of God. That we may be made worthy of the promises of Christ.

Let us pray: Pour forth, we beseech Thee, O Lord, Thy grace into our hearts, that we to whom the Incarnation of Christ Thy Son was made known by the message of an angel, may by His Passion and Cross be brought to the glory of His Resurrection. Through the same Christ Our Lord. Amen.

Most Sacred Heart of Jesus, Have mercy on us.
Immaculate Heart of Mary, Pray for us.
Our Lady of Sorrows, Pray for us.
Mother of the Church, Pray for us.
St. Joseph, Pray for us.
All the Holy Angels and Saints, Pray for Us.
Queen of Peace, Pray for us who have recourse to thee.

Visit, we beg You, O Lord (Visita, quaesumus, Domine)

Visit, we beg You, O Lord, this dwelling, and drive from it all snares of the enemy: let your holy Angels dwell herein, to keep us in peace; and let your blessing be always upon us. Through Christ our Lord. Amen.

𝔓𝔯𝔞𝔶𝔦𝔫𝔤 𝔥𝔞𝔫𝔡𝔰
by Albrecht Dürer

THE FIFTEEN PRAYERS
revealed by
OUR LORD to ST. BRIGIT

in the
CHURCH of ST. PAUL in ROME

Imprimatur: Ý V. Germond,
Vicar General, Niciae, September 23, 1940

The Promises:

Saint Brigit prayed for a long time to know how many blows Our Lord suffered during His terrible Passion. Rewarding her patience, one day He appeared to her and said:

"I received 5475 blows upon My Body. If you wish to honor them in some way, recite fifteen Our Fathers and fifteen Hail Mary with the following Prayers, which I Myself shall teach you, for an entire year. When the year is finished, you will have honored each of My Wounds."

Magnificent Promises to Saint Brigit of Sweden

Our Lord grants these promises to all who devoutly recite the 15 Saint Brigit Prayers every day for a year:

1. I will deliver 15 souls of his lineage from Purgatory.

2. 15 souls of his lineage will be confirmed and preserved in grace.

3. 15 sinners of his lineage will be converted.

Whoever recites these Prayers will attain the first degree of perfection.

4. 15 days before his death I will give him My Precious Body in order that he may escape eternal starvation; I will give him My Precious Blood to drink lest he thirst eternally.

5. 15 days before his death he will feel a deep contrition for all his sins and will have a perfect knowledge of them.

6. I will place before him the sign of My Victorious Cross for his help and defense against the attacks of his enemies.

7. Before his death I shall come with My Dearest Beloved Mother.

8. I shall graciously receive his soul, and will lead it into eternal joys.

9. And having led it there I shall give him a special draught from the fountain of My Deity, something I will not for those who have not recited My Prayers.

10. Let it be known that whoever may have been living in a state of mortal sin for 30 years, but who will recite devoutly, or have the intention to recite these Prayers, the Lord will forgive him all his sins.

11. I shall protect him from strong temptations.

12. I shall preserve and guard his 5 senses.

13. I shall preserve him from a sudden death.

14. His soul will be delivered from eternal death.

15. He will obtain all he asks for from God and the Blessed Virgin.

16. If he has lived all his life doing his own will and he is to die the next day, his life will be prolonged.

17. Every time one recites these Prayers he gains 100 days indulgence.

18. He is assured of being joined to the supreme Choir of Angels.

19. Whoever teaches these Prayers to another, will have continuous joy and merit which will endure eternally.

20. There where these Prayers are being said or will be said in the future God is present with His grace.

The 15 Prayers of Saint Brigit

First Prayer: *Our Father - Hail Mary*

O Jesus Christ! Eternal Sweetness to those who love Thee, joy surpassing all joy and all desire, Salvation and Hope of all sinners, Who hast proved that Thou hast no greater desire than to be among men, even assuming human nature at the fullness of time for the love of men, recall all the sufferings Thou hast endured from the instant of Thy conception, and especially during Thy Passion, as it was decreed and ordained from all eternity in the Divine plan.

Remember, O Lord, that during the Last Supper with Thy disciples, having washed their feet, Thou gavest them Thy Most Precious Body and Blood, and while at the same time Thou didst sweetly console them, Thou didst foretell them Thy coming Passion.

Remember the sadness and bitterness which Thou didst experience in Thy Soul as Thou Thyself bore witness saying: "My Soul is sorrowful even unto death."

Remember all the fear, anguish and pain that Thou didst suffer in Thy delicate Body before the torment of the crucifixion, when, after having prayed three times, bathed in a sweat of blood, Thou wast betrayed by Judas, Thy disciple, arrested by the people of a nation Thou hadst chosen and elevated, accused by false witnesses, unjustly judged by three judges during the flower of Thy youth and during the solemn Paschal season.

Remember that Thou wast despoiled of Thy garments and clothed in those of derision; that Thy Face and Eyes were veiled, that Thou wast buffeted, crowned with thorns, a reed placed in Thy Hands, that Thou was crushed with blows and overwhelmed with affronts and outrages. In memory of all these pains and sufferings which Thou didst endure before Thy Passion on the Cross, grant me before my death true contrition, a sincere and entire confession, worthy satisfaction and the remission of all my sins. Amen.

Second Prayer: *Our Father - Hail Mary*

O Jesus! True liberty of angels, Paradise of delights, remember the horror and sadness which Thou didst endure when Thy enemies, like furious lions, surrounded Thee, and by thousands of insults, spits, blows, lacerations and other unheard-of-cruelties, tormented Thee at will. In consideration of these torments and insulting words, I beseech Thee, O my Savior, to deliver me from all my enemies, visible and invisible, and to bring me, under Thy protection, to the perfection of eternal salvation. Amen.

Third Prayer: *Our Father - Hail Mary*

O Jesus! Creator of Heaven and earth whom nothing can encompass or limit, Thou Who dost enfold and hold all under Thy Loving power, remember the very bitter pain Thou didst suffer when the Jews nailed Thy Sacred Hands and Feet to the Cross by blow after blow with big blunt nails, and not finding Thee in a pitiable enough state to satisfy their rage, they enlarged Thy Wounds, and added pain to pain, and with indescribable cruelty stretched Thy Body on the Cross, pulled Thee from all sides, thus dislocating Thy Limbs.

I beg of Thee, O Jesus, by the memory of this most Loving suffering of the Cross, to grant me the grace to fear Thee and to Love Thee. Amen.

Fourth Prayer: *Our Father - Hail Mary*

O Jesus! Heavenly Physician, raised aloft on the Cross to heal our wounds with Thine, remember the bruises which Thou didst suffer and the weakness of all Thy Members which were distended to such a degree that never was there pain like unto Thine. From the crown of Thy Head to the Soles of Thy Feet there was not one spot on Thy Body that was not in torment, and yet, forgetting all Thy sufferings, Thou didst not cease to pray to Thy Heavenly Father for Thy enemies, saying: "Father forgive them for they know not what they do."

Through this great Mercy, and in memory of this suffering, grant that the remembrance of Thy Most Bitter Passion may effect in us a perfect contrition and the remission of all our sins. Amen.

Fifth Prayer: *Our Father - Hail Mary*
O Jesus! Mirror of eternal splendor, remember the sadness which Thou experienced, when contemplating in the light of Thy Divinity the predestination of those who would be saved by the merits of Thy Sacred Passion, Thou didst see at the same time, the great multitude of reprobates who would be damned for their sins, and Thou didst complain bitterly of those hopeless lost and unfortunate sinners.

Through the abyss of compassion and pity, and especially through the goodness which Thou displayed to the good thief when Thou saidst to him: "This day, thou shalt be with Me in Paradise." I beg of Thee, O Sweet Jesus, that at the hour of my death, Thou wilt show me mercy. Amen.

Sixth Prayer: *Our Father - Hail Mary*
O Jesus! Beloved and most desirable King, remember the grief Thou didst suffer, when naked and like a common criminal, Thou was fastened and raised on the Cross, when all Thy relatives and friends abandoned Thee, except Thy Beloved Mother, who remained close to Thee during Thy agony and whom Thou didst entrust to Thy faithful disciple when Thou saidst to Mary: "Woman, behold thy son!" and to Saint John: "Son, behold thy Mother!"

I beg of Thee O my Savior, by the sword of sorrow which pierced the soul of Thy holy Mother, to have compassion on me in all my affliction and tribulations, both corporal and spiritual, and to assist me in all my trials, and especially at the hour of my death. Amen.

Seventh Prayer: *Our Father - Hail Mary*
O Jesus! Inexhaustible Fountain of compassion, Who by a profound gesture of Love, said from the Cross: "I thirst!" suffered from the thirst for the salvation of the human race. I beg of Thee O my Savior, to inflame in our hearts the desire to tend toward perfection in all our acts; and to extinguish in us the concupiscence of the flesh and the ardor of worldly desires. Amen.

Eighth Prayer: *Our Father - Hail Mary*
O Jesus! Sweetness of hearts, delight of the spirit, by the bitterness of the vinegar and gall which Thou didst taste on the Cross for Love of us, grant us the grace to receive worthily Thy Precious Body and Blood during our life and at the hour of our death, that they may serve as a remedy and consolation for our souls. Amen.

Ninth Prayer: *Our Father - Hail Mary*
O Jesus! Royal virtue, joy of the mind, recall the pain Thou didst endure when plunged in an ocean of bitterness at the approach of death, insulted, outraged by the Jews, Thou didst cry out in a loud voice that Thou was abandoned by Thy Father, saying: "My God, My God, why hast Thou forsaken me?"

Through this anguish, I beg of Thee, O my Savior, not to abandon me in the terrors and pains of my death. Amen.

Tenth Prayer: *Our Father - Hail Mary*
O Jesus! Who art the beginning and end of all things, life and virtue, remember that for our sakes Thou was plunged in an abyss of suffering from the soles of Thy Feet to the crown of Thy Head. In consideration of the enormity of Thy Wounds, teach me to keep, through pure love, Thy Commandments, whose way is wide and easy for those who love Thee. Amen.

Eleventh Prayer: *Our Father - Hail Mary*

O Jesus! Deep abyss of mercy, I beg of Thee, in memory of Thy Wounds which penetrated to the very marrow of Thy Bones and to the depth of Thy being, to draw me, a miserable sinner, overwhelmed by my offenses, away from sin and to hide me from Thy Face justly irritated against me, hide me in Thy Wounds, until Thy anger and just indignation shall have passed away. Amen.

Twelfth Prayer: *Our Father - Hail Mary*

O Jesus! Mirror of Truth, symbol of unity, link of Charity, remember the multitude of wounds with which Thou was covered from head to foot, torn and reddened by the spilling of Thy adorable Blood. O Great and Universal Pain which Thou didst suffer in Thy virginal Flesh for Love of us! Sweetest Jesus! What is there that Thou couldst have done for us which Thou hast not done! May the fruit of Thy sufferings be renewed in my soul by the faithful remembrance of Thy Passion, and may Thy Love increase in my heart each day, until I see Thee in eternity, Thou Who art the treasury of every real good and every joy, which I beg Thee to grant me, O Sweetest Jesus, in Heaven. Amen.

Thirteenth Prayer: *Our Father - Hail Mary*

O Jesus! Strong Lion, Immortal and Invincible King, remember the pain which Thou didst endure when all Thy strength, both moral and physical, was entirely exhausted, Thou didst bow Thy Head, saying: "It is consummated!"

Through this anguish and grief, I beg of Thee Lord Jesus, to have mercy on me at the hour of my death when my mind will be greatly troubled and my soul will be in anguish. Amen.

Fourteenth Prayer: *Our Father - Hail Mary*

O Jesus! Only Son of the Father, Splendor and figure of His Substance, remember the simple and humble recommendation Thou didst make of Thy Soul to Thy Eternal Father, saying: "Father, into Thy Hands I commend My Spirit!" And with Thy Body all torn, and Thy Heart Broken, and the bowels of Thy Mercy open to redeem us, Thou didst Expire. By this Precious Death, I beg of Thee O King of Saints, comfort me and help me to resist the devil, the flesh and the world, so that being dead to the world I may live for Thee alone. I beg of Thee at the hour of my death to receive me, a pilgrim and an exile returning to Thee. Amen.

Fifteenth Prayer: *Our Father - Hail Mary*

O Jesus! True and fruitful Vine! Remember the abundant outpouring of Blood which Thou didst so generously from Thy Sacred Body as juice from grapes in a wine press.

From Thy Side, pierced with a lance by a soldier, blood and water issued forth until there was not lift in Thy Body a single drop, and finally, like a bundle of myrrh lifted to the top of the Cross Thy delicate Flesh was destroyed, the very Substance of Thy Body withered, and the Marrow of Thy Bones dried up. Through this bitter Passion and through the outpouring of Thy Precious Blood, I beg of Thee, O Sweet Jesus, to receive my soul when I am in my death agony. Amen.

Conclusion

O Sweet Jesus! Pierce my heart so that my tears of penitence and love will be my bread day and night; may I be converted entirely to Thee, may my heart be Thy perpetual habitation, may my conversation be pleasing to Thee, and may the end of my life be so praiseworthy that I may merit Heaven and there with Thy saints, praise Thee forever. Amen.

The Crucifixion - by Albrecht Dürer, 1511

Invocations in Honor of the Holy Wounds of Our Lord Jesus Christ
Eternal Father I offer Thee the Wounds of Our Lord Jesus Christ to heal the
wounds of our souls. My Jesus, pardon and mercy through the merits of Thy
Sacred Wounds.

Miscellaneous Prayers

A Short Way of the Cross
As used by The Franciscan Fathers on their Missions

First Station - Jesus Condemned to Death
O Jesus! so meek and uncomplaining, teach me resignation in trials.

Second Station - Jesus Carries His Cross
My Jesus, this Cross should be mine, not Thine; my sins crucified Thee.

Third Station - Our Lord Falls the First Time
O Jesus! by this first fall, never let me fall into mortal sin.

Fourth Station - Jesus Meets His Mother
O Jesus! may no human tie, however dear, keep me from following the road of the Cross.

Fifth Station - Simon the Cyrenean Helps Jesus Carry His Cross
Simon unwillingly assisted Thee; may I with patience suffer all for Thee.

Sixth Station - Veronica Wipes the Face of Jesus
O Jesus! Thou didst imprint Thy sacred features upon Veronica's veil; stamp them also indelibly upon my heart.

Seventh Station - The Second Fall of Jesus
By Thy second fall, preserve me, dear Lord, from relapse into sin.

Eighth Station - Jesus Consoles the Women of Jerusalem
My greatest consolation would be to hear Thee say: "Many sins are forgiven thee, because thou hast loved much."

Ninth Station - Third Fall of Jesus
O Jesus! when weary upon life's long journey, be Thou my strength and my perseverance.

Tenth Station - Jesus Stripped of His Garments
My soul has been robbed of its robe of innocence; clothe me, dear Jesus, with the garb of penance and contrition.

Eleventh Station - Jesus Nailed to the Cross
Thou didst forgive Thy enemies; my God, teach me to forgive injuries and FORGET them.

Twelfth Station - Jesus Dies on the Cross
Thou art dying, my Jesus, but Thy Sacred Heart still throbs with love for Thy sinful children.

Thirteenth Station - Jesus Taken Down from the Cross
Receive me into thy arms, O Sorrowful Mother; and obtain for me perfect contrition for my sins.

Fourteenth Station - Jesus Laid in the Sepulchre
When I receive Thee into my heart in Holy Communion, O Jesus, make it a fit abiding place for thy adorable Body. Amen.

The Madonna - by Albrecht Dürer

Chaplet of The Seven Sorrows of Our Lady

This devotion originated in the thirteenth century. It recalls the Sorrows which the Virgin Mother of God endured in compassion for the suffering and death of her Divine Son. The seven Sorrows chaplet consists of one Our Father followed by seven Hail Mary's for each of the Seven Sorrows. At the end, three Hail Mary's are said in honor of the Tears of our Sorrowful Mother.

The 1st Sorrow: The Prophecy of Holy Simeon

The prophecy of Simeon foretold of the bitter passion and death of Jesus, including the piercing of Mary's heart with a sword.

The 2nd Sorrow: The Flight into Egypt

This sorrow recalls how the Holy Family is forced to flee into Egypt from the death decree of Herod, and the slaughter of the Innocents.

The 3rd Sorrow: The Loss of the Child Jesus

Our Sorrowful Mother is separated from Jesus for three long days while He is lost in Jerusalem.

The 4th Sorrow: The Encounter of Jesus and Mary along the way of the Cross

Our Sorrowful Mother meets her son Jesus on the road to Calvary and sees Him fall under the weight of the cruel Cross.

The 5th Sorrow: Jesus dies on the Cross

Our Sorrowful Mother watches her Son die on the Cross.

The 6th Sorrow: Mary Receives the Body of Jesus

Our Sorrowful Mother takes the dead body of Her Son in Her arms as He is taken down from the Cross.

The 7th Sorrow: The Burial of Jesus

Our Sorrowful Mother sees Jesus placed in the tomb.

(Three Hail Mary's in Honor of the Tears of our Sorrowful Mother)
Our Father / Hail Mary / Glory Be - for the intentions of the Holy Father

For Enlightenment

O Holy Ghost, divine Spirit of light and love, I consecrate to Thee my understanding, my heart and my will, my whole being for time and for eternity. May my understanding be always obedient to Thy heavenly inspirations and the teachings of the holy Catholic Church, of which Thou art the infallible Guide; may my heart be ever inflamed with love of God and of my neighbor; may my will be ever conformed to the divine will, and may my whole life be a faithful following of the life and virtues of Our Lord and Savior Jesus Christ, to whom with the Father and Thee be honor and glory for ever. Amen.

The Divine Praises

Blessed be God.
Blessed be His Holy Name.
Blessed be Jesus Christ, true God and true Man.
Blessed be the Name of Jesus.
Blessed be His Most Sacred Heart.
Blessed be His Most Precious Blood.
Blessed be Jesus in the Most Holy Sacrament of the Altar.
Blessed be the Holy Spirit, the Paraclete.
Blessed be the great Mother of God, Mary most Holy.
Blessed be her Holy and Immaculate Conception.
Blessed be her Glorious Assumption.
Blessed be the Name of Mary, Virgin and Mother.
Blessed be St. Joseph, her most chaste spouse.
Blessed be God in His Angels and in His Saints.

Prayer for Pope Benedict XVI

Lord, source of eternal life and truth, give to your shepherd Benedict a spirit of courage and right judgement, a spirit of knowledge and love. By governing with fidelity those entrusted to his care may he, as successor to the apostle Peter and vicar of Christ, build your Church into a sacrament of unity, love, and peace for all the world.

We ask this through our Lord Jesus Christ, your Son, who lives and reigns with you and the Holy Spirit, one God for ever and ever. Amen.

Prayer for My Heart

Jesus, meek and humble of heart, make my heart like Your heart.
Mary, Mother of God, show yourself a mother to me.
Saint Joseph, protector of the Holy Family, protect me in all dangers.
Jesus, Mary and Joseph, I give you my heart and my soul.

Prayers for a Fallen Warrior

A Prayer for Help from a Weakened Soul

Dear Lord, my smallness and weakness are perfectly known to You.

Have pity on me. Pull me out of the mud of self, so that I may not be stuck in it forever. Consider the labors and trials of my daily life. Please stand by me in my efforts. Strengthen me in my resolutions. I have often failed because I depended on myself alone. Now, however, I shall seek advice and direction as often as I need it. Only in this way can I hope to make progress in true and solid virtue. Make me wise and honest in my daily efforts, so that I may no longer waste valuable time. I hope to become at least the kind of person You want me to be. Without You I can do nothing. Lord, help me! Amen

A Plea to God

Dear Lord, Please help me.

Time and again I give in to temptation and evil, the sins of lust. Time and again I offend You, my Savior, deepening Your already painful and bloody wounds. I give my 'yes', my will to Satan and to You, my loving God, I turn my back.

Time and again I find myself face down in the mud, crushed under the weight of my vileness and sins, while the force of my own destruction bears down on my soul.

Please forgive me, Lord, and help me to do better.

I am so weak that I feel helpless and defenseless, unable to stand, unworthy of Your love and support.

Cleanse me of self-loathing that I may see Your presence always within me and the countenance of Your loving Face in those whom I have desecrated, offended or injured.

Cleanse me of the spirit of addiction that I may take back control of myself, and please, once and for all, loosen the grasp that sin and Satan have over me.

Be victorious over my enemies, O Lord, for I alone cannot defeat them. Grant me the grace and strength of self-control, so that my spirit holds dominion over my weak and selfish flesh unto my dying breath.

Help me, O Lord, to discipline myself through prayer and fasting.

Let me never lose sight of You – for You, my God, are all that I truly seek.

I pray that in my weakness, Your strength, love and mercy may be shown to all, and I pray that somewhere, somehow, someday, I may come to give You glory by my life. Amen.

Prayer with a Remorseful Heart

Lord Jesus, before you I kneel, a sinful wretch, outcast and apart from You at no one's hand but mine, guilty by my own admission, in misery, humiliated, ashamed and sorrowful.

In sincere repentance, I beg You, Lord Jesus, turn not Your Glorious Face from me in the hideousness of my sins, but grant me the fullness of Your infinite mercy, Your unfathomable love, that I may draw from You all of the healing graces that I need to overcome my failings and vanquish the demons that torment me.

Channel Your strength to me, O Lord, so that, through You, I may defeat my own desires, imperfections and weaknesses, confront and conquer my tormentors, make worthy restitution to You for my sins and offenses, and give You glory by my life. Amen.

Perfect Trust

Oh, for the peace of a perfect trust, My loving God, in thee;
Unwavering faith that never doubts, Thou chooses best for me!
Best, though my plans be all upset; Best, though the way be rough;
Best, though my earthly store be scant; In Thee I have enough.
Best, though my health and strength be gone, Though weary days be mine,
Shut out from much that others have; Not my will, Lord, but Thine!
And even though disappointments come, They, too, are best for me,
To wean me from this changing world, And lead me nearer Thee.
Oh, for the peace of a perfect trust, That looks away from all;
That sees thy hand in everything, In great events or small.
That hears Thy voice - A Father's voice - Directing for the best.
Oh, for the peace of a perfect trust, A heart with Thee at rest.

Prayer Of Confession And Taking Back Ground From Satan

[This prayer may be used to confess venial sins, or for mortal sins until such time as confession is made in the Sacrament of Reconciliation. Catholic must bring all mortal sins to the Sacrament of Confession. See Page 26]

Lord, I confess that I have sinned by _____. I ask Your forgiveness, and I renounce _____ and take back the ground in my life gained by Satan through his sin. I reclaim this ground and my life for Christ. Amen.

Act of Contrition

O my God, I am heartily sorry for having offended Thee,
and I detest all of my sins because of Your just punishment,
but most of all, because they offend Thee, my God,
who are all good and deserving of all my love.
I firmly resolve, with the help of Thy grace,
to sin no more and to avoid the near occasion of sin.
Amen.

Anytime a Warrior has fallen in battle...he needs to see the doctor as soon as possible. Jesus Christ is our doctor and he can be found in confession. *Get to confession ASAP and do not delay!* **(See page 28)**

Appendix I

7 Steps to Freedom and Purity

1. Abandon Your Will to God!

2. Repent and Amend Your Life.

3. Daily Prayer and Devotion.

4. Live a Sacramental Life.

5. Consecrate Your Life to Christ and His Mother.

6. Practice Fasting and Mortification.

7. Replace Vice with Virtue.

True Knights Code of Chivalry

Our Holy Rule of Life - The Call for Men of Honour, Virtue and Purity to transform an Impure World.

The True Knights Code of Chivalry is not easy to follow, just as following Christ in any area of life takes one down a narrow road. The broad way appears easy. In reality, it only serves to lure the unsuspecting down the path of heartache and overwhelming hardship. Watered-down attempts to prop up contemporary family life are doomed in the face of modern pressures against marriage and the family. The solution to the family needs of our day begins with a call to husbands and fathers to follow the high calling of Christian fatherhood.

First: The True Knight shall always seek to love and serve the Lord thy God, with all his heart, mind and soul.

Second: The True Knight shall abandon his own will to the holy and divinely superior will of God.

Third: The True Knight shall always seek a greater union to God in His Holy Trinity, the Father, the Son and the Holy Spirit, though prayer and sacrifice, especially in participation of all of the Sacraments and contemplative prayer in Adoration of the True Presence of Jesus Christ, fully present body, blood, soul and divinity in the Holy Eucharist.

Fourth: The True Knight shall always seek to devote himself to the Mother of God, thy Holy Mother, the most Pure and Immaculate Virgin Mary as God's most perfect creature and the example of the perfect follower of Jesus Christ.

Fifth: The True Knight shall believe all the true teachings of the Holy Catholic Church in accordance with Holy Scripture, Sacred Tradition and the Magisterium in union with the Holy Father, the Holy Roman Pontiff.

Sixth: The True Knight shall always fight for True Christian Faith always ready to defend and give a reason to everyone who asks for the hope that abides within him.

Seventh: The True Knight shall always defend the Holy Catholic Church and the teachings of our faith against all attacks, slanders and outright lies.

Eighth: The True Knight shall unite himself with the communion of saints in the holy cloud of witnesses.

Ninth: The True Knight shall embrace all penance given to him by God for reparation of his own sins or the sins of others as deigned by God.

Tenth: The True Knight shall always defend those whom God has placed in his charge, not only against physical danger, but mental and more importantly spiritual danger and harm.

Eleventh: The True Knight shall always instruct those whom God has placed in his charge in the Truths of Jesus Christ and His Holy Catholic Church and uphold his God given responsibility to lead them into eternity in heaven.

Twelfth: The True Knight shall show regard for the weak and defend them. A True Knight is forbidden to ever harm, abuse or profane the dignity and purity of any woman or child. He must never stand by and allow a woman or child to be harmed in any way, always upholding the divine right to life of every human being, born or unborn.

Thirteenth: The True Knight shall never face the enemy alone, calling upon the strength of Our Lord and King, Jesus Christ.

Fourteenth: The True Knight shall make war against evil without cessation. Evil is not to be tolerated in any form. Doing things for the greater good is not synonymous with choosing the lesser of two evils. To show tolerance to the smallest of evils, will invite other evils. The True Knight is to behave in a manner that is above reproach at all times, and in all places. He shall always and in any places be champion of good and justice against evil and iniquity.

Fifteenth: The True Knight shall always avoid the near occasion of sin and do his best to avoid all occasions to sin within his means and the sublime grace of God. The True Knight shall never presume upon the grace of God to rescue him from his own carelessness or rebelliousness.

Sixteenth: The True Knight shall avoid avarice like the deadly pestilence and shall embrace its opposite.

Seventeenth: The True Knight shall keep himself chaste and pure in body, mind and soul for the sake of almighty God, the sanctification of his own soul and if married, for the dignity and fidelity of his wife and helpmate.

Eighteenth: The True Knight shall seek modesty in all things.

Nineteenth: The True Knight shall never use another, in any way, for his own selfish desires or advancement.

Twentieth: The True Knight shall always respect all human beings as true children of God.

Twenty-First: The True Knight shall seek to exhibit self-control in all matters by drawing upon the ever-present grace of God.

Twenty-Second: The True Knight shall never tell a lie and shall stay true to his word.

Twenty-Third: The True Knight shall seek prowess, to seek excellence in all endeavors expected of a True Knight, seeking strength to be used in the service of justice, rather than in personal aggrandizement.

Twenty-Fourth: The True Knight shall always seek Justice and seek always the path of 'right', unencumbered by bias or personal interest. Recognize that the sword of justice can be a terrible thing, so it must be tempered by the love of God, humanity and mercy.

Twenty-Fifth: The True Knight shall be known for unwavering loyalty to God and the people and ideals he chooses to live by.

Twenty-Sixth: The True Knight shall always be courageous which may mean choosing the more difficult path, the personally expensive one and always taking the side of truth in all matters.

Twenty-Seventh: The True Knight shall always be prepared to make personal sacrifices in service of God, the Holy Catholic Church, his family and for the good of all people.

Twenty-Eighth: The True Knight shall seek God's eternal truth and wisdom in all things.

Twenty-Ninth: The True Knight shall place his faith in God above all others, for faith roots him and gives hope against the despair that human failings create.

Thirtieth: The True Knight shall seek humility in all things. Value first the contributions of others; not boasting of his own accomplishments, by letting others do this for him. He shall hold up the deeds of others before his own, according them the renown rightfully earned through virtuous deeds. In this way the office of knighthood is well done and glorified, helping not only the gentle spoken of but also all who call themselves knights, recognizing that all glory ultimately is to be given to God almighty.

Thirty-First: The True Knight shall be generous and charitable in so far as his resources allow; largesse used in this way counters gluttony. Giving of his tithe to the Church, feeding and clothing the poor and to help the continued preservation of the Brotherhood of True Knights; generosity also makes the path of mercy easier to discern when a difficult decision of justice is required.

Thirty-Second: The True Knight shall seek virtue in all things. It is by virtue alone that he is made noble. He shall seek great stature of character by holding to the virtues and duties of a True Knight, realizing that though the ideals cannot be reached, the quality of striving towards them ennobles the spirit, growing the character from dust towards the heavens. Nobility also has the tendency to influence others, offering a compelling example of what can be done in the service of rightness.

Thirty-Third: The True Knight shall seek to emulate everything spoken of here as sincerely as possible, not for the reason of personal gain but because it is right in the eyes of God. He must not restrict his exploration to a small world, but seek to infuse every aspect of his life with these qualities. Should he succeed in even a tiny measure always remember that if not for the Grace of God, then none of these virtues would be possible. In all things give thanks to God and live for His greater Glory.

10 PROMISES OF A TRUE KNIGHT

1. Respect everyone - Christ lives in everyone. Be sensitive to others - they are your brothers and sisters.

2. Think well of everyone - think ill of no one. Try to find something good even in the worst circumstances.

3. Always speak well of others - do not cast a slur on anyone. Repair any harm resulting from an uttered word. Do not provoke strife between people.

4. Speak to everyone in the language of love. Do not raise your voice. Do not swear. Do not vex others. Do not provoke tears. Reassure others. Show a kind heart.

5. Forgive everyone everything. Do not hold grudges. Always be the first to extend your hand as a sign of reconciliation.

6. Act always to your neighbor's advantage. Do good things to others, as you would like them done to you. Never give a thought to what others owe you, but always to what you owe them.

7. Be actively compassionate in time of suffering. Be quick to offer consolation, council, assistance, kindness.

8. Work conscientiously - others benefit from the fruits of your labor, just as you benefit from the labor of others.

9. Be active in your community. Be open to the poor and the sick. Share your goods. Try to see the needs of those around you.

10. Pray for <u>everyone</u>, even your enemies.

Appendix II

Lust Kills...*the Soul!*
by Kenneth Henderson
Originally Published March 14, 2006 on CatholicExchange.com

I'm sure that everyone reading this article knows someone, either a friend or family member who struggles with sexual impurity. This problem is widespread and in a society that is so preoccupied with sex and sexual pleasure, many people, even good Catholics, can become ensnared in the trap of slavery to sex... through addiction. Lust in all its forms, including masturbation, pornography, promiscuity or adulterous relationships, is all a part of the attack on our society in what I call the **"Trinity of Evil."** It includes abortion homosexuality and sexual lust. All of these are intrinsically linked to the preoccupation with sex and the selfish, contraceptive mindset of our modern society; a mindset that is destroying our culture at the very foundation.

We have been told by the spirit of the age, the Zeitgeist, predominately through the media, that it's what you "get," that makes you who you are. All human beings are born into this world with certain innate needs that are instilled in us at birth. However, because of the effect of Original Sin, our broken nature, these needs can become twisted and disordered. We seek to fulfill these disordered needs with "things." However, these things — money, material items, food or sex — are only an attempt to fill the emptiness in our hearts where God should be. Saint Augustine, who also struggled with promiscuity and lust before his conversion, understood this when he finally came to know the Lord and said "You have made us for Yourself, O Lord, and our hearts are restless, until they rest in You."

Lust is a huge problem in our world and is probably the greatest contributor to the destruction of marriages and families. With the abundance of technological advances and media outlets, the selling of the human body has become big, big business and it feeds on the brokenness of men and women. Lust is an inordinate desire for sexual pleasure and involves engaging in the sexual act outside the context of God's intended purpose of marital communion. Saint Augustine teaches us that when we indulge in the sins of the flesh, as with any mortal sin, the intellect becomes darkened and God cannot be seen or recognized as Truth. In fact, the allure of lust will lead people to commit a wide variety of subsequent sins.

When a person is lost in lust, they become enslaved to this obsessive desire and their understanding of good becomes obscured. In his Summa Theologica, St. Thomas Aquinas said "this act (simple understanding) is hindered by lust, according to Daniel 13:56, 'Beauty hath deceived thee, and lust hath perverted thy heart.' In this respect we have 'blindness of mind.'." Because lust clouds even simple understanding, this blindness will affect every aspect of a person's life.

To illustrate this point, people often wonder how anyone could commit the sin of sexually abusing a child. But since lust cuts a person off from God and their intellect becomes blinded, that person loses their ability to correctly judge right and wrong. He (or she) acts out for one purpose — that of sexual pleasure. As in any addiction, the addict will often neglect family, job, and any other responsibility in order to pursue the distorted desire, even when he recognizes the destructive nature of his compulsion. Simply put, lust destroys a person's humanity.

It is important to point out that a person enslaved to this sexual sin does not start out to become as sexual addict nor do all who lust become sexual predators. Yet, even a person who only indulges in lust occasionally can have his life and relationships negatively affected.

To quote Catholic Pro-life speaker, Barbara McGuigan, host of the show Voices on Virtue on EWTN,

> "Satan, the master deceiver, loves to feed himself on the hearts of children, as well as, the hearts of young people and adults. He knows the intensity of the sexual appetite, and how sexual impurity can prevent us from seeing the truth by clouding the intellect through sensuality. The deadly sin of lust is deadly because it kills our ability to truly love. How Satan loves to corrupt a soul by lust! He knows with his angelic intellect that lust causes a blindness of understanding. Fr. John Hardon explained, 'When man is brought down to the level of a brute beast, he no longer possesses a sense of law, or conscience, or honor, or gratitude, or fidelity or friendship. When lust quenches the light of the soul, any advice, counsel, warning, or authority of parents is disregarded. The heart becomes hardened. A person steeped in lust has a hatred of all spiritual things, such as, prayer, sacraments, the Word of God, Catholicism and all who teach how to be holy. A lustful person has a hatred of all that is holy, which leads him to infidelity. He know longer believes in the God who loves him, in Heaven and Hell, and eternity. There is no God to judge him'.
>
> "It's not hard to understand that darkness of the mind, hardness of the heart, hatred of religion, and disbelief, lead to despair and sometimes to final impenitence, which of course, is a serious sin against the Holy Spirit. Could this be why our Blessed Mother at Fatima said that 'More souls go to hell for sins of the flesh than any other reason'?"

And I couldn't agree more! The time is NOW for all True Knights to rise up and spread the saving message of Jesus Christ and His Church. Only the Catholic Church, as established by Jesus Christ himself, has the means that can truly save marriages and families from the clutches of the devil. There is only one thing that can fill the emptiness that resides in the hearts of all men and women who struggle with lust... Jesus Christ, the Truth that sets all men and women free.

Education is the key. We cannot just sit by quietly and do nothing. Each and every Catholic needs to do what they can to learn more about this issue and what we can do about it. Just some suggestions, take a class on "The Theology of the Body" or a class on how you can protect your family from internet pornography that your diocese may offer. If no class exists, suggest it to your pastor or bishop. You can also invite speakers who specialize in this issue, like Jason Evert, Steve Wood, Christopher West or even me to come and speak to your parish, diocese, or conference. Ask your pastor to address this issue more often from the pulpit. I realize that many pastors may be uncomfortable with this, to which I would also suggest that they too seek education on the severity of this concern. Additionally, come to TrueKnights.org and learn of ways to get help. There are many articles, resources, and materials available to help educate you.

If you suffer from addiction to lust, the first thing you need to do is go to Confession... as soon as possible. Then find an accountability partner, someone you can call for help. At True Knights we have a recovery program available called Combat Training which is personal confidential purity coaching that includes accountability. However, space is limited for personal one-on-one purity coaching. To help reach even more people who suffer from this issue we have our Purity Corps recovery groups that are just in the beginning stages of being placed in parishes around the country. Perhaps you are called to form a group in your parish. Contact us to find out more.

The bottom line is that in this world of great darkness, it is imperative for all Christians to wake up, and by the grace of God, do what they can to bring the Truth of Christ to the world. We are called to intercede for and inform this world, a world that is so hungry for fulfillment, of God's divine and holy plan for human sexuality and destroy Satan's perverse and twisted grip on humanity. Lust is keeping many in the dark, perhaps even someone you know. We must shine the Light of Christ into this sick and dying world and send the devil running for cover into the pits of hell... like the nasty cockroach he is! The first move of any battle should always involve prayer. We are all called to pray, fast, offer up our sufferings and ask the communion of Saints to intercede for the lost souls of this world. Holy warriors, put on the Armor of God. Time is short and we have much work to do! Pray for God's grace, mercy and holy power in this War with eternal consequences!

Appendix iii

The Battle for Your Soul!

By Kenneth Henderson

We are at war! St. Paul said it like this in Ephesians 6:12

> *"We are not contending against flesh and blood, but against the principalities, against the powers, against the world rulers of this present darkness, against the spiritual hosts of wickedness in the heavenly places."*

This War is not a country, a government. The enemy is not visible. This is a spiritual war and the enemy is...Satan!

Satan's greatest lie is to have us believe that he doesn't exist, or that he is more powerful than he actually is.

In a well documented and witnessed event, on October 13, 1884, Pope Leo XIII stood motionless for several minutes after saying Mass and then collapsed to the floor. Immediately several observers rushed to his assistance. When asked what had happened he told them that he had just overheard a conversation between God and Satan. He said that Satan made a boast that he could destroy the Church and the world if he just had enough power and time to do so. So God granted Satan his request with the understanding that if the devil failed then he would be cast into Hell forever.

Why would God allow this? The Answer: To purge the world of the unfaithful. Man has turned his back on God. Through our Pride we have made ourselves into our own gods.

Take a look at this passage from the letter of St. Paul to the Romans 1:16-32:

> [16]I am not ashamed of the gospel. It is the power of God for the salvation of everyone who believes: for Jew first, and then Greek. [17]For in it is revealed the righteousness of God from faith to faith; as it is written, "The one who is righteous by faith will live." [18] The wrath of God is indeed being revealed from heaven against every impiety and wickedness of those who suppress the truth by their wickedness. [19]For what can be known about God is evident to them, because God made it evident to them. [20]Ever since the creation of the world, his invisible attributes of eternal power and divinity have been able to be understood and perceived in what he has made. *(Meaning in nature and the world around us.)* As a result, they have no excuse; [21]for although they knew God, they did not accord him glory as God or give him thanks. (Truth is relevant, You believe what you want and I'll believe what I want,

(Don't tell me about God, don't honor him anywhere, leave me alone, I want to do my own thing.) Instead, they became vain in their reasoning, and their senseless minds were darkened. [22]While claiming to be wise, they became fools *(Scientific revolution, Age of Enlightenment, Modern Arguments for Abortion, Euthanasia, etc.)* [23]and exchanged the glory of the immortal God for the likeness of an image of mortal man *(Music, Movie, and TV celebrities.)* or of birds or of four-legged animals or of snakes *(Bestiality).* [24]Therefore, God handed them over to impurity through the lusts of their hearts for the mutual degradation of their bodies. *(Pornography, hook-ups, etc.)* [25]They exchanged the truth of God for a lie and revered and worshiped the creature rather than the creator, who is blessed forever. Amen. [26]Therefore, God handed them over to degrading passions. Their females exchanged natural relations for unnatural, [27]and the males likewise gave up natural relations with females and burned with lust for one another. Males did shameful things with males and thus received in their own persons the due penalty for their perversity. *(Such as the rise of homosexuality, so-called homosexual marriage and all forms of sexual perversity today!)* [28]And since they did not see fit to acknowledge God, God handed them over to their undiscerning mind to do what is improper. [29]They are filled with every form of wickedness, evil, greed, and malice; full of envy, murder, rivalry, treachery, and spite. They are gossips [30]and scandalmongers and they hate God. They are insolent, haughty, boastful, ingenious in their wickedness, and rebellious toward their parents. [31]They are senseless, faithless, heartless, ruthless. *(Just by reading a newspaper, or watching the evening news...you can see this is the reality of our world TODAY!)* [32]Although they know the just decree of God that all who practice such things deserve death, they not only do them but give approval to those who practice them. *(A message to Believers who stand by and do nothing!)*

Paul's main point is that the wrath of God does not await the end of the world but goes into action at each present moment in humanity's history when misdirected piety serves as a facade for self-interest. In order to expose the depth of humanity's rebellion against the Creator, God handed them over to impurity through the lusts of their hearts. Instead of curbing people's evil interests, God abandoned them to self-indulgence, thereby removing the facade of apparent conformity to the divine will. Instead of bending the will of man, he allows man to exercise his freewill, even if it hurts us! Just as fathers try to guide their own children into adulthood, once they become old enough to make their own choices, inevitably they will make mistakes. But we have to allow them to make them, no matter how much it hurts us to watch. Thus, our Heavenly Father allows us to follow our own choices. And yes it hurts Him to watch us, all of his children in all the world!

That is the very reason for the exchange that Pope Leo was allowed to over hear. God is allowing Satan free reign in the world and thereby handing us over to our impurities. Since it's apparent we have no need of God and his laws. As is apparent by the attitude exhibited in our modern secular society. God is not politically correct these days. Since we would rather live with our own pride and live the ways of Satan, then Satan we shall have. And the war progresses.

So the question is, do you want to be victorious with the Church or do you want to be a casualty? It's your response to God that will make the difference. If you are not baptized, I would advise it so that you can be washed clean and born again as a child of God and obtain all the protections and benefits He gives you through baptism. If you are not Catholic then I encourage you to investigate for yourselves what I have shared with you about what I have discovered. If you are Catholic, it is time to devote yourself to living your faith in full. Don't be lukewarm! So many Catholics today are just so complacent in their faith. They are comfortable, thinking they are safe and sound as long as they just do what are the basic requirements for being a Catholic. The Truth is a different story altogether and Satan would like nothing better than for as many people as possible to remain ignorant of the Truth!

It's time to prepare for battle... so let's go to the armory!

Every knight needs a suit of armor - here is the Armor that every True Knight wears as described by Paul in Eph 6:10-20

[10]Finally, be strong in the Lord and in the strength of his might. [11]Put on the whole armor of God, that you may be able to stand against the wiles of the devil. [12]For we are not contending against flesh and blood, but against the principalities, against the powers, against the world rulers of this present darkness, against the spiritual hosts of wickedness in the heavenly places. [13]Therefore take the whole armor of God, that you may be able to withstand in the evil day, and having done all, to stand. [14]Stand therefore, having girded your loins with truth, and having put on the breastplate of righteousness, [15]and having shod your feet with the equipment of the gospel of peace; [16]besides all these, taking the shield of faith, with which you can quench all the flaming darts of the evil one. [17]And take the helmet of salvation, and the sword of the Spirit, which is the word of God. [18]Pray at all times in the Spirit, with all prayer and supplication. To that end keep alert with all perseverance, making supplication for all the saints, [19]and also for me, that utterance may be given me in opening my mouth boldly to proclaim the mystery of the gospel, [20]for which I am an ambassador in chains; that I may declare it boldly, as I ought to speak.

Appendix iv
The Armor of God

- The Sword Belt of Truth
- The Breastplate of Righteousness
- The Shoes, Boots and Footgear that are our readiness, our eagerness, to announce the Good News of Peace (the Gospel) to all the world
- The Shield of Faith...to quench all the flaming darts of the evil one
- The Helmet of Salvation
- The Sword of The Spirit, which is The Word of God
- Pray at ALL Times and Proclaim the Gospel boldly

Prayer for Putting on The Armor of God

That I may be able to stand firm against the devices of the devil,
I now put on the whole Armor of God.

I put on the helmet of Salvation.
Jesus, You are my Salvation!

I put on the breastplate of Righteousness, and the belt of Truth.
Jesus, You are my Righteousness, and my Truth!

I put on the shoes for spreading the Gospel of Peace.
Jesus, You are my Peace!

I carry the shield of Faith and the sword of the Spirit, the Word of God.
Jesus, You are my Faith! You are the Living Word!

And in You, O Lord, I place all my trust.
Amen.

Appendix v

The Armor of the Enemy

This is the armor worn by Satan and all of his demonic thugs:
- The Sword Belt of Lies.
- The Breastplate of Evil Deeds.
- The Shoes, Boots and Footgear that is their readiness to announce the Bad News of Hate, Distrust and Prejudice.
- The Shield of Doubt & Despair.
- The Helmet of Damnation.
- The Sword of the Evil Spirit, which is the Word (Lies) of Satan.

Satan's Great sin was Pride! He said, "I will not serve!"

The Five Ploys of Satan

Binding Satan is always a matter of faith and prayer, yet it also helps to be aware of his strategies, such as the following:

Doubt - Tempts us to question God's Word and his goodness, forgiveness, and love.

Discouragement - Tempts us to focus intently on our problems rather than entrusting them to God's care.

Diversion - Tempts us to see the wrong things as attractive so that we will want them more than the right things.

Defeat - Tempts us to feel like failure so that we don't even try.

Delay - Tempts us to procrastinate so that things never get done.

Application: Reflect on these ploys of Satan, and if you find that he has darkened your life on any of these counts, lift up the situation to Our Lady in prayer.

Recall her advice on binding the evil one:
"Put on the armor of God. With the rosary in your hand, defeat him!"

Appendix vi

Afraid of the Devil?

Saint Teresa of Jesus responds:

If this Lord is powerful, as I see that He is and I know that He is, and if the devils are His slaves (and there is no doubt about this because it's a matter of faith), what evil can they do to me since I am a servant of this Lord and King? Why shouldn't I have the fortitude to engage in combat with all of hell?

I took a cross in my hand, and it seemed to me truly that God gave me courage because in a short while I saw that I was another person and that I wouldn't fear bodily combat with them; for I thought that with that cross I would easily conquer all of them. So I said: "Come now all of you, for, being a servant of the Lord, I want to see what you can do to me."

There was no doubt, in my opinion, that they were afraid of me, for I remained so calm and so unafraid of them all. All the fears I usually felt left me – even to this day. For although I sometimes saw them, as I shall relate afterward, I no longer had hardly any fear of them; rather it seemed they were afraid of me. I was left with a mastery over them truly given by the Lord of all; I pay no attention to them than to flies. I think they're such cowards that when they observe they are esteemed but little, their strength leaves them.

These enemies don't know how to attack head – on, save those whom they see surrender to them, or when God permits them to do so for the greater good of His servants whom they tempt and torment. May it please His Majesty that we fear Him whom we ought to fear and understand that more can come to us from one venial sin than from all hell together – for this is so.

How frightened these devils make us because we want to be frightened through other attachments to honors, property, and delights! It is then that they do us great harm, when they are joined with us who loving and desiring what we ought to abhor are in contradiction with ourselves. For we make them fight against us with our own very weapons, handing over to them what we need for our own defense. This is a great pity. But if we abhor all for God and we embrace the cross and try truly to serve God, the devil will flee these truths like the plague. He is a friend of lies, and is the lie itself. He will make no pact with anyone who walks in truth. When he sees the intellect darkened, he subtly helps to blind the eyes. For if he sees people already blind by the fact that they place their trust in vain things (and so vain that these worldly things become like children's games), he concludes that they are then children, treats them as such, and dares to fight with them not once but many times.

May it please the Lord that I not be one of these but that His Majesty favor me so that I may understand by repose what repose is, by honor what honor is, and by delight what delight is – not the reverse; and a fig for all the devils, because they shall fear me. I don't understand these fears, "The devil! The devil!", when we can say "God! God", and make the devil tremble. Yes, for we already know that he cannot stir if the Lord doesn't permit him to. What is this? Without doubt, I fear those who have such great fear of the devil more than I do the devil himself, for he can't do anything to me. Whereas these others, especially if they are confessors, cause severe disturbance; I have undergone some years of such great trial that I am amazed now at how I was able to suffer it. Blessed be the Lord who has so truly helped me!

This passage is provided from the autobiography of St Teresa of Avila to counteract unjustified fear of the devil. It is an encouraging passage, unless we ourselves open the door to the devil. (For The Book of Her Life, chap. 25, nos. 19-22, in The Collected Works of St Teresa of Avila, trans. Kieran Kavanaugh, O.C.D., and Otilio Rodriguez, O.C.D., vol. 1, 2d ed. [Washington, D.C.: ICS Publications, 1987]).

Appendix vii

Spiritual Warfare : Exorcism, Deliverance & Healing

Adapted from www.theworkofgod.org

In the very beginning of man's history as we see in the Book of Genesis, we see how the serpent or demon began his work of temptation cheating our first parents. He made them distrust the Word of God, tempting them to "become like gods." This is what led them to sin, to be expulsed from Paradise and to suffer death. This is the very reason for our brokenness.

God in his great design has allowed the devil to be near us, in order to prove our fidelity to His Word and to demonstrate the great Power of His Infinite Mercy.

The devil can not make us sin, he can only tempt us to sin, so that finally we are responsible for our actions before God.

The wages of sin is death (Romans 6:23), but our redemption and salvation is found in the Grace of God, that gives us forgiveness and eternal life in Christ Jesus (Ephesians 2:5).

Jesus came to the world to die for the forgiveness of our sins and to give us eternal life, he also came to give us his testimony as the Son of God so that believing in Him, we can be saved and enjoy the gifts of God the Father. (John 3:16).

Jesus also came to demonstrate the supernatural power of God with His miracles: transforming water into wine, the multiplication of loaves and fishes, giving order to the storm to be calmed, all the physical, mental and spiritual healings, the expulsion of demons, the resurrection of the dead, his own resurrection and the promise of our resurrection.

A last miracle, but the greatest is the gift of his flesh and blood, in the bread and wine consecrated by his apostles and followers, which we must eat and drink if we want to be saved.

Jesus had his first encounter with the devil after receiving his baptism in the Jordan river and after fasting for forty days and nights.

Jesus was tempted by the three enemies of the soul: the world, the devil and the flesh.

The devil tempted him using the Word of God written in the Bible in the following manner:

In the flesh, he suggested that he could transform stones into bread in order to appease the hunger of his fast, but Jesus said to him: "It is written, man does not live on bread alone but on every word that comes from the mouth of God." The devil took him to the highest part of the temple suggesting him that if he would throw himself from there, the angels would protect him, but Jesus answered him: "It is also written you shall not put the Lord to the test". Finally the devil tempted Jesus with all the riches of the world in return for his worship but Jesus rebuked him saying "Be gone Satan, it is written: You shall worship the Lord your God and serve Him only "

This was the first exorcism of Jesus, casting out the tempter out of his life and demonstrating his power. This power of resisting the devil has been given to all of us by nature, because we have the option of being tempted and fall into sin or we can resist evil by the grace of God and our own will.

Our objective as we treat this subject, is to learn how to pray with humility and in obedience to the Church, in order to unleash the power of God and to obtain the expulsion of evil spirits from our lives and of those who suffer their dominion.

Some Definitions

Exorcism, Deliverance and Healing are the results of the same process of repentance, prayer and surrender to Jesus. No one can be exorcised, delivered or healed of the influence of the devil except in the name of Jesus and by his power. No one can receive any divine favor except through the goodness and grace of God in response to prayer.

Exorcism is the act of giving order to the devil or to evil spirits to come out of a person, a place, object or situation, adjuring them in the Holy Name of God the Father, the Son or the Holy Spirit.

Jesus, the Son of God or God the Son, has all the authority of the Supreme God, power that he used during his ministry of three years, which he delegated to his disciples, apostles and believers.

Deliverance is the result of the work of God in a person through prayers or through an exorcism, which frees him from the evil influence.

Physical Healing is the miraculous result of the prayers done in great faith that manifest a miracle of God.

Spiritual Healing is the result of renouncing sin, of giving oneself totally to Jesus Christ and of receiving the gift of Peace.

Who is The Enemy?

In the beginning God existed in His Glory, surrounded by all the angels, pure spirits created as an emanation of His Presence. There existed one who was adorned with outstanding attributes and who shone above all the others, his name was Lucifer, which means full of light or light bearer (Ezekiel 31:3-11) (Ezekiel 28:13-19)

God announced to his angels that he was going to create in the order of time creatures who would also participate in his Kingdom, and that he was going to share that human nature in the flesh, in order to become their Master and to deliver them from evil.

Lucifer in his pride defied the Divine Will and together with one third of all the angels disapproved the creation of man, refusing to give adoration to God in human form (Jesus) and to the woman who would have the privilege of being exalted above all the human race by becoming His Mother and the Queen of all creation. (The Blessed Virgin Mary)

A great spiritual battle commenced between those angels faithful to God, who were guided by the Archangel Michael. In humility they felt shame because of the defiance of Lucifer and began to worship God saying "Who can be like God"

Lucifer was cast out from Heaven as lighting (Ezekiel 28:17) (Luke 10:18), he received his punishment becoming the monarch of darkness because he opposed God who is Light. (Isaiah 14:12-15)

God permitted the human creation to coexist beside the fallen angels of darkness in order to put us to the test and in a certain way to fill the vacancies left in Heaven by the reprobate angels, with all the human beings who obtain Eternal Salvation.

The name Satan known in the Hebrew as Abaddon or in Greek as Apollyon means "destroyer". Other names given to Him are prince of darkness, adversary, accuser, deceiver, dragon, liar, leviathan, murderer, serpent, tormentor and god of this world.

In the final battle of the angels as revealed in the Apocalypse, St. Michael the Archangel will defeat Satan forever, who will be thrown in the lake of eternal fire with all his angels.

Being human beings, our fight with these evil spirits is not very fair, because we fall easily into sin and automatically give territory to the enemy. In order to fight with him, we must become people of God, we must overcome him personally first, as Jesus did in the desert, and then, together with the rest of the Church we have to fight spiritually through our prayers to be delivered from this mortal enemy.

Here is what Saint Paul says about the spiritual battle in Ephesians 6:12-18

> [12] For our wrestling is not against flesh and blood; but against principalities and power, against the rulers of the world of this darkness, against the spirits of wickedness in the high places. [13] Therefore take unto you the armor of God, that you may be able to resist in the evil day, and to stand in all things perfect. [14] Stand therefore, having your loins girt about with truth, and having on the breastplate of justice, [15] And your feet shod with the preparation of the gospel of peace: [16] In all things taking the shield of faith, wherewith you may be able to extinguish all the fiery darts of the most wicked one. [17] And take unto you the helmet of salvation, and the sword of the Spirit (which is the word of God). [18] By all prayer and supplication praying at all times in the spirit; and in the same watching with all instance and supplication for all the saints.

and Saint Peter in his first letter 5:8-9

> [8] Be sober and watch: because your adversary the devil, as a roaring lion, goes about seeking whom he may devour. [9] Resist him, strong in faith: knowing that the same affliction befalls your brethren who are in the world.

Why can the devil enter into a person

We have been created in the image and likeness of God. We are living temples of the Spirit of God. The life that runs through our veins is not ours, it is a divine gift, a little breath of God that sustains us.

Because of this, we must live our lives with great reverence before our creator, because in Him we live, move and have our being. (Acts 17:28)

When we decide to live a life of disobedience, we despise the spirit of God who lives within us, we don't listen to the voice of the conscience and we choose to defy God with our sin.

At that moment, we authorize the enemy, who with subtlety makes us fall into sin and little by little takes away our fear of God until we can even doubt his existence. God loves us so much, that He has sent his only begotten Son to forgive us our sins with his death on the cross, with the price of his suffering and with his precious blood.

When we harden our hearts and resist the call of God, or when we feel apathy for Him or for consecrated things or persons, we close the door completely to the Holy Spirit and we open it totally to the enemy who begins to influence our lives until we end up being governed by him.

At that stage, we can not call ourselves temples of the Holy Spirit but temples of Satan. There begins the great spiritual problem, of which only few can leave triumphantly.

Of course it is different in the case of innocent victims of influence or possession, there is no guilt from their part, this is a case in which we can act with mercy as children of God. This is the reason why we are determined to pray for deliverance for those who suffer this spiritual malady.

Influence and Demonic possession: What's the Difference?

According to the information in the New Testament, the devil used to take possession of a victim and caused madness in some cases, in others blindness or dumbness. This does not mean that all those who were mad, blind or dumb were possessed by the devil, but in some cases, the devil caused these diseases.

Many mental illnesses have nothing to do with diabolical influence, this is why we must look to other symptoms that are very common in those influenced or possessed by the devil.

Many diabolical possessions occur in innocent persons that are victims of the evil of other people, relatives inclusive. In other cases of influence and diabolic possession, the victim has contributed to his or her state because of disobedience to the laws of God and curiosity for the occult.

Possession: It is common in cases of those who are possessed to have certain supernatural signs such as to produce a very hoarse voice of such a low tone impossible to be imitated by human beings, they may show strength superior to any other human being, they know the sins of people present if they have not been confessed, they know the future, read minds and show a lot of pride when they speak, they can master other languages.

Those who are possessed by the devil are filled with hatred, blasphemy for holy things, they emit furious sounds, they move and act with weird behavior, they tend to hurt or to mutilate themselves, they enter into periods of trance, they may vomit and do biological functions as if they were animals, they become a threat to their families and those around them, they lose contact with society. In other words, they are described as mad and most likely end up in a mental hospital, where they are doped for life without any spiritual help.

Diabolical influence or possession may occur for different reasons:
- Damnations from the parents, many times from the mother's womb.
- Cases of incest or sexual abuse of children.
- Victims of witchcraft, hatred, evil eye, voodoo, etc.
- Participation in satanic cults, witchcraft, séances, magic, yoga, Ouija board, clairvoyance, divinations, superstitions, amulets, enchantments, crystals, new age; literatures, movies and impure, violent or satanic shows.

Demonic influence: This is a more subtle level of demonic or diabolical possession. He who suffers the influence of the evil one, ends up doing evil things without any explanation, he may blaspheme against God without knowing why, he may listen to voices that lead him to do undesirable things, he may become obsessed with suicide, he may kill himself or others.

These persons can specialize themselves in committing any of the capital sins: pride, greed, envy, anger, lust, gluttony and sloth. They do it being influenced by the evil one, as an escape to their frustration and for the lack of fear of God. In other words, they still acknowledge their behavior, they know that something is wrong and that they may do something about it. In some cases they lose courage when they try to be delivered because they feel that the enemy mistreat them and does not let them have peace. Some may go to confession, but don't have enough repentance to pray for themselves and be delivered. Others are people of the world who don't know God.

The demonic influence may begin by interest in the occult, consultations of horoscopes, reading of the hands, predictions of the future, Ouija board, witchcraft, enchantments, evil eye, damnations from other people, hatred, séances, magic, yoga, pendulum, communication with spirits through mediums, clairvoyance, tarot cards, divinations, superstitions, amulets, crystals, new age, literatures, movies and impure, violent or satanic shows.

He who is possessed loses control of his mental faculties, in so far as to come to a spirituality that allows him to pray for himself, because the devil has received total dominion over him. Only through a profound prayer of deliverance done by believers in Christ or an official exorcism of the Church, can he be delivered.

He who is being influenced by the devil still has the opportunity to pray for himself or to ask others to pray for him, but first he has to repent of his sin, go to confession with a humble and contrite heart and to beg the divine mercy through the Precious Blood of Christ and the Power of the Holy name of Jesus who has guaranteed deliverance in his name. A lot of preparation, prayer and struggle is required to overcome the devil, but it is not impossible.

Blessed be the Lord who has given us the means to be saved from the evil one. In this treatise on exorcism, deliverance and healing, we find the solution to these spiritual problems.

Jesus asserts his authority over Satan

Jesus was tempted three times in the desert. In all these temptations, he overcame the devil with the sanctity of the Word of God in the Holy Scriptures. The same authority has been given to all of us human beings when we reject sin and choose the grace of God. This divine gift continues in every one of us, it is the right to use our free will to decide between good or evil.

During the three years of the ministry of Jesus, he demonstrated his power over evil spirits as we can see in some Bible passages:

Matthew 8:16 And when evening was come, they brought to him many that were possessed with devils: and he cast out the spirits with his word: and all that were sick he healed:

Matthew 8:28-32
28 And when came to the other side of the water, into the country of the Gerasens, there met him two that were possessed with devils, coming out of the sepulchres,

exceeding fierce, so that none could pass by that way. [29] And behold they cried out, saying: What have we to do with thee, Jesus Son of God? art thou come hither to torment us before the time? [30] And there was, not far from them, an herd of many swine feeding. [31] And the devils besought him, saying: If thou cast us out hence, send us into the herd of swine. [32] And he said to them: Go. But they going out went into the swine, and behold the whole herd ran violently down a steep place into the sea: and they perished in the waters.

Matthew 12:22

Then was offered to him one possessed with a devil, blind and dumb: and he healed him, so that he spoke and saw.

Matthew 17:14-20

[14] And when he was come to the multitude, there came to him a man falling down on his knees before him, saying: Lord, have pity on my son, for he is a lunatic, and suffers much: for he falls often into the fire, and often into the water. [15] And I brought him to thy disciples, and they could not cure him. [16] Then Jesus answered and said: O unbelieving and perverse generation, how long shall I be with you? How long shall I suffer you? Bring him hither to me. [17] And Jesus rebuked him, and the devil went out of him, and the child was cured from that hour. [18] Then came the disciples to Jesus secretly, and said: Why could not we cast him out? [19] Jesus said to them: Because of your unbelief. For, amen I say to you, if you have faith as a grain of mustard seed, you shall say to this mountain, Remove from hence hither, and it shall remove; and nothing shall be impossible to you. [20] But this kind is not cast out but by prayer and fasting.

Mark 1:23-27

[23] And there was in their synagogue a man with an unclean spirit; and he cried out, [24] Saying: What have we to do with thee, Jesus of Nazareth? Art thou come to destroy us? I know who thou art, the Holy One of God. [25] And Jesus threatened him, saying: Speak no more, and go out of the man. [26] And the unclean spirit tearing him, and crying out with a loud voice, went out of him. [27] And they were all amazed, insomuch that they questioned among themselves, saying: What thing is this? What is this new doctrine? For with power he commands even the unclean spirits, and they obey him.

Authority to perform exorcisms given by Jesus

Jesus gave authority to the apostles, disciples and believers as we see in the New Testament. This authority was received first by the apostles and disciples directly from Christ. After the descent of the Holy Spirit on the apostles in the form of tongues of fire, the authority was passed to the new believers through the word and the imposition of the hands by those who had the Holy Spirit.

Apostles. Matthew 10:8 Jesus sent the twelve apostles to preach the Good News that the Kingdom of Heaven was close at hand, he commissioned them to heal the sick, to cleanse the lepers, to resurrect the dead and to expulse evil spirits.

Disciples. Luke 10:17 The seventy two disciples returned to the Lord telling him how they had expulsed evil spirits in his name.

Believers. Mark 16:17 These are the signs that accompany believers, in my name they will cast out devils, they will speak in strange tongues, they will pick up serpents and won't be harmed if they drink their poison, they will lay their hands on the sick who will recover.

The believers mentioned in Mark 16:17, who fall in the category of faithful, disciples and apostles of Christ, shared something in common in the primitive Church, the fire of the Holy Spirit was upon them and the signs that accompanied them were prophecy, healing of the sick, speaking in strange tongues, discernment, faith in the name of Jesus, the gift of casting out evil spirits, the gift of preaching the Word of God, etc.

These signs are still present in our own time, their manifestation is visible in the charismatic movement. However, the Church has forbidden the use of exorcisms or to give orders to the enemy in the name of God except by qualified priests.

Because of this restriction imposed by the hierarchy of the Church to the believers who desire to be liberated or to do prayers against Satan, the only solution that allows us to act, remaining faithful to the Catholic Faith, is the prayer of deliverance that all the faithful can do, we will explain more about it further on.

Exorcisms that failed - A Warning

Mark 9:17-29

> The Apostles, even using the authority given to them were not able to cast out a demon from a possessed boy, Jesus had to do the exorcism personally, he criticized the lack of faith and explained that some evil spirits could only come out through prayer and fasting.

Acts 19:13-17

> Some Jews and the seven sons of Sceva tried to exorcise a man in the name of Jesus, who was preached by the Apostle Paul, but to their disappointment, the possessed man jumped over them giving them such a beating that they left the place naked and bleeding.

First we realize that to exorcise is a difficult job even for the apostles themselves who were authorized by Jesus personally. Now regarding those who are not genuine believers, to try to give orders to an evil spirit is a very high risk that may even cause the evil spirit to take possession of them or any one present.

Authority to perform exorcisms, given by the Catholic Church

Only priests authorized by a Bishop may officially do the solemn rite of Exorcism to persons who after psychological examination are accepted as being influenced or possessed by evil spirits and are in need of an exorcism.

Types of Exorcism and Deliverance

Solemn. This term is applied to an exorcism done officially under the authority of the Catholic Church to a person possessed by evil spirits. A rigorous psychological evaluation must be conducted on the victim, to establish if this is a case of possession, diabolical influence or to determine if it is a fraud.

The victim must show the typical signs that accompany those who are possessed, among them the knowledge of other languages, prediction of the future, blasphemies and abhorrence of holy things such as holy water, salt or blessed oil, he may display supernatural strength, levitation, etc.

Only an authorized priest can do the exorcism following the official rite of the Church. The devil or devils present in the possessed person receive orders from the exorcist to leave and never to come back, in the name of Jesus Christ and the Church in general, which received from Christ the promise that the gates of hell would not prevail against it. (Matthew 16:18)

According to Canon 1172 of the Code of Canon Law no one may licitly perform exorcisms on those who are possessed, unless he has obtained particular and express permission from the local ordinary (section 1), and it decrees that this permission is to be granted by the Ordinary only to priests who are outstanding in piety, knowledge, prudence, and integrity of life (section 2).

Private. The faithful of the Church may say prayers of deliverance, in which they ask divine intervention to cast out the evil influence on any person, place or object. Because of the extreme danger involved, and the lack of knowledge about the enemy, it is very important to know more deeply all about the devil and his angels, and this is why the Church doesn't allow exorcisms to be done by any one, except by a priest officially qualified by a Bishop.

In 1 Peter 5:8-9 Saint Peter, the head of the apostles exhorts us to have discipline and to be alert, because the devil, our adversary is like a roaring lion who is prowling around seeking for someone to devour. Saint Peter tells us to resist him by remaining firm in our faith.

Let us then be armed with great faith in God, let us grow in spiritually, so that God will listen to our prayers of deliverance.

Weapons of the exorcism

The weapon used to cast out an evil spirit of a person influenced or possessed by the devil is only the holy name of God, either the Father, the Son or the Holy Spirit, and the Precious Blood of Christ.

The weapon in the cases of deliverance is the prayer done to God the Father in the name of Jesus and by the power of his Precious Blood, the petitions of intercession done by the Virgin Mary in response to our prayers, especially the Holy Rosary, and also the prayers directed to San Michael the Archangel, the angels and the saints.

According to Canon 1172 of the Code of Canon Law no one may licitly perform exorcisms on those who are possessed, unless he has obtained particular and express permission from the local ordinary (section 1), and it decrees that this permission is to be granted by the Ordinary only to priests who are outstanding in piety, knowledge, prudence, and integrity of life (section 2).

Therefore, the *lay faithful are forbidden to do exorcisms*.

How can we the faithful and also believers in Christ then make use of the Holy Name of Christ without disobeying the Church?

How can we have recourse to the Holy Name of Christ, when we find ourselves affected by evil spirits?

The answer is our *"prayer of deliverance"*

Let us not do any exorcism, that is to say, let us not give orders to the devil, let us not enter into a dialog with him in any way whatsoever, so that we don't have to suffer the consequences. Let us allow the Holy Name of Jesus obtain from God the Father the power to cast out Satan from our world, let us invoke the Precious Blood of Jesus to cover us and to protect us every moment, let us permit our faith to flourish in praise and supplication before the only God, who has offered us His protection.

Because of the restrictions imposed upon the believers by the authority of the Church to exorcise, we are left with our prayers of deliverance in which we can ask God the Father in the name of Jesus, through the intercession of the Blessed Virgin Mary and the saints and by the power of Saint Michael the Archangel. This doesn't mean that we are going to lose the battle, on the contrary, we are going to let the Lord do the battle for us with the assurance of victory, just as when Moses said to the Israelites before crossing the red sea. Exodus 14:14 "The Lord will fight for you, and you have only to keep still."

The weapon of our deliverance is our own faith, and in the same way that Christ resisted the devil in the desert, now we are in the desert of this world, where we only have one powerful weapon which is the Holy Name of Jesus. Through his Holy Name, we are filled with power before the enemy, not in direct form, but seeking refuge in the protection that Christ gives us and in the promises that he has given us:

Matthew 7:7-8
   [7] Ask and you will receive, search and you will find, knock and the door will be open. [8] Because everyone who asks receives, everyone who searches finds and for everyone who knocks, the door will be open.

Matthew 18:18-20
   [18] Amen I say to you, whatsoever you shall bind upon earth, shall be bound also in heaven; and whatsoever you shall loose upon earth, shall be loosed also in heaven. [19] Again I say to you, that if two of you shall consent upon earth, concerning any thing whatsoever they shall ask, it shall be done to them by my Father who is in heaven. [20] For where there are two or three gathered together in my name, there am I in the midst of them.

John 14:13-14
   [13] Because I go to the Father: and whatsoever you shall ask the Father in my name, that will I do: that the Father may be glorified in the Son. [14] If you shall ask me any thing in my name, that I will do.

Preparation before the Prayer of Deliverance

Just as when we are about to begin a battle, we must sit and study our intelligence on the enemy, we must analyze our weapons and our capacity, we must be totally sure that our battle will lead us to victory. To try to fight the devil without knowing the necessary tactics to defeat him, is like being unprotected and placing our hands in a beehive, or like playing with fire.

First of all we must be clear about the notion that God is the only one who can overcome the enemy, since He alone is superior to the devil, who has been created according to his designs.

Here we really must make use of the Work of God, nor our own, since God definitively is the only way for our deliverance.

Again, an exorcism is an exclusive matter for a priest duly authorized by the Church according to Canon 1172 of the Code of Canon Law.

I repeat, *we are not going to do an exorcism*, we are going then to prepare ourselves for a profound *prayer of deliverance*, which involves the knowledge of all that is mentioned previously above and of the prayers recommended.

We may also make use of sacramentals such as a crucifix containing wood (it must not be all plastic or metallic), holy water, holy salt and holy oil.

The influenced person may pray these prayers although, it is probable that the enemy will distract him and he may end up doing something else, this is why it is recommended that at least two people who are faithful to the Church, preferably who attend mass daily say the prayers.

The day of the prayers, they must get together in a place where there won't be other persons who may interrupt or become influenced by the evil one. First of all they must talk about God, read the Holy Bible and make available at least two or three hours to avoid any haste.

It is a good idea for all to be in a state of grace, and to have confessed their sins recently, to avoid the risk of being scandalized by knowledge of the evil one.

During some moments in our prayers we should kneel down, although it is also good to be comfortable and serene during most of the time.

It is recommended to anoint the influenced person with holy oil during the prayer of deliverance, especially when we start to ask the Lord to cast out the enemy. It is also recommended to sprinkle holy water in the place and also to make the sign of the cross.

In the sections where appears the sign of the cross, we must pause, bless ourselves and bless those we praying for.

It is advisable to make copies of the prayers for every one present, this way there is more concentration, although only one person should read the prayers loudly and clearly, but every one must live them in their hearts.

We must read very slowly, as if waiting for a response to our prayer after every sentence.

Those who have received the gift of tongues, may praise God in tongues during the prayers, remembering the words of Jesus about not worrying in court, that is being before the accuser, since the Holy Spirit will speak for us, and our Heavenly Father will command the enemy to go out of the situation or person we are praying for.

These prayers may be repeated as often as possible, until obtaining total deliverance. Whenever a priest exorcises in cases of possession, very seldom, the devil leaves in the first session, unless it is a case of influence which only requires faith and determination from the influenced person.

Here we may understand better Mark 16:15 when Jesus gives the believers the power to cast out devils, as a sign accompanied by the gift of tongues and the gift of healing. Since it is the Spirit that commands and not ourselves, we are never contradicting the Church during these prayers. He who prays for the benefit of his brother is giving glory to God. See James 5:19-20

Warnings

The devil knows beforehand that we are preparing a prayer to this end, normally unexpected things may occur, like problems and misunderstandings that perturb those who are going to do the prayer, cars don't start, unexpected programs, lock that don't open, keys that brake, and other incredible things may happen to cancel the prayer meeting. It is recommended that those taking part in the prayers attend mass during that day, and with anticipation offer holy masses offering the Precious Blood of Jesus for the deliverance of the person who requires it.

When we start the prayers, we must not pay attention to the enemy if there is a manifestation, especially with lies or blasphemies. Our prayers are directed to God, not to the devil, our conversation is with God, we can not interrupt it by having a dialog with the devil.

We must not be afraid by any noises, movements or gestures made by the one being prayed over, we must not be afraid even if our legs are trembling, this is natural to feel, but we must not interrupt our prayer by having a dialog with the enemy.

Our faith must remain firm in the power of God that is going to bring deliverance to a suffering soul.

It is advisable to speak with the person in question and make him feel repentance for his sins and to confirm his faith in the power of Christ for his deliverance, at the same time these prayers can be said at any distance, with the same effectiveness, since we don't have any power or sanctity, it is God who is doing his work by listening to our sincere prayer full of faith.

We must not allow ourselves to be taken away by curiosity of having this encounter with the devil, after all we are children of God, created in his image; the devil is also his creation and we must not be too impressed, he is acting according to his evil nature, we are praying according to the Spirit of God who leads us to seek his Glory.

Appendix viii
Important Sacramentals

What are Sacramentals?

This is from the Catechism of the Catholic Church

CHAPTER FOUR

OTHER LITURGICAL CELEBRATIONS

ARTICLE 1 - SACRAMENTALS

1667 "Holy Mother Church has, moreover, instituted sacramentals. These are sacred signs which bear a resemblance to the sacraments. They signify effects, particularly of a spiritual nature, which are obtained through the intercession of the Church. By them men are disposed to receive the chief effect of the sacraments, and various occasions in life are rendered holy."[171]

The characteristics of sacramentals

1668 Sacramentals are instituted for the sanctification of certain ministries of the Church, certain states of life, a great variety of circumstances in Christian life, and the use of many things helpful to man. In accordance with bishops' pastoral decisions, they can also respond to the needs, culture, and special history of the Christian people of a particular region or time. They always include a prayer, often accompanied by a specific sign, such as the laying on of hands, the sign of the cross, or the sprinkling of holy water (which recalls Baptism).

1669 Sacramentals derive from the baptismal priesthood: every baptized person is called to be a "blessing," and to bless.[172] Hence lay people may preside at certain blessings; the more a blessing concerns ecclesial and sacramental life, the more is its administration reserved to the ordained ministry (bishops, priests, or deacons).[173]

1670 Sacramentals do not confer the grace of the Holy Spirit in the way that the sacraments do, but by the Church's prayer, they prepare us to receive grace and dispose us to cooperate with it. "For well-disposed members of the faithful, the liturgy of the sacraments and sacramentals sanctifies almost every event of their lives with the divine grace which flows from the Paschal mystery of the Passion, Death, and Resurrection of Christ. From this source all sacraments and sacramentals draw their power. There is scarcely any proper use of material things which cannot be thus directed toward the sanctification of men and the praise of God."[174]

Various forms of sacramentals

1671 Among sacramentals blessings (of persons, meals, objects, and places) come first. Every blessing praises God and prays for his gifts. In Christ, Christians are blessed by God the Father "with every spiritual blessing."[175] This is why the Church imparts blessings by invoking the name of Jesus, usually while making the holy sign of the cross of Christ.

1672 Certain blessings have a lasting importance because they consecrate persons to God, or reserve objects and places for liturgical use. Among those blessings which are intended for persons - not to be confused with sacramental ordination - are the blessing of the abbot or abbess of a monastery, the consecration of virgins, the rite of religious profession and the blessing of certain ministries of the Church (readers, acolytes, catechists, etc.). The dedication or blessing of a church or an altar, the blessing of holy oils, vessels, and vestments, bells, etc., can be mentioned as examples of blessings that concern objects.

1673 When the Church asks publicly and authoritatively in the name of Jesus Christ that a person or object be protected against the power of the Evil One and withdrawn from his dominion, it is called exorcism. Jesus performed exorcisms and from him the Church has received the power and office of exorcizing.[176] In a simple form, exorcism is performed at the celebration of Baptism. The solemn exorcism, called "a major exorcism," can be performed only by a priest and with the permission of the bishop. The priest must proceed with prudence, strictly observing the rules established by the Church. Exorcism is directed at the expulsion of demons or to the liberation from demonic possession through the spiritual authority which Jesus entrusted to his Church. Illness, especially psychological illness, is a very different matter; treating this is the concern of medical science. Therefore, before an exorcism is performed, it is important to ascertain that one is dealing with the presence of the Evil One, and not an illness.[177]

Popular piety

1674 Besides sacramental liturgy and sacramentals, catechesis must take into account the forms of piety and popular devotions among the faithful. The religious sense of the Christian people has always found expression in various forms of piety surrounding the Church's sacramental life, such as the veneration of relics, visits to sanctuaries, pilgrimages, processions, the stations of the cross, religious dances, the rosary, medals,[178] etc.

1675 These expressions of piety extend the liturgical life of the Church, but do not replace it. They "should be so drawn up that they harmonize with the liturgical seasons, accord with the sacred liturgy, are in some way derived from it and lead the people to it, since in fact the liturgy by its very nature is far superior to any of them."[179]

1676 Pastoral discernment is needed to sustain and support popular piety and, if necessary, to purify and correct the religious sense which underlies these devotions so that the faithful may advance in knowledge of the mystery of Christ.[180] Their exercise is subject to the care and judgment of the bishops and to the general norms of the Church.

At its core the piety of the people is a storehouse of values that offers answers of Christian wisdom to the great questions of life. The Catholic wisdom of the people is capable of fashioning a vital synthesis.... It creatively combines the divine and the human, Christ and Mary, spirit and body, communion and institution, person and community, faith and homeland, intelligence and emotion. This wisdom is a Christian humanism that radically affirms the dignity of every person as a child of God, establishes a basic fraternity, teaches people to encounter nature and understand work, provides reasons for joy and humor even in the midst of a very hard life. For the people this wisdom is also a principle of discernment and an evangelical instinct through which they spontaneously sense when the Gospel is served in the Church and when it is emptied of its content and stifled by other interests.[181]

IN BRIEF

1677 Sacramentals are sacred signs instituted by the Church. They prepare men to receive the fruit of the sacraments and sanctify different circumstances of life.

1678 Among the sacramentals blessings occupy an important place. They include both praise of God for his works and gifts, and the Church's intercession for men that they may be able to use God's gifts according to the spirit of the Gospel.

1679 In addition to the liturgy, Christian life is nourished by various forms of popular piety, rooted in the different cultures. While carefully clarifying them in the light of faith, the Church fosters the forms of popular piety that express an evangelical instinct and a human wisdom and that enrich Christian life.

The Miraculous Medal & Consecration to Our Lady

It is highly recommended that every True Knights wear the Miraculous Medal and Consecrate himself to Our Lady.

The Miraculous Medal is a "spiritual bullet" in the war to win souls, said St. Maximiian of the medal given to us by Our Lady of Rue du Bac in 1830. Front proclaims Mary as Immaculate Conception and Mediatrix of All Graces; back as Coredemptrix.

The Miraculous Medal owes its origins to the apparitions of the Blessed Virgin Mary in the chapel of the Rue du Bac, Paris, in 1830. She appeared to Catherine Labouré, showing the young nun and future saint the design of a medal that serves as a mini-catechism of the Church's teaching on Our Lady.

In a vision, Mary stood on a globe with brilliant light streaming from her jeweled fingers. "Behold the symbol of graces shed upon those who ask for them," she said, representing herself as Mediatrix of All Graces. Surrounding her a banner read, "O Mary, conceived without sin, pray for us who have recourse to you," symbolizing her Immaculate Conception. The vision reversed, showing the letter 'M' entwined with a cross above the Sacred Hearts. This image represents Mary as Coredemptrix, a unique participator in Jesus' saving act of redemption.

Millions of medals have been distributed and untold graces given "to those who wear it around the neck" as the Virgin promised to St. Catherine. Hearing of the miraculous conversion of the agnostic Alphonse Ratisbonne through the medal, St. Maximilian made wearing it and giving it away an integral part of his movement. He called the Miraculous Medal "a 'bullet' with which the faithful soldier hits the enemy, that is evil, and thus rescues souls."

What is Consecration to Our Lady (From www.consecration.com)

We can consecrate ourselves to Our Lady in various ways and this consecration can be formulated in different words; indeed, a simple interior act of the will is sufficient, since in this is included the essence of our consecration to the Immaculata. But for greater facility there exists a short formula that expresses the spirit of the Militia of the Immaculata (www.Consecration.com).

How to Consecrate Yourself and Enroll in the MI *(Militia of the Immaculata)*

A. Select the date on which you want your name recorded in the official register of the MI, preferably a Marian feast day. Please select from the list of dates here below or choose your own special feast date. Then go to the MI Consecration website and fill out the enrollment application.

Marian Feast Days

Jan 1	Solemnity of the Mother of God	Aug 22	Queenship of Mary
Feb 11	Our Lady of Lourdes	Sept 8	Birth of the Blessed Virgin Mary
Mar 25	Annunciation	Sept 15	Our Lady of Sorrows
May 13	Our Lady of Fatima	Oct 7	Our Lady of the Rosary
May 31	Visitation	Nov 21	Presentation of Mary
June 27	Our Lady of Perpetual Help	Nov 27	Our Lady of the Miraculous Medal
July 1	Immaculate Heart of Mary	Dec 8	Immaculate Conception
July 16	Our Lady of Mt. Carmel	Dec 12	Our Lady of Guadalupe
Aug 15	Assumption		

B. Prepare yourself for the day of consecration by daily Mass if possible, the Rosary, spiritual reading and receive the Sacrament of Reconciliation on or before the day of your consecration.

C. On the day of your enrollment, recite the official act of consecration. Renounce attachment to sin and if possible attend Mass. (A Plenary Indulgence is granted by the Church under the usual conditions: Confession, Communion, a visit to a Church and prayers for the intentions of the Holy Father, must be included. It may be satisfied on the day of your enrollment or within the following eight days.) In this way you will be making an effort to remove all obstacles to Our Lady making you her own in the Holy Spirit.

D. Finally, ask Our Lady and St. Maximilian to show you how you can best serve the Lord from this moment on.

Prayer of Total Consecration By St. Maximilian Kolbe

O Immaculata, Queen of heaven and earth, refuge of sinners and our most loving Mother, God has willed to entrust the entire order of mercy to you. I, N..., a repentant sinner, cast myself at your feet humbly imploring you to take me with all that I am and have, wholly to yourself as your possession and property. Please make of me, of all my powers of soul and body, of my whole life, death and eternity, whatever most pleases you.

If it pleases you, use all that I am and have without reserve, wholly to accomplish what was said of you: "She will crush your head," and, "You alone have destroyed all heresies in the world." Let me be a fit instrument in your immaculate and merciful hands for introducing and increasing your glory to the maximum in all the many strayed and indifferent souls, and thus help extend as far as possible the blessed kingdom of the most Sacred Heart of Jesus. For wherever you enter you obtain the grace of conversion and growth in holiness, since it is through your hands that all graces come to us from the most Sacred Heart of Jesus.

V. Allow me to praise you, O sacred Virgin.
R. Give me strength against your enemies.

Commentary on the Consecration Prayer
by St. Maximilian Kolbe

This act of consecration includes three parts: an invocation; a request that she may deign to accept us as her property; and a please that she may deign to make use of us to conquer other souls for her. In the invocation we first say,

O Immaculata

We turn to her under this name, because she herself deigned to give herself this name at Lourdes: "the Immaculate Conception." God is immaculate, but God is not conceived. Angels are immaculate, but there is no conception with them. The first parents were immaculate before sinning, but neither were they conceived. Jesus was immaculate and conceived, but he was not a conception, for as God he already existed before and to him also applied the words of the name of God as revealed to Moses: "I am who am, who always is and does not begin to be." Other people are conceptions, but stained. She alone is not only conceived, but also a conception and immaculate. This name conceals many more mysteries, which will be discovered in time. Thus she indicates that the Immaculate Conception belongs to her essence.

This name must be dear to her, because it signifies the first grace she received in the first moment of her existence. The first gift is the dearest one. This name is ratified by her life, because she was always unspotted. Hence she was also full of grace and God was always with her, even to the degree that she became the Mother of the Son of God.

Queen of heaven and earth

In a family, the loving parents fulfill the will of the children as much as they are able, insofar as it is not harmful for them. So much more does God, the Creator and prototype of earthly parents, desire to fulfill the will of his creatures, insofar as it is not harmful for them, that is, insofar as it is conformable with his will. The Immaculata did not bend away from the will of God in anything. In all things she loved the will of God, loved God. Hence she is justly called the Omnipotent Beggar. She has influence upon God himself, on the entire world; she is the Queen of heaven and earth. In heaven everyone acknowledges the rule of her love. That group of the first angels that did not want to acknowledge her reign lost its place in heaven.

She is queen also of earth because she is the Mother of God himself, but she both desires and has a right to be freely acknowledged by every heart, be loved as the Queen of every heart, so that through her that heart might become immaculate, similar to her heart and more worthy of union with God, with the love of God, with the Sacred Heart of Jesus.

Refuge of sinners

God is merciful, infinitely merciful, nevertheless just and infinitely just. He cannot bear the least sin and must demand full satisfaction for it. The stewardess of the infinite value of the Precious Blood of Jesus that washes away sin, the Immaculata, is the personification of God's mercy. Therefore she is rightly called the refuge of sinners, of all sinners regardless of the number and greatness of their sins - even though the sinner would think there is no more mercy left for him. Indeed, every cleansing of the soul is for her a new confirmation of her title of Immaculate Conception. The more deeply the soul is plunged into sin, the more does the power of her immaculateness show itself, by the fact that she gives snowy whiteness to such a soul.

Our most loving Mother

The Immaculata is the mother of our entire supernatural life because she is the Mediatrix of the grace of God, hence our mother in the sphere of grace, in the supernatural sphere. She is a most loving mother, because you do not have any mother so affectionate, so loving, so godlike, so Immaculate, so wholly divine.

God has willed to entrust the entire order of mercy to you

In a family, the father is glad at times that the mother stays his punishing hand over the child by her intercession, because justice is satisfied and mercy is shown. Not without cause is justice suspended. Similarly God, in order not to punish us, gives us a spiritual mother, whose intercession he never opposes. Hence the saints claim that Jesus reserved for himself the order of justice, giving to the Immaculata the whole order of his mercy.

Go to www.consecration.com for more information or write to:
MI National Center
1600 West Park Avenue
Libertyville, IL 60048
847-367-7800 Fax 847-367-7831

(NEW MEMBERS will receive a free miraculous medal, a frameable MI enrollee certificate, and information on living out your Marian consecration.)

The Brown Scapular of Our Lady of Mount Carmel

It is recommended that all True Knights wear the Brown Scapular as a powerful defense in the spiritual war that we are battling everyday. By doing so we call for the intercession of Our Lady constantly in return for our devotion to her. The following information is from http://carmelnet.org/scapular/scapular.htm.

The world in which we live is full of material things that have symbolic meaning: light, fire, water... there are also, in everyday life, experiences of relationships between human beings, which express and symbolize deeper realities such as taking part in a protest march (as a sign of solidarity), joining together in a national celebration (as a sign of identity).

We need signs and symbols to help us understand what is happening at present, or what happened before, and to give us an awareness of who we are, as individuals and as groups.

Jesus is the great sign of the Father's love. He founded the Church as a sign and instrument of His love. Christian life also has its signs. Jesus used bread, wine, water to help us understand higher things, which we can neither see or touch.

In the celebration of the Eucharist and the other sacraments (baptism, confirmation, reconciliation, matrimony, orders, the sacrament of the sick) the symbols, (water, oil, the laying on of hands, the rings,) all have their own meaning and bring us into.

As well as liturgical signs, the Church has others related to some event, to some tradition or some person. One of these is the Brown Scapular of Our Lady of Mount Carmel.

A Sign of Mary

One of the signs in the tradition of the Church from many centuries ago is the Brown Scapular of Our Lady of Mount Carmel. It is a sign approved by the Church and accepted by the Carmelite Order as an external sign of love for Mary, of the trust her children have in her, and of commitment to live like her.

The word scapular indicates a form of clothing, which monks wore when they were working. With the passage of time, people began to give symbolic meaning to it: the cross to be borne every day as disciples and followers of Christ. In some religious orders, such as the Carmelites, the Scapular turned into a sign of their way of life. The Scapular came to symbolize the special dedication of Carmelites to Mary, the Mother of God, and to express trust in her motherly protection as well as the desire to be like her in her commitment to Christ and to others. Thus it became a sign of Mary.

In the Middle Ages many Christians wanted to be associated with the orders founded at that time: Franciscans, Dominicans, Augustinians, and Carmelites. Groups of lay people began to emerge in associations such as confraternities and sodalities.

All the religious orders wanted to give these lay people a sign of affiliation and of participation in their spirit and apostolate. That sign was often a part of their habit: a cloak, a cord, a scapular.

Among the Carmelites, the stage came when a smaller version of the Scapular was accepted as the sign of belonging to the Order and an expression of its spirituality.

Value and Meaning

The Blessed Virgin teaches us:
- To be open to God, and to his will, shown to us in the events of our lives;
- To Listen to the Word of God in the Bible and in life, to believe in it and to put into practice its demands;
- To pray at all times, as a way of discovering the presence of God in all that is happening around us;
- To be involved with people, being attentive to their needs.

The Scapular finds its roots in the tradition of the Order, which has seen in it a sign of Mary's motherly protection. It has therefore, a centuries old spiritual meaning approved by Church.
- It stands for a commitment to follow Jesus, like Mary, the perfect model of all the disciples of Christ. This commitment finds its origin in baptism by which we become children of God.
- It leads us into the community of Carmel, a community of religious men and women, which has existed in the Church for over eight centuries.
- It reminds us of the example of the saints of Carmel, with whom we establish a close bond as brothers and sisters to one another.
- It is an expression of our belief that we will meet God in eternal life, aided by the intercession and prayers of Mary.

Rules and Rituals

- People are enrolled in the Scapular only once by a priest or authorized person.
- The Scapular can be replaced afterwards by a medal, which has on one side the image of the Sacred Heart of Jesus and on the other, the image of Mary.
- The Scapular holds us to live as authentic Christians in line with the teaching of the Gospel, to receive the sacraments, to profess our special devotion to the Blessed Virgin, which should be expressed each day, at least by saying the Hail Mary three times.

Short form of giving the scapular

Receive this Scapular, a sign of your special relationship with Mary, the Mother of Jesus, whom you pledge to imitate. May it be a reminder to you of your dignity as a Christian in serving others and imitating Mary. Wear it as a sign of her protection and of belonging to the family of Carmel, voluntarily doing the will of God and devoting yourself to building a world true to his plan of community, justice and peace.

The Brown Scapular is not:
- a magical charm to protect you
- an automatic guarantee of salvation
- an excuse for not living up to the demands of the Christian life

It is a sign:
- which has been approved by the Church for over seven centuries;
- which stands for the decision to
    - follow Jesus like Mary:
    - be open to God and to his will
    - be guided by faith, hope, and love
    - to pray at all times
    - to discover God present in all that happens around us.

The Medal or Crucifix of Saint Benedict

It is recommended that all True Knights wear the Medal or Crucifix of St. Benedict as a powerful defense in the spiritual war that we are battling everyday. By doing so we call for the intercession of St. Benedict, who is a powerful ally in spiritual warfare. The St. Benedict Medal is the only medal in the church that has an exorcism pray placed on it.

The following information is from http://www.osb.org/gen/medal.html.

Medals, crosses, rosaries, statues, paintings and other religious articles have long been used as a means of fostering and expressing our religious devotion to God and the saints. Icons, or painted images of Christ and the saints, are especially popular among Eastern Christians as an aid to Christian piety and devotion.

The use of any religious article is therefore intended as a means of reminding us of God and of stirring up in us a ready willingness and desire to serve God and our neighbor. With this understanding we reject any use of religious articles as if they were mere charms or had some magic power to bring us good luck or better health. Such is not the Christian attitude.

Origin of the Medal of Saint Benedict

For the early Christians, the cross was a favorite symbol and badge of their faith in Christ. From the writings of St. Gregory the Great (540-604), we know that St. Benedict had a deep faith in the Cross and worked miracles with the sign of the cross. This faith in, and special devotion to, the Cross was passed on to succeeding generations of Benedictines.

Devotion to the Cross of Christ also gave rise to the striking of medals that bore the image of St. Benedict holding a cross aloft in his right hand and his Rule for Monasteries in the other hand. Thus, the Cross has always been closely associated with the Medal of St. Benedict, which is often referred to as the Medal-Cross of St. Benedict.

In the course of time, other additions were made, such as the Latin petition on the margin of the medal, asking that by St. Benedict's presence we may be strengthened in the hour of death, as will be explained later.

We do not know just when the first medal of St. Benedict was struck. At some point in history a series of capital letters was placed around the large figure of the cross on the reverse side of the medal. For a long time the meaning of these letters was unknown, but in 1647 a manuscript dating back to 1415 was found at the Abbey of Metten in Bavaria, giving an explanation of the letters. They are the initial letters of a Latin prayer of exorcism against Satan, as will be explained below.

The Cross of Eternal Salvation

On the face of the medal is the image of Saint Benedict. In his right hand he holds the cross, the Christian's symbol of salvation. The cross reminds us of the zealous work of evangelizing and civilizing England and Europe carried out mainly by the Benedictine monks and nuns, especially for the sixth to the ninth/tenth centuries.

Rule and Raven

In St. Benedict's left hand is his Rule for Monasteries that could well be summed up in the words of the Prolog exhorting us to "walk in God's ways, with the Gospel as our guide."

On a pedestal to the right of St. Benedict is the poisoned cup, shattered when he made the sign of the cross over it. On a pedestal to the left is a raven about to carry away a loaf of poisoned bread that a jealous enemy had sent to St. Benedict.

C. S. P. B.

Above the cup and the raven are the Latin words: Crux s. patris Benedicti (The Cross of our holy father Benedict). On the margin of the medal, encircling the figure of Benedict, are the Latin words: Eius in obitu nostro praesentia muniamur! (May we be strengthened by his presence in the hour of our death!). Benedictines have always regarded St. Benedict as a special patron of a happy death. He himself died in the chapel at Montecassino while standing with his arms raised up to heaven, supported by the brothers of the monastery, shortly after St. Benedict had received Holy Communion.

Monte Cassino

Below Benedict we read: ex SM Casino MDCCCLXXX (from holy Monte Cassino, 1880). This is the medal struck to commemorate the 1400th anniversary of the birth of Saint Benedict.

Reverse Side of the Medal

Crux mihi lux

On the back of the medal, the cross is dominant. On the arms of the cross are the initial letters of a rhythmic Latin prayer: Crux sacra sit mihi lux! Nunquam draco sit mihi dux! (May the holy cross be my light! May the dragon never be my guide!).

In the angles of the cross, the letters C S P B stand for Crux Sancti Patris Benedicti (The cross of our holy father Benedict).

Peace

Above the cross is the word pax (peace), that has been a Benedictine motto for centuries. Around the margin of the back of the medal, the letters V R S N S M V - S M Q L I V B are the initial letters, as mentioned above, of a Latin prayer of exorcism against Satan: Vade retro Satana! Nunquam suade mihi vana! Sunt mala quae libas. Ipse venena bibas! (Begone Satan! Never tempt me with your vanities! What you offer me is evil. Drink the poison yourself!)

Use of the Medal

There is no special way prescribed for carrying or wearing the Medal of St. Benedict. It can be worn on a chain around the neck, attached to one's rosary, kept in one's pocket or purse, or placed in one's car or home. The medal is often put into the foundations of houses and building, on the walls of barns and sheds, or in one's place of business.

The purpose of using the medal in any of the above ways is to call down God's blessing and protection upon us, wherever we are, and upon our homes and possessions, especially through the intercession of St. Benedict. By the conscious and devout use of the medal, it becomes, as it were, a constant silent prayer and reminder to us of our dignity as followers of Christ.

The medal is a prayer of exorcism against Satan, a prayer for strength in time of temptation, a prayer for peace among ourselves and among the nations of the world, a prayer that the Cross of Christ be our light and guide, a prayer of firm rejection of all that is evil, a prayer of petition that we may with Christian courage "walk in God's ways, with the Gospel as our guide," as St. Benedict urges us.

A profitable spiritual experience can be ours if we but take the time to study the array of inscriptions and representations found on the two sides of the medal. The lessons found there can be pondered over and over to bring true peace of mind and heart into our lives as we struggle to overcome the weaknesses of our human nature and realize that our human condition is not perfect, but that with the help of God and the intercession of the saints our condition can become better.

The Medal of St. Benedict can serve as a constant reminder of the need for us to take up our cross daily and "follow the true King, Christ our Lord," and thus learn "to share in his heavenly kingdom," as St. Benedict urges us in the Prolog of his Rule.

Two Special Uses of the Medal

By a rescript of the Sacred Congregation of Religious (4 May 1965) lay Oblates of St. Benedict are permitted to wear the Medal of St. Benedict instead of the small black cloth scapular formerly worn.

By a decree of the Sacred Congregation of Rites (6 March 1959), the Blessing of St. Maur over the sick is permitted to be given with a Medal of St. Benedict instead of with a relic of the True Cross, since the latter is difficult to obtain.

Approved Blessing of the Medal of St. Benedict

Medals of Saint Benedict are sacramentals that may be blessed legitimately by any priest or deacon -- not necessarily a Benedictine (Instr., 26 Sept. 1964; Can. 1168). The following English form may be used.

V. Our help is in the name of the Lord.

R. Who made heaven and earth.

In the name of God the Father + almighty, who made heaven and earth, the seas and all that is in them, I exorcise these medals against the power and attacks of the evil one. May all who use these medals devoutly be blessed with health of soul and body. In the name of the Father + almighty, of the Son + Jesus Christ our Lord, and of the Holy + Spirit the Paraclete, and in the love of the same Lord Jesus Christ who will come on the last day to judge the living and the dead, and the world by fire.

Amen.

Let us pray. Almighty God, the boundless source of all good things, we humbly ask that, through the intercession of Saint Benedict, you pour out your blessings + upon these medals. May those who use them devoutly and earnestly strive to perform good works be blessed by you with health of soul and body, the grace of a holy life, and remission of the temporal punishment due to sin.

May they also with the help of your merciful love, resist the temptation of the evil one and strive to exercise true charity and justice toward all, so that one day they may appear sinless and holy in your sight. This we ask though Christ our Lord. Amen.

The medals are then sprinkled with holy water.

The Cord of Saint Joseph for Purity

It is recommended that all True Knights wear the Cord of the Confraternity of Saint Joseph in honor of our perfect example of a husband, father and man, and as a powerful defense in the spiritual war that we are battling everyday. By doing so we call for the intercession of St. Joseph constantly in return for our devotion to him. Cords are available at: http://www.inhisname.com/Scapulars5.htm or call In His Name Catholic Store Toll-Free 1-800-735-4566.

What are Cords & Cinctures

The wearing of a cord or cincture has always been a sign of chastity as well as mortification and humility for the laity as well as the religious.

The wearing of a cord in honor of a saint goes back to the very early Church. We find the first instance mentioned in the life of St Monica. In a vision from the Blessed Virgin, she received a black leathern belt, and assured that those who wore it in her honor would be under her protection. And there are many other instances.

The wearing a cord to honor St. Michael was general throughout France. After his conversion St. Francis of Assisi girded himself in rough cords in honor of the cords that bound Our Lord during His passion. St Dominic received his cord from St Francis & wore it out of sight in devotion to St. Francis. The cord of St. Philomena was a pious practice after many miracles & her confraternity was raised to an Archconfraternity. The miraculous cure of an Augustinian nun of St Joseph's Archconfraternity gave rise to the pious wearing of the cincture of St. Joseph.

Cords worn around the waist are for additional grace to live a life of purity & chastity, among other graces. When worn sash style across one shoulder, it is for obedience.

The Cord of Saint Joseph

The cord of Saint Joseph originated in Antwerp, Belgium, in 1657 with the miraculous cure of a devoted Augustinian nun, Sister Elizabeth. After a three year severe and painful illness, the physicians had given up hope of curing her and expected her death. But the nun made a cord and had it blessed in the Saint's honour and put it around her waist. A few days later when praying before St Joseph's statue she was suddenly freed from the pain. Her recovery was considered miraculous and the devotion spread. Numerous special graces were obtained through it's use. It was not used merely as a remedy against bodily ailments but also as a spiritual aid to preserve the virtue of purity. The devotion was approved by the Sacred Congregation of rights on September 19, 1859. It was also blessed and approved by Pope Pius IX who approved a spacial formula for the blessing of the cord of St Joseph.

The cord was invoked, not merely as a remedy against physical ailments, but also as a preservative of the virtue of purity.

The Bishop of Verona became aware of the necessity of addressing a supplication to the Congregation of Rites, which he did by letter on January 14, 1859. After a mature examination the Sacred Congregation, in accordance with the request, approved on September 19 of that year, the new formula of blessing and permitted its solemn and private use. Finally the Bishop obtained for the Association of the Cord the privilege of being declared 'primarie," and at the same time His Holiness, Pope Pius IX enriched it with special indulgences.

Graces Attached to the Wearing of the Cord

Graces precious to the piety of St. Joseph's servants are attached to the wearing of this cord. They are:

1. St. Joseph's special protection;
2. Purity of soul;
3. The grace of chastity;
4. Final perseverance;
5. Particular assistance at the hour of death.

Nature of the Cord and the Manner of Wearing it

The Cord of St. Joseph should be of thread or cotton, ending at one extremity in seven knots, indicative of the Seven Joys and Sorrows of St. Joseph. It is worn as a girdle for purity or chastity and humility and around the shoulders for obedience. It ought to be blessed by a priest with the faculties for this blessing. Pius IX approved a special formula for the blessing of the cord of St. Joseph.

Plenary Indulgences Attached to the Cord

1. On the day of entrance into the Association.

2. On the day of the Feast of the Espousals of the Blessed Virgin and St. Joseph (Jan. 23).

3. On the 19th of March, the Feast of St. Joseph, and on one of the seven days which immediately follow.

4. On the Feast of the Patronage of St. Joseph (3rd Sunday after Easter).

5. Upon death for members of the Association who are truly penitent, have confessed their sins and received Holy viaticum; or not being able to do, having invoked by mouth or in the heart, the Name of Jesus.

Conditions for Gaining the Indulgences

1. Be truly contrite, confess and communicate the day of investiture or wearing it for the first time.

2. If possible visit the church of the Association or an other oratory, if not, and to pray for peace between Christian princes or rulers, the extirpation of heresies, and the exaltation of Holy Mother Church.

3. Must be affiliated with the Church of San Rocco at Rome. We do not know how binding this is for Americans or how to contact them. We have provided a link to the Company that distributes the Cord in the U.S. Someone one there may know how to contact that church. All the indulgences are applicable to the Holy Souls.

Recite Daily Seven Times the Glory Be, Together with the following prayer, which is the Prayer for Purity *(See page 4 for the Prayers in honor of the 7 Sorrows and Joys of Saint Joseph.)*

O GUARDIAN of Virgins and holy Father St. Joseph, into whose faithful keeping were entrusted Christ Jesus, Innocence Itself, and Mary, Virgin of virgins, I pray and beseech thee by these dear pledges, Jesus and Mary, that, being preserved from all uncleanness, I may with spotless mind, pure heart and chaste body, ever serve Jesus and Mary most chastely all the days of my life. Amen.

Blessing the Cord To be worn in honour of Saint Joseph

[Approved by the congregation of Sacred Rites, 19 September 1859.]

The priest, vested in surplice and white stole, says;

V. Our help is in the name of the Lord.   R. Who made heaven and earth.
V. The Lord be with you.   R. May He also be with you.
Let us pray.

O Lord Jesus Christ, who inculcated the counsel and love of virginity, and gave the precept of chastity, we appeal to Thy kindness, asking that Thou bless and hallow this cincture as a token of purity. Let all who gird themselves with it as a safeguard of chastity be enabled, by the prayers of Saint Joseph, spouse of Thy holy Mother, to practise that continence which is so pleasing to Thee, and to live in obedience to Thy commandments. May they also obtain pardon of their sins, health in mind and body, and finally attain everlasting life. We ask this of Thee who lives and reigns with God the Father, in the unity of the Holy Ghost, God, forever and ever. R. Amen.

Let us pray.

Almighty and everlasting God, grant, we pray, that those who revere the inviolate virginity of the most pure Virgin Mary and of Saint Joseph, her spouse, may by their prayers be pure in mind and body; through Christ our Lord. R. Amen.

Let us pray.

Almighty and everlasting God, who committed the boy Jesus and the most pure Mary, ever a Virgin, to the care of the chaste man Saint Joseph, we humbly entreat Thee that those who are girded with this cincture in honour of Saint Joseph and under his patronage may, by Thy help and his prayers, persevere in holy chastity for all time; through Christ our Lord. R. Amen.

Let us pray.

God, the lover and restorer of innocence, we pray that Thy faithful who are to wear this cincture may, by the prayers of Saint Joseph, spouse of Thy holy Mother, have their loins girded and hold burning lamps in their hands, and thus be likened to men who wait for their Lord when He shall return for a wedding, that when He comes and knocks they may open to Him, and be found worthy of being taken into everlasting joys; through Thee who lives and reigns forever and ever. R. Amen.

Then the priest puts incense into the censer, sprinkles the cincture with holy water, saying:

Sprinkle me with hyssop, Lord, and I shall be clean of sin. Wash me, and I shall be whiter than snow.

After this he incenses the cincture, and then continues:

V. Save Thy servants.   R. Who trust in Thee, my God.
V. Lord, send them aid from Thy holy place. R. And watch over them from Sion.
V. Lord, heed my prayer.   R. And let my cry be heard by Thee.
V. The Lord be with you.   R. May He also be with you.
Let us pray.

O God of mercy, God of goodness, Thou are pleased with all good things, and without whom no good work is begun, no good work is finished; kindly hear our prayers, and defend Thy faithful, who are to wear this blessed cincture in honour of Saint Joseph and under his protection, from the snares of this world and all its lusts. Help them to persist in their holy resolution and to obtain pardon of their sins, and thus merit to be numbered amongst Thy elect; through Christ our Lord. R. Amen.

The Angelic Warfare Confraternity

It is recommended that all True Knights wear the Cord of the Angelic Warfare Confraternity as a powerful defense in the spiritual war that we are battling everyday for Holy Chastity. By doing so we call for the intercession of St. Thomas Aquinas constantly in return for our devotion to him. Cords are available at: http://www.newhope-ky.org or call New Hope Publications at 1-270-325-3061.

What is the Angelic Warfare Confraternity?

The Angelic Warfare is an International Confraternity open to Catholics of all ages. It was founded to grant special graces and indulgences to help members resist temptations of impurity and sexual immorality.

Who was the Inspiration for the Confraternity?

The Angelic Warfare Confraternity was inspired by St. Thomas Aquinas, which is why it is sometimes called "The Guild of the Cord of St. Thomas". When Thomas was a young man in Italy, over 700 years ago, he decided to enter the priesthood in the new begging Order of Preachers (the Dominicans). His wealthy family was so infuriated at his decision that they kidnapped him and locked him in a tower.. His stubborn refusal to leave the Dominicans was met by an equally stubborn effort on the part of his family. They went so far as to send a prostitute into his room in order to tempt Thomas to break his vow of chastity! However, Thomas took up a firebrand and drove the woman from his room. He was shaken by this temptation and began to pray for the strength to remain pure. Appearing at that moment, two angels put a cord around his waist, saying "On God's behalf, we clothe you with the cord of chastity, a cord which no attack will ever destroy." Thomas became a great theologian and writer in the Church and he remained sexually moral for the rest of his life. From this came the tradition of wearing a cord and praying to St. Thomas for his intercession in order to live a chaste life.

How did the Confraternity Start?

Soon after the death of St. Thomas Aquinas it was a fairly common devotion for people to wear a cord in his honour and to seek the grace of purity through his intercession. The first local associations were founded in Spain and Italy in the fifteenth and sixteenth centuries, mainly in schools and universities. Fr. Duerwerdes, a Dominican priest, established the Confraternity in the.1600's as it exists today. About 100 years later the Dominican Pope Benedict XIII made the Angelic Warfare an official, apostolic Confraternity under the direction of the Master General of the Dominicans and granted special indulgences to members of the Confraternity.

The Purpose of the Angelic Warfare Confraternity

The purpose of the Angelic Warfare Confraternity includes the following:

- Imitation and veneration of St. Thomas Aquinas himself
- Imitation of St. Thomas' life long chastity
- Study of the special connection of Thomas' chastity with all his other infused and acquired virtues.
- Chastity is the key to St. Thomas' marvelous wisdom and charity.

The AWC aims at the veneration and imitation of St. Thomas' chastity. Here, we note the important words of John Chrysostom that "we ought not to praise the saints unless we are prepared to imitate them".

Membership and Organization

Membership into the AWC is open to anyone who is a baptized Christian, and fervently desires to be outstanding in purity as a witness to the world in the way of St. Thomas. It is desirable that members be at least in their last years of primary school (primary 5 or 6) The AWC is a Confraternity of the Dominican Order. Thus, it is an association of lay people who are joined together by a special gift of God in the apostolic spirit of St. Dominic. Besides taking very seriously their personal sanctification and holiness, they must aim to achieve their salvation and that of others by the profession of the evangelical life according to their state in life (LCO 149, I). It is the duty and concern of the AWC as a Dominican confraternity, to foster renewal of Christian life among God's people, especially in the area of chastity, serve the spiritual welfare of young and old, and provide collaboration with the Order in some particulars apostolate. The organization and government of the AWC is determined by their own rule which is according to the legislation of Canon Law for lay confraternities and associations. The AWC is intended to be organized with officers and regular meetings. Private members may also be admitted without affiliation to any AWC group. An official register must be kept wherever the AWC is canonically established. Valid and actual membership consist necessarily in having one's name registered in the official book of the confraternity. All such members share the benefits of the AWC. The ritual for solemn enrolment is not required for valid reception into the AWC. It is most desirable that some ceremony be held when a group of members are being enrolled. St. Thomas Aquinas is the patron of AWC.

There is no prayer obligation attached to membership in the AWC. The rosary and the 2 prayers for purity (indulgenced for members) are highly recommended as special devotions of the AWC,

What are the Benefits of Joining?

Members of the Confraternity share, during their lives and after their death, in the graces of the entire Order of Preachers (the Dominicans), including their good works, spiritual goods, and prayers. These graces are supernatural helps from God for us to succeed in our intention of being pure.

Members of the Angelic Warfare also receive many indulgences, which are pardons of the temporal punishments still left from sins after the priest has absolved you in Confession. In other words, through indulgences you can get time off from purgatory after your death! Indulgences are granted on the day of your enrollment in the Confraternity, and for attending monthly meetings of your local Angelic Warfare Chapter.

By attaining personal purity you free yourself to become stronger in the other virtues Pope Pius XI said in the encyclical Studiorum Ducem:

> "If anyone refrains from bodily delights in order more freely to yield himself to the contemplation of truth, this belongs to the rectitude (correctness) of reason."

This means that our own personal purity will be a powerful weapon in the midst of a corrupt world. Our chastity will enable us to better fight the evils of this world, and especially to stop pornography.

An additional benefit of joining the confraternity is that you can become friends with other members in local Angelic Warfare Chapters, and strengthen each other as believers in purity in a very impure world.

Enrollment in the Confraternity consists of signing and sending in the Enrollment Form available from the St. Martin de Porres Dominican Community at 270-325-3061 or www.newhope-ky.org.

The Cord of Saint Philomena

It is recommended that all True Knights wear the Cord of Saint Philomena in honor of chastity and martyrdom, and as a powerful defense in the spiritual war that we are battling everyday. By doing so we call for the intercession of St. Philomena constantly in return for our devotion to her. The below information from http://www.saintphilomena.com.

The Story of St. Philomena

On May 25, 1802, excavators in the ancient Catacomb of St. Priscilla in Rome came upon a well-preserved shelf tomb sealed with terra-cotta slabs in the manner usually reserved for nobility or great martyrs. The tomb was marked with three tiles, inscribed with the following confusing words: LUMENA / PAXTE / CUMFI. However, if one places the first tile last and separates the words properly, the very intelligible sentence emerges: Pax tecum, Filumena, which is "Peace be with you, Philomena." Also inscribed on the tiles were symbols: a lily, arrows, an anchor and a lance, which would appear to indicate virginity and martyrdom. Inside the coffin there were discovered the remains of a girl of about twelve or thirteen years of age, along with a vial or ampulla of her dried blood.

Transferred to the Treasury of the Rare Collections of Christian Antiquity in the Vatican, the remains were soon forgotten by the public, especially since no record existed of a virgin martyr named Philomena. But in 1805, a Neapolitan priest, Don Francesco di Lucia, traveling to Rome with his newly appointed bishop, requested and, after a brief delay, received the relics of this martyr "Philomena" to enshrine in his village church at Mugnano, near Naples.

Immediately upon the official donation of St. Philomena's sacred remains, signal favors began to be granted through her intercession and unusual events to occur. The favors, graces and even miracles started to increase, even before her enshrinement at Mugnano, and they steadily grew in number thereafter - such that this virgin martyr soon earned the title, "Philomena, Powerful with God". In 1837, only 35 years after her exhumation, Pope Gregory XVI elevated this "Wonder-Worker of the Nineteenth Century" to sainthood. In an act unprecedented in the history of Catholicism, she became the only person recognized by the Church as a Saint solely on the basis of her powerful intercession, since nothing historical was known of her except her name and the evidence of her martyrdom.

St. Philomena has been successfully invoked by her supplicants in every sort of needed, such that she has become another patron of "hopeless" and "impossible" cases, like St. Jude or St. Rita, but she is known to be especially powerful in cases involving conversion of sinners, return to the Sacraments, expectant mothers, destitute mothers, problems with children, unhappiness in the home, sterility, priests and their work, help for the sick, the missions, real estate, money problems, food for the poor and mental illness. But truly, as her devotees discovered, no case, of whatever matter, is too trivial or too unimportant to concern her.

The Saints & St. Philomena

Among her most devout clients was St. John Vianney (the Cure' of Ars), whose childlike devotion to this virgin Saint played an intimate part in his daily life. Other Saints who were always devoted to her prayed to her and sang her praises were St. Peter Julian Eymard, St. Peter Chanel, St. Anthony Mary Claret, St. Madeleine Sophie Barat, St. Euphrasia Pelletier, St. Francis Xavier Cabrini, St. John Nepomucene Neumann, Blessed Anna Maria Taigi and Ven. Pauline Jaricot.

The Popes & St. Philomena

A number of Popes have also shown remarkable devotion to St. Philomena as well: Pope

Leo XII (1823-1829) expressed the greatest admiration for this unknown child-saint and gladly gave his permission for the erection of altars and churches in her honor. Pope Gregory XVI (1831-1846), who authorized her public veneration, showed his esteem and devotion to the Saint by giving her the title of "Patroness of the Living Rosary". A Mass and proper Office in her honor were approved by him in 1834 or 1835. This is an extraordinary privilege granted to comparatively few Saints. Pope Pius IX (1846-1878) proclaimed her "Patroness of the Children of Mary." Pope Leo XIII (1878-1903) made two pilgrimages to her shrine before his election to the papacy. After he had become the Vicar of Christ, he gave a valuable cross to the sanctuary. He approved the Confraternity of St. Philomena and later raised it to an Archconfraternity (which is still headquartered at her shrine at Mugnano, Italy). Pope St. Pius X (1903-1914) spoke warmly of her and manifested his devotion to her in various ways. Costly gifts were given by him to her shrine.

Truly, St. Philomena is a powerful intercessor - seemingly held quietly in reserve by Our Divine Lord during these many centuries - for especially strong help in our times, when so much confusion and absence of faith are manifest. Her principal feast day is August 11.

What is the Cord of Saint Philomena- the history and meaning:

The wearing of a cord in honor of a saint is an ancient tradition of the Church. In the early Church virgins wore cords/cinctures as a sign or emblem of purity. Very few saints have the extraordinary privilege of a cord. Devotion of the Cord of St. Philomena came into being as a result of the innumerable graces obtained through her intercession. The Cure of Ars who had so many times experienced the power of this saint loved to see the faithful wear the precious Cord. Pope Leo XIII blessed and approved the Cord and attached many privileges and indulgences to the wearing of it.

St. Philomena Cords are white and red and are to be made of either linen, wool or cotton threads so interwoven as to give an almost equal preponderance to the two colors which represent virginity and martyrdom. The two knots on the one end of the Cord honor her double title of virgin and martyr.

Why wear the Cord?

The use of the St. Philomena Cord is one of the ways we honor her and secure protection from her. The Cord is a sign of devotion to St. Philomena and an action prayer of petition seeking through her intercession health of body and protection of soul. She is model and powerful intercessor of two greatly needed virtues in our time - steadfast faith and courageous chastity.

Who should wear the Cord?

"All the baptized are called to chastity. The Christian has 'Put on Christ,' the model for all chastity. All Christ's faithful are called to lead a chaste life in keeping with their particular states of life. At the moment of his Baptism, the Christian is pledged to lead his affective life in chastity." (Catechism of the Catholic Church CCC: 2348) Note this includes: Married, singles and the consecrated. This cord is a perfect sacramental for us all, with many graces and blessings.

How is the Cord to be used?

It is normally worn around the waist under one's clothing. The Cord should be properly blessed (as the enclosed Cord is). No ceremony is required in conferring it. In putting on the Cord we should commit to constantly honoring St. Philomena in order to merit her protection against all evils of soul and body and also to obtain through her intercession perfect chastity and the spirit of faith necessary in these most challenging times. One who wears the Cord should recite the accompanying prayer each day.

Much of the above and additional information can be found in: Saint Philomena: The Wonder-Worker, by Fr. Paul O'Sullivan, OP & Saint Philomena: Powerful with God, by Sr. Marie Helene Mohr, SC. Both can be obtained from Tan Books, PO Box 424, Rockford, IL 61105.

The Cord of Saint Philomena is available online at: http://www.saintphilomena.com

or: The Saint Philomena Foundation
        Suite 140 – 15774 S. LaGrange Rd
        Orland Park, IL 60462-4766
        (815) 462-3809

Appendix ix
Holy Water & Blessed Salt

Holy Water - A Means of Spiritual Wealth

Imprimatur: Albert G. Meyer, Archbishop of Milwaukee, Jan. 13, 1958

Holy water is a sacramental that remits venial sin. Because of the blessing attached to it, Holy Church strongly urges its use upon her children, especially when dangers threaten, such as fire, storms, sickness and other calamities. Every Catholic home always should have in it a supply of holy water. We do not take advantage of the benefits derived from holy water.

Let Us Cultivate Its Use

Untold spiritual wealth is concentrated in a tiny drop of blessed water. And we give it so little thought! Did we realize now, as we shall realize after death, the many benefits which may be derived from holy water, we would use it far more frequently, and with greater faith and reverence. Holy Water has its great power and efficacy from the prayers of the Church, which its Divine Founder always accepts with complacency.

Following Are Some of the Petitions the Priest Makes to God When He Blesses Water

"O God, ...grant that this creature of Thine (water) may be endowed with divine grace to drive away devils and to cast out diseases, that whatever in the houses or possessions of the faithful may be sprinkled by this water, may be freed from everything unclean, and delivered from what is hurtful...Let everything that threatens the safety or peace of the dwellers therein be banished by the sprinkling of this water; so that the health which they seek by calling upon Thy Holy Name may be guarded from all assault."

Prayers Effective

These prayers ascend to heaven each time you take holy water and sprinkle a drop either for yourself or for another, whether he be present or absent; and God's blessings descend for soul and body.

Dispel the Devil

The devil hates holy water because of its power over him. He cannot long abide in a place or near a person that is often sprinkled with this blessed water.

Do Your Dear Ones Live at a Distance?

Holy water, sprinkled with faith and piety, can move the Sacred Heart to bless your loved ones and protect them from all harm of soul and body, when worry and fear take possession of your heart, hasten to your holy water font, and give your dear ones the benefit of the Church's prayers.

The Holy Souls Long For It

Only in Purgatory can one understand how ardently a poor soul longs for holy water. If we desire to make a host of intercessors for ourselves, let us try to realize now some of their yearnings, and never forget them at the holy water font. The holy souls nearest to Heaven may need the sprinkling of only one drop to relieve their pining souls.

Remits Venial Sins

Because Holy Water is one of the Church's sacramentals, it remits venial sin. Keep your soul beautifully pure in God's sight by making the Sign of the Cross carefully saying, "By this holy water and by thy Precious Blood wash away all my sins, O Lord."

Blessed Salt - A Powerful Sacramental of the Catholic Church

This information is taken from a pamphlet written by Fr. Hampsch. You can obtain the entire pamphlet, tapes, and books by contacting his ministry at Claretian Tape Ministry, P.O. Box 19100, Los Angeles, CA 90019

ABOUT BLESSED SALT

Blessed salt is an instrument of grace to preserve one from the corruption of evil occurring as sin, sickness, demonic influence, etc.

As in the case of all sacramentals, its power comes not from the sign itself, but by means of the Church's official (liturgical, not private) prayer of blessing -- a power the Church derives from Christ Himself. (see Matt. 16:19 and 18:18). As the Vatican II document on the Liturgy states, both Sacraments and sacramentals sanctify us, not of themselves, but by power flowing from the redemptive act of Jesus, elicited by the Church's intercession to be directed through those external signs and elements. Hence sacramentals like blessed salt, holy water, medals, etc., are not to be used superstitiously as having self-contained power, but as 'focus points' funneling one's faith toward Jesus, just as a flag is used as a focus point of patriotism, or as handkerchiefs were used to focus faith for healing and deliverance (Acts 19:12).

Thus, used non-superstitiously, modest amounts of blessed salt may be sprinkled in one's bedroom, or across thresholds to prevent burglary, in cars for safety, etc. A few grains of blessed salt in drinking water or used in cooking or as food seasoning often bring astonishing spiritual and physical benefits. As with the use of Sacraments, much depends on the faith and devotion of the person using salt or any sacramental. This faith must be Jesus-centered, as was the faith of the blind man in John 9; he had faith in Jesus, not in the mud and spittle used by Jesus to heal him.

Blessed salt is not a new sacramental, but the Holy Spirit seems to be leading many to a new interest in its remarkable power as an instrument of grace and healing. Any amount of salt may be presented to a priest for his blessing using the following official prayer from the Roman Ritual:

> "Almighty God, we ask you to bless this salt, as once you blessed the salt scattered over the water by the prophet Elisha. Wherever this salt (and water) is sprinkled, drive away the power of evil, and protect us always by the presence of your Holy Spirit. Grant this through Christ our Lord. Amen"

If you are interested in getting blessed salt, print this information out and present the blessing prayer to your parish priest. Ask him to bless the salt for you using the official prayer from the Roman Ritual printed above, (get a large amount - it will last a long time and you won't have to bother him again!)

Appendix X

The Sign of the Cross

Some things become so familiar that we can take them for granted. Stop and think about what we're doing when we make the Sign of the Cross. The Cross is the center of Christianity; it signifies the deepest surrender to God's will. As we recall at the Baptismal ceremony, "We die with Christ to rise again in Him." When I make the sign of the Cross, I affirm our own surrender to God's will. While tracing the sign over my body, I pray that I will live as a member of God's kingdom.

How to make the Sign of the Cross:

1. Father, Son and Holy Spirit (With the thumb and first 2 fingers of the right hand).

2. One God (bring fingers together - index, middle finger and thumb).

3. Jesus came down to earth to save us (from head to stomache). Roman Guardini the great theologian prior to Vatican II stated: "Cross yourself from head to stomach, from shoulder to shoulder."

4. God saved us through the cross and transferred us from left to right (Matt 25). Pope Innocent III (13th century) said: "Make the sign of the cross from left to right, which means from death to life, from misery to glory." The saints also teach that the left signifies 'justice' the right sighifies 'mercy.'

5. We love God with all our mind, heart, soul and strength (touch head, shoulders, and heart, which is the first and greatest commandment).

6. We belong to the Lord Jesus Christ and are sealed with the sign of the cross and nothing will ever separate us from his love (were sacramentally branded).

7. We worship God through the blood of His Son Jesus Christ, which was shed on the cross, with our mind, heart and body.

8. Holy water is a reminder that we are under oath, it reminds us of our baptismal promises and our oath of Christian citizenship.

CCC 1235 – The sign of the cross, on the threshold of the celebration, marks with the imprint of Christ the one who is going to belong to him and signifies the grace of the redemption Christ won for us by his cross.

Why do we make the sign of the Cross? Probably no action identifies a person as a Catholic Christian so easily as the Sign of the Cross. From the earliest times of the Church, this sign of the cross was used in all the Sacraments, and as a means of recognizing other Christians in time of persecution. In the earliest times of the Church, the sign of the cross was drawn by the thumb on the forehead, in much the same way as Catholics cross themselves on the forehead, lips and breast, before the reading of the Gospel at Holy Mass.

The Christian writer **Tertullian** (160 A.D.- 225 A.D) wrote for Fathers to teach sons: *"In all our travels, in our coming in and going out, in putting on our clothes and our shoes, at table, in going to rest, whatever we are doing we mark our forehead with the sign of the cross."*

Saint Ephrem the Syrian (306 A.D. - 373 A.D.) wrote: *"My son, mark all you do with the sign of the life giving cross. Do not go out from the door of your house until you have signed yourself with the sign of the cross. Do not neglect to make that sign whether you are eating or drinking, or going to sleep, whether you are at home, or going on a journey. There is no habit to be compared with it. Let it be like a wall that protects you and your conduct; teach it to your children so that they may faithfully learn the custom."*

Saint Augustine of Hippo (Sermon on Psalm 141) said: *"Let me not have my forehead bare - let the cross of my Lord cover it."*

Ezekiel 9: 4 *"'Go through the city, through Jerusalem, and put a mark upon the foreheads of the men who sign and groan over all the abominations that are committed in it.' And to the others he said in my hearing, 'Pass through the city after him, and smite; your eyes shall not spare, and you shall show no pity; slay old men outright, young men and maidens, little children and woman, but touch no one upon whom is the mark.'"*

Judgement always begins in the house of God (1 Peter 4:17) and those Israelites in the days of Ezekiel who were engaged in idolatry and abused the holy things of God incurred His judgement. The Israelites that were spared were those that did not worship false gods, they were sealed with the Hebrew letter 'Tau' which is the form of a cross. This sign (the cross) was the mark that singled out the ones who were to be spared out of the destruction of Jerusalem the first time it was destroyed in 587 B.C. In Revelation 7:3, John the Evangelist alludes to those servants of God in the 'New Jerusalem' as being marked with the sign of the cross that Ezekiel spoke about.

Appendix xi

Releasing the Grip of Addiction
by Much Prayer and Fasting
by Kenneth Henderson
Originally Published March 21, 2006 on CatholicExchange.com

The season of Lent always brings with it questions about fasting and why "Catholics" have to fast. It's not so much that Catholics "have to fast" as some kind of meaningless obedience to the laws of the Church, but in fact we are commanded by God Himself to fast and deny our very selves in response to the fleshly ways of the world and the grip of sin in our lives.

Making a Gift of Yourself

There are seventy-four biblical references to fasting, and Jesus Himself said when you fast and not if you fast, so fasting must be very important for our spiritual growth. In our modern self-centered, self-indulgent, all-about-me world, this concept of fasting is very foreign and many Christians resist it. But according to Scripture and many historic Christian writings, fasting is supposed to be a normal part of our spiritual life here on earth, and the benefits that come from it are wonderful.

In the first few hundred years of the Church, Christians fasted regularly on Wednesdays and Fridays as evidenced in the Didache — essentially the first Catechism of the Catholic Church — written between 50 and 90AD. This was a carrying on of the Jewish tradition of fasting. However, the Christians of the first century took to fasting on Wednesday and Friday to set themselves apart from the Pharisees who fasted on Mondays and Thursdays.

The kind of fast that the first Christians practiced was a strict fast of bread and water only. Fasting is so important because it helps cleanse our souls and bring our fleshly appetites under control. Indeed, if we find it easy to indulge ourselves in food, then it is much easier for us to indulge ourselves in other "fleshly" appetites as well. By denying ourselves food, we help strengthen our wills — which is so important in conquering sinful addictions — and we facilitate self-mastery. We gain control over our flesh, or carnal nature, which all too often opposes God's Spirit and seeks to rebel against His Truth. We can not find our true spirituality unless we bring the flesh under submission. Saint Paul tells us in Romans 8:7-8: "For the concern of the flesh is hostility toward God; it does not submit to the law of God, nor can it; and those who are in the flesh cannot please God." Saint Paul continues by saying that we must allow the Spirit of God to dwell within us. Only then can we be freed from slavery to sin.

Through fasting we can gain that freedom and a deeper spirituality, a greater hunger for God. It is a tool that helps us obtain a closer walk with God. Through God's grace it has the power to break the effect of concupiscence — the tendency to sin — and brings our flesh under submission. Prayer and fasting are largely overlooked as weapons to conquer addictions. But if you are struggling with persistent sins such as lust or gluttony, fasting is an effective way to help you rid these sins from your life.

Fasting has stopped wars, healed the terminally ill and has even brought about conversions. If you have a loved one who is mired in a powerful sin, praying and fasting can be the means to bring about God's saving power in his or her life. By doing this, you are indeed, in one sense, living out the meaning of love as our late Holy Father John Paul II said, by "giving the gift of self."

Fasting in humility is a powerful means of conquering selfishness and pride in your life, and both are at the root of all addiction. In addition to the many gifts that our Lord has given us through His Church to grow in holiness, primarily through Confession and the Eucharist, fasting loosens the grip of sinful addictions and thus freedom can be achieved.

Getting Beyond the Minimum

True biblical fasting is, in essence, more than what the guidelines of the Church prescribe for a Lenten fast. What the Church gives us is a minimal guideline to serve as an introduction to fasting, or as a reminder of the place that fasting has in the Christian life — and the Lenten fasts are something we do as a community. By giving us this guideline, the Church is not telling us that this is the only time we should fast.

Fasting means to abstain from food either partially or completely. We starve our flesh, so that we may feed our spirit. The Bible promises that when we deny ourselves, whether by fasting or other acts of sacrifice, then God will feed us with something far superior to our earthly food. Jesus calls us to deny our flesh so that we may take up our crosses, follow Him, and thus be united with Him.

To fast you must voluntarily abstain from food, either partially or completely for a period of time. You may fast for 24 hours or fast for a few days. However, I encourage you pray to find out what kind of fast the Lord is calling you to. Please check with your doctor and spiritual advisor (if you have one) before fasting for more than a few days. Some have found that to break the grip of sin in their lives, fasting every Wednesday and Friday on bread and water is effective. This imitates the practice of the early Christians. Most importantly, approach your fasting with "JOY" — Jesus first, Others second, Yourself last. If you approach fasting as a chore or with apprehension, you will not succeed and will become discouraged. This is exactly what the devil wants to happen! Remain faithful and persevere until you can faithfully fast.

Combating the temptation to give up fasting, even before you start, takes prayer, constant prayer. Prayer must always be a part of fasting. Pray for the grace to fast. Pray that your fast will be effective. Pray that your fast will move mountains in your life and the lives of others. Perhaps praying the Rosary and mediating on the Sorrowful Mysteries would be helpful to you. Some people who have made a successful practice of fasting recommend 30 minutes every day of prayer with the fasting. That can seem like a lot of time, but getting used to praying and fasting takes time and practice. Maybe that is why they call it a spiritual practice — because you get better at it over time. You begin to desire to spend more time in prayer. You begin to look forward to fasting, especially as you begin to see the grip of sin being loosened.

The use of caffeine beverages is widespread in our culture. If you often drink coffee or other caffeinated drinks, you might experience some discomfort, possibly headaches or even nausea when you first begin to fast if you have decided to fast on bread and water.

This can be caused by what is known as caffeine withdrawal and is normal. If that is the fast that you have chosen, then pray through this and unite the pain with Christ and His Passion. I have personally experienced this and from my experience I have found when the pain comes I need to pray right then and there for God to provide the grace to endure the pain. When I do, the pain subsides. In any event it is temporary, and if that is the fast you are offering, then God will give you all the grace you need to embrace whatever suffering comes with it. Look at it as an opportunity to offer reparation for the times you turned your back on God and said "yes" to the devil.

Note: If you are pregnant, nursing or suffer from illness, do not attempt a full fast. Instead, consider fasting in other ways. You can fast from sweets, snacking or television (perhaps permanently) or some other "non-essential." Realize there are many different types of "fasts" you can do. However, bread-and-water fasts are the most sacrificial and advisable if your health is good. If for some reason you feel too weak to carry out your daily duties or you work at a job were you must stay alert, add what you need to carry out your duties — perhaps juice or maybe peanut butter on bread to add some protein to your fast. Please check with your doctor if you have any questions about your health and the effect fasting may have on it.

Fasting "Supercharges" Our Prayer

What are some of the reasons given for fasting in the Bible? Esther fasted for protection and divine favor. Ezra fasted for direction and protection. Elijah fasted to combat spiritual enemies. Daniel fasted to overcome the flesh and for spiritual breakthrough. The disciples fasted for a powerful ministry. Even Jesus Himself "fasted forty days and forty nights" (Mt 4:1-2). By doing this, our Lord was preparing Himself for the great demand His public ministry would make on His life. He knew He would face temptation and persecution, and by denying Himself He showed us that we too must rely on God for all we do. This is where the Church derives the forty days for Lent, and indeed, this is the purpose of Lent: to help us deny ourselves and draw us to a greater dependence on God in our own lives.

There are many biblical reasons to fast. In fact, our Lord showed the disciples that it was the only way to overcome certain, more powerful demons in our lives. You know the story from Mark 9: Jesus saw the disciples return from a mission. They had been healing the sick, crippled, and blind, all by God's grace, and they were very pleased to be doing His work. But one day they came upon a man whose son was tormented by a demon, and they were not able to cast the demon out. Jesus rebuked the disciples and cast the demon out. The astonished disciples asked, "Why could we not cast him out?" (Mk 9:27b), to which Jesus replies "This kind can only come out by much prayer and fasting" (Mk 9:29). In that same passage (as well as the same story related in Matthew 17), Jesus emphasizes the necessity of faith, a faith that can move mountains. When complete faith and trust in God is combined with prayer and fasting from the heart, the devil is rendered powerless. St. John Vianney, the patron of parish priests, once was explaining to a young priest the secret of his success in healing and spiritual warfare. He said prayer and fasting was the key. He also said that when we deny ourselves food and drink the devil can be beaten. This is what helped him to save many people from the power of sin.

It's important to note that fasting does not "add" anything to God's power; nothing we can do will "add" to the power of God. But fasting, joined together with fervent prayer from the heart, demonstrates just how serious our prayer is. When a Christian practices the sacrifice of self-denial, he is joining himself to the sacrifice of the Cross, and by joining our prayer to the sacrifice of the Cross, the power for good is unleashed and miracles are allowed to happen where half-hearted prayer alone could not succeed.

Spiritual fasting is undoubtedly powerful. Through spiritual fasting, we can receive healing, gain spiritual protection, combat spiritual enemies, and overcome the sinful desires of the flesh. It helps when we intercede for our loved ones and can gain for us spiritual breakthroughs and clarity in prayer. To sum it up, fasting is a way for us to "work" with God's grace received through prayer in faith. This dispels the notion that we are "saved" by "faith alone" or "works alone," but as the Catholic Church has plainly taught for 2000 years, we are saved by God's grace with faith that works through love as we read in Galatians 5:6. In these very wise words, Saint Ignatius of Loyola sums up the attitude in which we should always approach fasting: "Work as if everything depends on you, and pray as if everything depends on God."

When you undertake your fast prayerfully and fervently you will notice miracles and breakthroughs in your life where before you may have experienced all kinds of road blocks to spiritual progress. Be amazed as miracles unfold and God blesses your life.

The Scriptures on Fasting - from www.scripturecatholic.com

Matt. 9:15; Mark 2:20; Luke 5:35 - many non-Catholics frown upon the Church's pious practice of fasting, and say that fasting went away after the resurrection of Christ. But Jesus Himself says that His followers will fast once He is gone and does not object.

Matt. 6:16-18 - in fact, Jesus even gives instructions on how to fast. Jesus says, "Do not look dismal like the hypocrites, but look clean and refreshed."

Matt. 17-21; Mark 9:29 - Jesus teaches that only prayer and fasting had special power to cure a man possessed by a demon. Jesus teaches about the efficacy of fasting and how fasting, coupled with prayer, is acceptable and pleasing to God.

Luke 2:37 - Anna the widow worshiped God with fasting and prayer night and day. The Church has always taught that, by virtue of our priesthood conferred in baptism, our fasting participates in the priesthood of Christ by atoning for the temporal punishments due to our and other people's sins.

Acts 13:2-3; 14:23 - the apostles engaged in prayer and fasting in connection with ordaining leaders of the Church. Prayer and fasting have always been the practice of the Church.

1 Tim. 4:3 - when Paul refers to doctrines that require abstinence from foods, some Protestants refer to this verse to condemn the Catholic Church's practice of fasting. But Paul is referring to abstinence and any other practice that is performed apart from Christ's teachings. Fasting, on the other hand, is done in obedience to Christ's teachings of taking up our cross and following Him, by participating in His sufferings so we can share in His glory. When citing this verse, these Protestants do not explain why Jesus prophesied that his followers would fast and why Jesus gave instructions on how to fast.

Ez. 8:21-23 - Ezra proclaims a fast as a prayer for humility and self-mortification and God responds. Our fasting is performed to remind us of our absolute reliance upon God.

Neh. 1:4; 9:1 - these texts also show the historical practice of fasting. Fasting atones for temporal punishment due to sin and repairs our relationship with God.

Tobit 12:8 - prayer is good when accompanied by fasting. Throughout salvation history, God has encouraged fasting to be coupled with prayer.

Judith 4:9-13 - the people of Israel humbled themselves with fasting and the Lord Almighty responds.

Esther 4:3,16 - people fasted for days to atone for sin. Although Jesus remits the eternal penalty of our sin, we can atone for temporal penalties due to our sin.

Psalm 35:13 - David says, "I afflicted myself with fasting." David recognized that fasting drew him closer to God. Fasting makes us aware of our dependency on God.

Psalm 69:10 - the Psalmist writes, "I humbled my soul with fasting." Fasting helps us become humble, and in our humility we unit ourselves with our humble God.

Jer. 36:9 - the peoples of Jerusalem and Judah declared a fast before the Lord.

Baruch 1:5 - they wept, fasted, and prayed before the Lord.

Dan. 9:3; 10:2-3 - Daniel sought God through fasting, and abstained from choice foods and wine for three weeks.

Joel 1:14; 2:12,15 - fasts are called to sanctify and turn oneself toward the Lord.

Jonah 3:5,10 - people of Nineveh proclaim a fast to appease God and God responds favorably.

1 Macc. 3:47; 2 Macc. 13:12 - Judas and his army fasted in prayer.

Appendix xii
Mortification

The Spirit of Mortification

*I come back to Your feet, O Crucified Jesus, desirous of understanding more
thoroughly the spirit of mortification.*

The spirit of mortification has more than a purely physical aspect of mortification; it also includes
renunciation of the ego, the will, and the understanding. Just as in our body and in our senses
we have unruly tendencies toward the enjoyment of material things, so also in our ego there are
inordinate tendencies toward self-assertion. Love of self and complacency in our own excellence
are often so great that, even unconsciously, we tend to make "self" the center of the universe.

The spirit of mortification is really complete when, above all, we seek to mortify self-love in all
its many manifestations. The Pharisee who fasted on the appointed days, but whose heart was so
puffed up with pride that his prayer amounted to nothing more than praise of himself and scorn
of his neighbor did not have the spirit of mortification and hence was not justified before God.
There is little value in imposing corporal mortifications on ourselves if we then refuse to yield our
opinion in order to accommodate ourselves to others, if we cannot be reconciled with our enemies,
or bear an injury and a cutting word with calmness, or hold back a sharp answer.

"Why," asks St. Teresa of Jesus, "do we shrink from interior mortification [of our ego, our will,
and judgment] since this is the means by which every other kind of mortification may become
much more meritorious and perfect, and may be practiced with greater tranquility and ease?"
(Way of Perfection, 12). As long as mortification does not strike at our pride, it remains at the
halfway mark and never reaches its goal.

The true spirit of mortification embraces, in the first place, all the occasions for physical or moral
suffering permitted by divine Providence. The sufferings attendant on illness or fatigue; the efforts
required by the performance of our duties or by a life of intense labor; the privations imposed by
the state of poverty - all are excellent physical penances. If we sincerely desire to be guided by
divine Providence in everything, we will not try to avoid them, or even to lighten them, but will
accept wholeheartedly whatever God offers us. It would be absurd to refuse a single one of those
providential opportunities for suffering and to look for voluntary mortifications of our own choice.
Likewise, it would be foolish for those in religious life to omit the least exercise imposed by the
Rule in order to do a penance of their own choosing.

It is exactly the same in the moral order. Do we not sometimes try to avoid a person whom we
do not like, but with whom the Lord has brought us into contact? Do we look for every means of
avoiding a humiliation or an act of obedience which is painful to nature? If we do, we are running
away from the best opportunities for sacrificing ourselves and for mortifying our self-love; even
if we substitute other mortifications, they will not be as effective as those which God Himself
has prepared for us. In the mortifications offered to us by divine Providence, there is nothing
of our own will or liking; they strike us just where we need it most, and where, by voluntary
mortification, we could never reach.

In order to arrive at sanctity, a certain specified amount of voluntary penance is not required of
all; this varies according to the inspiration of the Holy Spirit, the advice of superiors, and each

one's physical strength. All, however, must have that truly deep spirit of mortification which can embrace with generosity every opportunity for renunciation prepared or permitted by God.

Prayer

O Lord, You who have sought for adorers in spirit and in truth, preserve me, I beg You, from the pharisaic spirit against which You fought while on earth, and which is so opposed to You, who are infinite Truth and Simplicity. Grant that while mortifying my body, I may mortify my pride even more, or better, mortify it Yourself.

You who know the secret places in my heart, the most deeply hidden instincts of my self-love, prepare for me the most effective medicine for purifying, healing, and transforming me. You alone know where this most harmful microbe nests; You alone can destroy it. But how often, alas, in the varying circumstances of my life, I have not recognized Your hand, Your work; and I have tried in so many ways to escape the physical and moral sufferings, the mortifications, humiliations, and difficulties which You Yourself had prepared for me.

How blind I am, O Lord, and how poorly do I recognize Your ways, which are so different and remote from my limited human views. Give me, O God, that supernatural sight which can judge events in Your light, and which can penetrate the true meaning of the sufferings which You place in my path. Intensify this light in proportion to the obstacles You prepare for me to strike my "ego", my pride, my opinions, my rights, because it is then above all that I am terribly blind, and groping in the dark, I reject the medicine You offer. I may lack, O Lord, the means of carrying out the purification of my ego, so foolish and so proud. But nothing is lacking to You, You who are the All, and whose finite mercy utterly surpasses my misery. I confess, O Lord, that I have often strayed like a lamb which, leaving its shepherd, has taken a wrong path. But I desire to return once more, and I come back with complete confidence because I know that You never tire of waiting and of pardoning. Here I am, Lord; I place myself in Your hands. Mortify me, purify me as You wish, for whenever You afflict, it is to heal, and wherever You mortify, life increases.

Suggestions for Mortification

In overcoming sins of the flesh, mortification is a very powerful weapon. Ways of mortification could include: Take a cold shower while praying three Hail Mary's. Put the needs of others first before yourself. Make a kind gesture for someone, but do it without them knowing it. Offer up all your daily sufferings, from your minor aches and pains to accepting rude behavior from others, as a sacrifice in reparation for your sins and the sins of the world. Unite your daily sufferings with the sufferings of Christ.

The Scriptures on Suffering and Mortification - from www.scripturecatholic.com

Matt. 10:38 - Jesus said, "he who does not take up his cross and follow me is not worthy of me." Jesus defines discipleship as one's willingness to suffer with Him. Being a disciple of Jesus not only means having faith in Him, but offering our sufferings to the Father as He did.

Matt. 16:24; Mark 8:34 - Jesus said, "if any man would come after me, let him deny himself and take up his cross and follow me." Jesus wants us to empty ourselves so that God can fill us. When we suffer, we can choose to seek consolation in God and become closer to Jesus.

Luke 9:23 - Jesus says we must take up this cross daily. He requires us to join our daily temporal sacrifices (pain, inconvenience, worry) with His eternal sacrifice.

Luke 14:27 - Jesus said, "whoever does not bear his own cross and come after me, cannot be my disciple." If we reject God because we suffer, we fail to apply the graces that Jesus won for us by His suffering.

John 7:39 - Jesus was first glorified on the cross, not just the resurrection. This text refers to John 19:34, when Jesus was pierced on the cross by the soldier's lance.

John 12:24 - unless a grain of wheat falls into the earth and dies, it remains alone and bears no fruit. Jesus is teaching that suffering and death are part of every human life, and it is only through suffering and death that we obtain the glory of resurrection.

Rom. 5:2-3 - Paul says that more than rejoicing in our hope, we rejoice in our sufferings which produces endurance, character and hope. Through faith, suffering brings about hope in God and, through endurance, salvation.

Rom. 8:17 - Paul says that we are heirs with Christ, but only if we suffer with him in order that we may also be glorified with Him. Paul is teaching that suffering must be embraced in order to obtain the glory that the Father has bestowed upon Jesus.

Rom. 8:18 - the sufferings of the present time are not worth comparing with the glory that is to be revealed to us. We thus have hope that any sufferings we or others endure, no matter how difficult, will pale in comparison to the life of eternal bliss that awaits us.

1 Cor. 1:23- Paul preaches a Christ crucified, not just risen. Catholic spirituality focuses on the sacrifice of Christ which is the only means to the resurrection. This is why Catholic churches have crucifixes with the corpus of Jesus affixed to them. Many Protestant churches no longer display the corpus of Jesus (only an empty cross). Thus, they only preach a Christ risen, not crucified.

1 Cor. 2:2 - Paul preaches Jesus Christ and Him crucified. While the cross was the scandal of scandals, and is viewed by the non-Christian eye as defeat, Catholic spirituality has always exalted the paradox of the cross as the true tree of life and our means to salvation.

2 Cor. 1:5-7- if we share abundantly in Christ's sufferings, so through Christ we share abundantly in comfort as well. If we unite our sufferings with His, we will be comforted by Him.

2 Cor. 4:10 – Paul writes that we always carry in the body the death of Jesus so that the life of Jesus may also be manifested in our bodies. Christ has allowed room in His Body for our sufferings, and our sufferings allow room for Christ to bring us to life.

2 Cor. 4:11 - while we live we are always being given up to death for Jesus' sake so that His life may be manifested in our flesh. This proves the Catholic position that our sufferings on earth are united with Jesus in order to bring about Jesus' life in us.

2 Cor. 12:9-10 - Jesus' grace is sufficient, for His power is made perfect in weakness. If we are weak, we are strong in Christ. Our self-sufficiency decreases, so Christ in us can increase.

Eph. 3:13 - Do not to lose heart over my sufferings for your glory. Our suffering also benefits others in the mystical body of Christ.

Phil. 1:29 - for the sake of Christ we are not only to believe in Him but also to suffer for His sake. Growing in holiness requires more than having faith in God and accepting Jesus as personal Lord and Savior. We must also willfully embrace the suffering that befalls us as part of God's plan. Thus, Christ does not want our faith alone, but our faith in action which includes faith in suffering.

Phil. 3:10 - Paul desires to share in Christ's sufferings in order to obtain the resurrection. Paul recognizes the efficacy of suffering as a means of obtaining holiness which leads to resurrection and eternal life. There is no Easter Sunday without Good Friday.

Col. 1:24 - Paul rejoices in his sufferings and completes what is lacking in Christ's afflictions for the sake of His body. This proves the Catholic position regarding the efficacy of suffering. Is there something lacking in Christ's sufferings? Of course not. But because Jesus loves us so much, He allows us to participate in His redemptive suffering by leaving room in His mystical body for our own suffering. Our suffering, united with our Lord's suffering, furthers the work of His redemption.

2 Thess. 1:5 - we may be made worthy of the kingdom of God for which we are suffering. This is because suffering causes us to turn to God and purifies us from sin.

2 Tim. 1:8 - Paul instructs Timothy to share in suffering for the Gospel. Suffering is not to be asked for, but it is also not to be avoided. For the sake of the Gospel, it is to be embraced.

2 Tim. 2:3 - Paul says to take our share of sufferings as a good soldier in Christ. Sufferings atone for the temporal effects of our sin.

2 Tim. 3:12 - all who desire to live a godly life in Christ Jesus will be persecuted. But this persecution unites us more closely to Jesus and repairs our relationship with God.

2 Tim. 4:5 - Paul instructs Timothy to endure suffering to fulfill his ministry. As evangelists, we suffer with Christ for the Gospel.

Heb. 12:5-7 - do not lose courage when you are punished, for the Lord disciplines whom He loves. The Lord loves each one of us more than we love ourselves, and will only permit suffering if it brings about our salvation.

Heb. 12:11 - this discipline seems painful rather than pleasant, but it brings the peaceful fruit of righteousness.

James 4:8-10 - we must purify our hearts and grieve, mourn and wail, changing our laughter into morning and joy to gloom.

1 Peter 1:6 - Peter warns us that we may have to suffer various trials. Peter does not want us to be discouraged by this reality, but understand that such suffering purifies us and prepares us for union with God.

1 Peter 2:19-21 - Peter instructs that we have been called to endure pain while suffering for Christ, our example. God actually calls us to suffer as His Son did, and this is not to diminish us, but to glorify us, because it is by our suffering that we truly share in the eternal priesthood of Jesus Christ.

1 Peter 4:1-2 - Peter says whoever has suffered in the flesh has ceased from sin to live not by the flesh but by the will of God. Our suffering furthers our growth in holiness which is the aim of Catholic life.

1 Peter 4:13 - Peter says to rejoice in Christ's sufferings in order to rejoice and be glad when Christ's glory is revealed. Those who suffer with faith in Christ will rejoice in His glory.

1 Peter 4:16 - if we suffer as Christians, we should not be ashamed but glorify God.

1 Peter 5:10 - after we have suffered, the God of all grace will restore, establish and strengthen us. God promises us that our suffering will ultimately be followed by glory.

Rev. 11:3 - Jesus gives power to His witnesses clothed in sackcloth. By virtue of our priesthood, we suffer to repair our relationship with God for sins that He has already forgiven us. As priests, we atone for the temporal punishments due to our sin.

Appendix xiii
Contemplative Prayer:
The Lifeline, Healing and Strength of a True Knight
by Kenneth Henderson

Why is prayer so vital to our ever hoping to be set free from slavery to sin? When I say that a person must pray to be set free, many people will tell me "I do pray. I pray a Rosary everyday" or "I pray a novena" or "I pray everyday...in fact I beg God to set me free from my problems, but He doesn't seem to be listening." The problem is that this is only one part of prayer. Praying like this is like having a one sided conversation. Imagine how you would feel if a friend of yours called you up, told you about all his problems, complained, and then hung up...without ever giving you a chance to speak? I know how I would feel, I would feel a bit used maybe. A bit incomplete. Perhaps I could have said something to help. But, they never gave me a chance to say anything...they never listened. They just spoke.

I often wonder if God feels like this sometimes. We come to Him with our issues, our problems, our frustrations, our wants, desires, etc. But, do we ever give Him a chance to answer us? Maybe we expect that God will just chime in when He's ready...or by divine intervention He will answer us. But, there is something else we must do to really hear Him. We must listen.

Listen
Listening is a vital part of prayer. This is called Contemplative Prayer. In fact without this listening, Contemplative Prayer we never really engage in any authentic prayer at all.

What is Contemplative Prayer and how do we get there?
Here's what the *Catechism of the Catholic Church* has to say:

III. CONTEMPLATIVE PRAYER

2709 What is contemplative prayer? St. Teresa answers: "Contemplative prayer [oracion mental] in my opinion is nothing else than a close sharing between friends; it means taking time frequently to be alone with him who we know loves us."6 Contemplative prayer seeks him "whom my soul loves."7 It is Jesus, and in him, the Father. We seek him, because to desire him is always the beginning of love, and we seek him in that pure faith which causes us to be born of him and to live in him. In this inner prayer we can still meditate, but our attention is fixed on the Lord himself.

2710 The choice of the time and duration of the prayer arises from a determined will, revealing the secrets of the heart. One does not undertake contemplative prayer only when one has the time: one makes time for the Lord, with the firm determination not to give up, no matter what trials and dryness one may encounter. One cannot always meditate, but one can always enter into inner prayer, independently of the conditions of health, work, or emotional state. The heart is the place of this quest and encounter, in poverty ant in faith.

2711 Entering into contemplative prayer is like entering into the Eucharistic liturgy: we "gather up:" the heart, recollect our whole being under the prompting of the Holy Spirit, abide in the dwelling place of the Lord which we are, awaken our faith in order to enter into the presence of him who awaits us. We let our masks fall and turn our hearts back to the Lord who loves us, so as to hand ourselves over to him as an offering to be purified and transformed.

2712 Contemplative prayer is the prayer of the child of God, of the forgiven sinner who agrees to welcome the love by which he is loved and who wants to respond to it by loving even more.8 But he knows that the love he is returning is poured out by the Spirit in his heart, for everything is grace from God. Contemplative prayer is the poor and humble surrender to the loving will of the Father in ever deeper union with his beloved Son.

2713 Contemplative prayer is the simplest expression of the mystery of prayer. It is a gift, a grace; it can be accepted only in humility and poverty. Contemplative prayer is a covenant relationship established by God within our hearts.9 Contemplative prayer is a communion in which the Holy Trinity conforms man, the image of God, "to his likeness."

2714 Contemplative prayer is also the pre-eminently intense time of prayer. In it the Father strengthens our inner being with power through his Spirit "that Christ may dwell in [our] hearts through faith" and we may be "grounded in love."10

2715 Contemplation is a gaze of faith, fixed on Jesus. "I look at him and he looks at me": this is what a certain peasant of Ars in the time of his holy curé used to say while praying before the tabernacle. This focus on Jesus is a renunciation of self. His gaze purifies our heart; the light of the countenance of Jesus illumines the eyes of our heart and teaches us to see everything in the light of his truth and his compassion for all men. Contemplation also turns its gaze on the mysteries of the life of Christ. Thus it learns the "interior knowledge of our Lord," the more to love him and follow him.11

2716 Contemplative prayer is hearing the Word of God. Far from being passive, such attentiveness is the obedience of faith, the unconditional acceptance of a servant, and the loving commitment of a child. It participates in the "Yes" of the Son become servant and the Fiat of God's lowly handmaid.

2717 Contemplative prayer is silence, the "symbol of the world to come"12 or "silent love."13 Words in this kind of prayer are not speeches; they are like kindling that feeds the fire of love. In this silence, unbearable to the "outer" man, the Father speaks to us his incarnate Word, who suffered, died, and rose; in this silence the Spirit of adoption enables us to share in the prayer of Jesus.

2718 Contemplative prayer is a union with the prayer of Christ insofar as it makes us participate in his mystery. The mystery of Christ is celebrated by the Church in the Eucharist, and the Holy Spirit makes it come alive in contemplative prayer so that our charity will manifest it in our acts.

2719 Contemplative prayer is a communion of love bearing Life for the multitude, to the extent that it consents to abide in the night of faith. The Paschal night of the Resurrection passes through the night of the agony and the tomb - the three intense moments of the Hour of Jesus which his Spirit (and not "the flesh [which] is weak") brings to life in prayer. We must be willing to "keep watch with [him] one hour."14

The key here is "our attention is fixed on the Lord himself." Sec. 2709. We are not thinking about Jesus, or about what he said and did. We are not imagining what he looks like, nor what he might say in conversation. We are not pleading with him for help for ourselves or others. What we do is say to him:

> "This little bit of time is my gift to you. I will simply sit here in your presence, focus my attention on you, and direct my love toward you. I will not allow anything to distract me, not anxiety about my future, not worry for the sick, not even a vision of angels. This time in silence is my gift to you."

The silence is an interior silence as well as exterior. The use of conscious breathing can help one get to the point of inner peacefulness so that attention can be fully directed to the Lord. We can also use a "prayer word" to help bring our attention back if we become distracted. Distractions will come, but we choose to let the thoughts and images go by rather than give them center stage. Don't let yourself become frustrated, that is an emotion that will just pull you away from contemplation. If needed, use breathing or a prayer word to bring you back to the inner peacefulness and silence, so you can make yourself present to God. (This is not Quietism or Centering Prayer which is condemned, but an inner silence with attention focused on God present and love of Him present. We believe God is present through faith but this can become the Prayer of Quiet through grace, a step towards mystical union in the traditional understanding of contemplation.)

"2710 The choice of the time and duration of the prayer arises from a determined will, revealing the secrets of the heart. One does not undertake contemplative prayer only when one has the time: one makes time for the Lord, with the firm determination not to give up, no matter what trials and dryness one may encounter. One cannot always meditate, but one can always enter into inner prayer, independently of the conditions of health, work, or emotional state. The heart is the place of this quest and encounter, in poverty and in faith." *Catechism of the Catholic Church.*

This is the form of prayer encouraged by the great mystics, St. John of the Cross and Teresa of Avila. The following text is quoted by St. John Cassian (Fourth Century) whose writings had a vast impact on the monastic movement in the Middle Ages. He in turn is quoting Abba Isaac one of the "Fathers of the Desert".

> "I think it will be easy to bring you to the heart of true prayer. . . . The man who knows what questions to ask is on the verge of understanding; the man who is beginning to understand what he does not know is not far from knowledge. I must give you a formula for contemplation. It you carefully keep this formula before you, and learn to recollect it at all times, it will help you to mount to contemplation of high truth. Everyone who seeks for continual recollection of God uses this formula for meditation, intent upon driving every other sort of thought from his heart. You cannot keep the formula before you unless you are free from all bodily cares.
>
> The formula was given us by a few of the oldest fathers who remained. They communicated it only to a very few who were athirst for the true way. To maintain an unceasing recollection of God, this formula must be ever before you. The formula is this: 'O God, come to my assistance; O Lord, make haste to help me.' (Psalm 69:2 DR; compare Ps 70:1 NIV; Cf Psalm 40:13 NIV.)

Rightly has this verse been selected from the whole Bible to serve this purpose. It suits every mood and temper of human nature, every temptation, every circumstance. It contains an invocation of God, an humble confession of faith, a reverent watchfulness, a meditation on human frailty, an act of confidence in God's response, an assurance of his ever-present support. The man who continually invokes God as his protector is aware that God is ever at hand.

I repeat: each one of us, whatever his condition in the spiritual life, needs to use this verse.

Perhaps wandering thoughts surge about my soul like boiling water, and I cannot control them, nor can I offer prayer without its being interrupted by silly images. I feel so dry that I am incapable of spiritual feelings, and many sighs and groans cannot save me from dreariness. I must needs say: "O God, come to my assistance; O Lord, make haste to help me."

The mind should go on grasping this formula until it can cast away the wealth and multiplicity of other thoughts, and restrict itself to the poverty of this single word. And so it will attain with ease that Gospel beatitude which holds first place among the other beatitudes: "Blessed are the poor in spirit, for theirs is the kingdom of heaven." Thus by God's light the mind mounts to the manifold knowledge of God, and thereafter feeds on mysteries loftier and more sacred....And thus it attains that purest of pure prayers..., so far as the Lord deigns to grant this favor; the prayer which looks for no visual image, uses neither thoughts nor words; the prayer wherein, like a spark leaping up from a fire, the mind is rapt upward, and, destitute of the aid of the senses or of anything visible or material pours out its prayer to God . . "

This is the Prayer of Contemplation.

The following is a teaching from Mother Nadine of the Intercessors of the Lamb*, from her writing on "Contemplation."

What is this life that comes through listening? "Listen that you might have life. Heed My word. Listen to it." Jesus was asked that question, "What is this life?" And He replied, "Eternal life is this: to know the Father and the One whom the Father has sent." Now, the word, "know" in the Bible, means to "experience." So, Jesus is telling us that eternal life is this: to experience the Father and to experience the one the Father has sent. "To experience Me." No wonder that when Jesus took Peter, James and John up to Mount Tabor to encounter the Father, the first thing we hear from the Father is, "Listen to Him!" Isn't that interesting?

In the Old Testament, we hear God speaking, "Sacrifice and oblation I do not desire. But love and knowledge of Me." There is that word, "knowledge." What He wants is love and experience of Himself. I was just delighted the first time I read that scripture. As a new convert, I was reading all the lives of the saints. They all were so penitential. They did severe fastings and went bare-foot in the snow! I remember thinking to myself, "Is that what I have to do to get to know God?" That is when the scripture came to me. "No! I do not want those sacrifices and oblations! But," He said, "I want you to love and have knowledge of Me!" I thought, "Lord, that means that You must reveal Yourself to me."

In the scripture with the woman at the well Jesus said, "If you but knew the gift of God." There it is! If you but knew! If you could experience this gift of God!" He said, "The Father is seeking those to worship Him in spirit and truth." These words set her on fire! She was having an experience right there at the well. Most of the women came to the well first thing in the morning. This woman was there at noon. Perhaps this was because she was not accepted by the others. She was on her fifth husband; so she came at noon. There He was – at high noon, right under the glory spout. When she had this experience and heard these words she ran back into the village and she told everyone, "I have met someone who told me everything I have ever done!" Isn't that what we, ourselves, want? Do we not want to have a relationship with someone who knows everything we have ever done, and every thought we have ever thought, no matter good or bad and loves us where we are and as we are? No conditions. No conditions.

Have you ever tried to go just one day and love somebody with no conditions? I tried it a couple of times. It is quite challenging! We will find ourselves complaining, "Lord, if she would just say something a little kinder, if she wouldn't have that frown on her face, if they wouldn't be so negative (and all these other little conditions we have) then we could love them more!" You know. But, try to love others with no conditions. Try to love them just as they are. That is the way God loves us. He loves us just as we are. We can be our best self. We can be our worst self. We can come just as we are. We can come apart and rest with Him.

In Psalm 46:10, we hear God saying, "Be still and know that I am God." Be still and experience Me. I am God." We want to know God and He knows we want to know Him. This is the first thing that Moses said when He came into God's presence on the mountaintop. "Who are You?" We ask that question, "Who are you?" God answers, "I am who I am!" I asked, "Where do we go from here?" That is when He gave me the scripture, "Just be still and experience who I am." He wants to reveal Himself to us in so many different ways. We can never exhaust all those ways. He wants us to know Him and He knows that this must come through an experience.

Look at the gospel account of the Annunciation. How silent it was; how quiet it was. We do not see anyone there with Our Lady. Then, the angel comes. Mary was having an experience of God when she gave her fiat, "Be it done unto me." The Word, this Word, that she wants to come into our hearts, became en-fleshed within her. She wants that for us! She wants His Word to become bone of our bone and flesh of our flesh. It is her Jesus. She wants us to experience Him.

In the gospel account of Bethlehem, the first ones that were summoned were the shepherds. They heard the message from the angel; they went to see the little baby. But there are no words. Scripture tells us that the world was in silence. It says, "The shepherds looked." They looked. That is a contemplative gaze. They looked and they must have understood because they went away exceedingly glad, rejoicing. They told everybody what they had seen. So you can see, it is gift. God is drawing us. But, He, ultimately, is the revealer of this very special presence.

Look at the Resurrection – this tremendous mystery – this Easter moment. No one is there. God seems to love the silence. He likes that intimacy. When Mary Magdalene came to the tomb, she did not see Him. She saw a gardener. He did not look like the Jesus she knew. It was when He spoke - when He spoke - that she knew. She knew! "Rabboni! Rabboni!" How did she know? She spent hours at His feet listening. She knew His voice. No matter what the disguise, no matter how He manifests Himself to you, once you know His voice, you will recognize it no matter who it comes through. If it comes through a child, through the TV, through the news, through anybody, you will know Him. When you can recognize His voice then you can discard anything else that is not the voice that you are used to. In John 10 Jesus tells us "I know My sheep." I experience them. "And," He said, "They know Me." They experience Me.

Once you begin to practice Contemplative Prayer faithfully, you will begin to see results. Maybe not right away, maybe not for several days, or weeks, but eventually you will. Will you "hear" the voice of God? Maybe not in words...but perhaps in an interior knowing. The feeling of the indwelling of the Holy Spirit, filling you with His love. I know that everyday that I pray this way, I have a power, strength and peace that is virtually impenetrable. Temptations bounce off my armor like spit wads against steel armor. I can treat people better, I have greater charity, I have greater peace.

Prayer is lifeline to the Graces. We can go to Mass everyday, pray 20 decades of the rosary everyday, go to confession every week, but if we are not practicing this kind of prayer, we are getting the maximum benefit from these graces. Prayer is absolutely essential to our life. In Genesis 19:17 God tells Abraham to "Flee into the hill country or you will die." We too must flee into the hill country of Contemplative Prayer or we too may die, our souls will suffer. Prayer is a matter of Life or Death. Prayer happens when we are in the hill country, because there is nobody else there but God. That is when we have the experience with Life!

* Intercessors of the Lamb, Contemplative Formation Center - http://www.bellwetheromaha.org

Appendix xiv

The True Knights Rosary for Purity

Sign of the Cross
In the Name of the Father, and of the Son, and of the Holy Spirit. Amen.

Opening Prayer
Queen of the Most Holy Rosary and Mother of us all, we come to you for help in our sorrows, trials and necessities. Sin leaves us weak and helpless but Divine Grace heals and strengthens.

We ask for the grace to love Jesus as you loved Him, to believe as you believed, to hope as you hoped; we ask to share your purity of mind and heart. Give us true sorrow for sin and make us love people as you and Jesus loved them. Obtain for us the gifts of the Holy Spirit that we may be wise with your wisdom, understand with your understanding, know with your knowledge, prudent with your prudence, patient with your patience, courageous with your fortitude and desire justice ardently for everyone with the all consuming desire of the Sacred Heart of Jesus your Son.

Open our minds that as we pray the Rosary we will understand the teachings of the Gospel contained in its mysteries.

We pray especially for True Knights, those men who wish to live a life of purity and chastity and be the holy husbands, fathers and sons that God Wills them to be. Help them wherever they may be; guide them, watch over them and make them strong in their trials and suffering. We pray for everyone who struggle with sins of the flesh, men and women. We are drawn together by a common bond of great charity for you and for each other; keep us faithful to your Son and to your Rosary till death.

Intercede for the souls in Purgatory, especially for the members of True Knights who have died. May they rest in peace. Finally we ask for the grace of final perseverance for ourselves and for our loved ones that we may all be reunited in heaven forever.

Mary, Mother of grace, Mother of mercy, Shield me from the enemy And receive me at the hour of my death.

Apostle's Creed
I believe in God, the Father almighty, Creator of Heaven and earth; and in Jesus Christ, his only Son, our Lord; who was conceived by the Holy Spirit, born of the Virgin Mary, suffered under Pontius Pilate, was crucified, died, and was buried. He descended into hell; the third day he rose again from the dead; he ascended into heaven, sits at the right hand of God, the Father almighty; from there he shall come to judge the living and the dead. I believe in the Holy Spirit, the Holy Catholic Church, the communion of saints, the forgiveness of sins, the resurrection of the body, and life everlasting. Amen.

Our Father
Our Father, who art in heaven, hallowed be thy name; thy kingdom come; thy will be done, on earth as it is in heaven. Give us this day our daily bread; and forgive us our

trespasses, as we forgive those who trespass against us; and lead us not into temptation, but deliver us from evil. Amen.

For Faith
I salute Thee as Daughter of God the Father, obtain for me and all whom I pray for, the gift of firm faith. Hail Mary...

For Hope
I salute Thee as Mother of God the Son, obtain for me and all whom I pray for, the gift of constant hope. Hail Mary...

For Love
I salute Thee as Spouse of God the Holy Spirit, obtain for me and all whom I pray for, the gift of an ardent charity. Hail Mary...

Glory Be
Glory be to the Father, and to the Son, and to the Holy Spirit. As it was in the beginning, is now, and ever shall be, world without end. Amen.

The Joyful Mysteries

The First Joyful Mystery - The Annunciation
I offer you, Lord Jesus, this first decade in honour of your Incarnation in Mary's womb; through this mystery and her intercession I ask for deep humility. By Your power rid me of all pride and provide for me the grace to come to you as a little child. Amen.

By thy Holy and Immaculate Conception, O Mary, purify my body and sanctify my soul.

Our Father

Hail Mary...blessed is the fruit of thy womb, Jesus who humbled Himself and become man.

> ...Holy Mary, Mother of God, Most Pure...
> ...Holy Mary, Mother of God, Most Prudent...
> ...Holy Mary, Mother of God, Most Humble...
> ...Holy Mary, Mother of God, Most Faithful...
> ...Holy Mary, Mother of God, Most Devout...
> ...Holy Mary, Mother of God, Most Obedient...
> ...Holy Mary, Mother of God, Most Poor...
> ...Holy Mary, Mother of God, Most Patient...
> ...Holy Mary, Mother of God, Most Merciful...
> ...Holy Mary, Mother of God, Most Sorrowful...

Glory be to the Father, and to the Son, and to the Holy Spirit. As it was in the beginning, is now, and ever shall be, world without end. Amen.

O my Jesus, forgive us our sins. Save us from the fires of hell. Lead all souls to heaven, especially those in most need of thy mercy.

Eternal Father, I offer You the most Precious Blood of Your Divine Son, Jesus, in union with the Masses said throughout the world today, for all the Holy Souls in Purgatory, for sinners everywhere, for sinners in the Universal Church, those in my own home and within my family. Amen.

The Second Joyful Mystery - The Visitation

I offer you, Lord Jesus, this second decade in honour of the Visitation of your holy Mother to her cousin Saint Elizabeth and of the sanctification of Saint John the Baptist; through this mystery and the intercession of your holy Mother I ask for charity towards our neighbor. Amen.

By thy Holy and Immaculate Conception, O Mary, purify my body and sanctify my soul.

Our Father

Hail Mary...blessed is the fruit of thy womb, Jesus sanctifying us.

> ...Holy Mary, Mother of God, Most Pure...
> ...Holy Mary, Mother of God, Most Prudent...
> ...Holy Mary, Mother of God, Most Humble...
> ...Holy Mary, Mother of God, Most Faithful...
> ...Holy Mary, Mother of God, Most Devout...
> ...Holy Mary, Mother of God, Most Obedient...
> ...Holy Mary, Mother of God, Most Poor...
> ...Holy Mary, Mother of God, Most Patient...
> ...Holy Mary, Mother of God, Most Merciful...
> ...Holy Mary, Mother of God, Most Sorrowful...

Glory be to the Father, and to the Son, and to the Holy Spirit. As it was in the beginning, is now, and ever shall be, world without end. Amen.

O my Jesus, forgive us our sins. Save us from the fires of hell. Lead all souls to heaven, especially those in most need of thy mercy.

Eternal Father, I offer You the most Precious Blood of Your Divine Son, Jesus, in union with the Masses said throughout the world today, for all the Holy Souls in Purgatory, for sinners everywhere, for sinners in the Universal Church, those in my own home and within my family. Amen.

The Third Joyful Mystery - The Nativity

I offer you, Lord Jesus, this third decade in honour of your Birth in the stable at Bethlehem; through this mystery and the intercession of your holy Mother, I ask for detachment from worldly things, contempt of riches and a love of poverty. Amen.

By thy Holy and Immaculate Conception, O Mary, purify my body and sanctify my soul.

Our Father

Hail Mary...blessed is the fruit of thy womb, Jesus being born.

> ...Holy Mary, Mother of God, Most Pure...
> ...Holy Mary, Mother of God, Most Prudent...
> ...Holy Mary, Mother of God, Most Humble...
> ...Holy Mary, Mother of God, Most Faithful...
> ...Holy Mary, Mother of God, Most Devout...
> ...Holy Mary, Mother of God, Most Obedient...
> ...Holy Mary, Mother of God, Most Poor...

...Holy Mary, Mother of God, Most Patient...

...Holy Mary, Mother of God, Most Merciful...

...Holy Mary, Mother of God, Most Sorrowful...

Glory be to the Father, and to the Son, and to the Holy Spirit. As it was in the beginning, is now, and ever shall be, world without end. Amen.

O my Jesus, forgive us our sins. Save us from the fires of hell. Lead all souls to heaven, especially those in most need of thy mercy.

Eternal Father, I offer You the most Precious Blood of Your Divine Son, Jesus, in union with the Masses said throughout the world today, for all the Holy Souls in Purgatory, for sinners everywhere, for sinners in the Universal Church, those in my own home and within my family. Amen.

The Fourth Joyful Mystery - The Presentation

I offer you, Lord Jesus, this fourth decade in honour of your presentation in the temple and the purification of Mary; through this mystery and her intercession we ask for the grace of obedience. Amen.

By thy Holy and Immaculate Conception, O Mary, purify my body and sanctify my soul.

Our Father

Hail Mary...blessed is the fruit of thy womb, Jesus sacrificed.

...Holy Mary, Mother of God, Most Pure...

...Holy Mary, Mother of God, Most Prudent...

...Holy Mary, Mother of God, Most Humble...

...Holy Mary, Mother of God, Most Faithful...

...Holy Mary, Mother of God, Most Devout...

...Holy Mary, Mother of God, Most Obedient...

...Holy Mary, Mother of God, Most Poor...

...Holy Mary, Mother of God, Most Patient...

...Holy Mary, Mother of God, Most Merciful...

...Holy Mary, Mother of God, Most Sorrowful...

Glory be to the Father, and to the Son, and to the Holy Spirit. As it was in the beginning, is now, and ever shall be, world without end. Amen.

O my Jesus, forgive us our sins. Save us from the fires of hell. Lead all souls to heaven, especially those in most need of thy mercy.

Eternal Father, I offer You the most Precious Blood of Your Divine Son, Jesus, in union with the Masses said throughout the world today, for all the Holy Souls in Purgatory, for sinners everywhere, for sinners in the Universal Church, those in my own home and within my family. Amen.

The Fifth Joyful Mystery - The Finding of Jesus in the Temple

I offer you, Lord Jesus, this fifth decade in honour of your being found in the temple by Mary; through this mystery and her intercession I ask for grace of Joy in my life. Amen.

By thy Holy and Immaculate Conception, O Mary, purify my body and sanctify my soul.

Our Father

Hail Mary...blessed is the fruit of thy womb, Jesus Holy of holies.

...Holy Mary, Mother of God, Most Pure...

...Holy Mary, Mother of God, Most Prudent...

...Holy Mary, Mother of God, Most Humble...

...Holy Mary, Mother of God, Most Faithful...

...Holy Mary, Mother of God, Most Devout...

...Holy Mary, Mother of God, Most Obedient...

...Holy Mary, Mother of God, Most Poor...

...Holy Mary, Mother of God, Most Patient...

...Holy Mary, Mother of God, Most Merciful...

...Holy Mary, Mother of God, Most Sorrowful...

Glory be to the Father, and to the Son, and to the Holy Spirit. As it was in the beginning, is now, and ever shall be, world without end. Amen.

O my Jesus, forgive us our sins. Save us from the fires of hell. Lead all souls to heaven, especially those in most need of thy mercy.

Eternal Father, I offer You the most Precious Blood of Your Divine Son, Jesus, in union with the Masses said throughout the world today, for all the Holy Souls in Purgatory, for sinners everywhere, for sinners in the Universal Church, those in my own home and within my family. Amen.

The Five Luminous Mysteries

The First Luminous Mystery – The Baptism in the Jordan

I offer you, Lord Jesus, this sixth decade in honour of your Baptism in the River Jordan; through this mystery and the intercession of your holy Mother I ask, by virtue of my own baptism for the grace of a clean heart. Amen.

By thy Holy and Immaculate Conception, O Mary, purify my body and sanctify my soul.

Our Father

Hail Mary...blessed is the fruit of thy womb, Jesus the Lamb of God.

...Holy Mary, Mother of God, Most Pure...

...Holy Mary, Mother of God, Most Prudent...

...Holy Mary, Mother of God, Most Humble...

...Holy Mary, Mother of God, Most Faithful...

...Holy Mary, Mother of God, Most Devout...

...Holy Mary, Mother of God, Most Obedient...

...Holy Mary, Mother of God, Most Poor...

...Holy Mary, Mother of God, Most Patient...

...Holy Mary, Mother of God, Most Merciful...

...Holy Mary, Mother of God, Most Sorrowful...

Glory be to the Father, and to the Son, and to the Holy Spirit. As it was in the beginning, is now, and ever shall be, world without end. Amen.

O my Jesus, forgive us our sins. Save us from the fires of hell. Lead all souls to heaven, especially those in most need of thy mercy.

Eternal Father, I offer You the most Precious Blood of Your Divine Son, Jesus, in union with the Masses said throughout the world today, for all the Holy Souls in Purgatory, for sinners everywhere, for sinners in the Universal Church, those in my own home and within my family. Amen.

The Second Luminous Mystery – The Miracle at the Wedding of Cana

I offer you, Lord Jesus, this seventh decade in honour of the start of your public ministry; through this mystery and the intercession of your holy Mother I ask for the grace to always follow your will. Amen.

By thy Holy and Immaculate Conception, O Mary, purify my body and sanctify my soul.

Our Father

Hail Mary...blessed is the fruit of thy womb, Jesus whom you tell us to follow.

>   ...Holy Mary, Mother of God, Most Pure...
>   ...Holy Mary, Mother of God, Most Prudent...
>   ...Holy Mary, Mother of God, Most Humble...
>   ...Holy Mary, Mother of God, Most Faithful...
>   ...Holy Mary, Mother of God, Most Devout...
>   ...Holy Mary, Mother of God, Most Obedient...
>   ...Holy Mary, Mother of God, Most Poor...
>   ...Holy Mary, Mother of God, Most Patient...
>   ...Holy Mary, Mother of God, Most Merciful...
>   ...Holy Mary, Mother of God, Most Sorrowful...

Glory be to the Father, and to the Son, and to the Holy Spirit. As it was in the beginning, is now, and ever shall be, world without end. Amen.

O my Jesus, forgive us our sins. Save us from the fires of hell. Lead all souls to heaven, especially those in most need of thy mercy.

Eternal Father, I offer You the most Precious Blood of Your Divine Son, Jesus, in union with the Masses said throughout the world today, for all the Holy Souls in Purgatory, for sinners everywhere, for sinners in the Universal Church, those in my own home and within my family. Amen.

The Third Luminous Mystery – The Proclamation of the Kingdom

I offer you, Lord Jesus, this eighth decade in honour of your proclaiming the coming of the Kingdom of God; through this mystery and the intercession of your holy Mother I ask for the grace of my own daily conversion. Amen.

By thy Holy and Immaculate Conception, O Mary, purify my body and sanctify my soul.

Our Father

Hail Mary...blessed is the fruit of thy womb, Jesus proclaiming the Kingdom of God.

>   ...Holy Mary, Mother of God, Most Pure...
>   ...Holy Mary, Mother of God, Most Prudent...
>   ...Holy Mary, Mother of God, Most Humble...
>   ...Holy Mary, Mother of God, Most Faithful...
>   ...Holy Mary, Mother of God, Most Devout...

...Holy Mary, Mother of God, Most Obedient...

...Holy Mary, Mother of God, Most Poor...

...Holy Mary, Mother of God, Most Patient...

...Holy Mary, Mother of God, Most Merciful...

...Holy Mary, Mother of God, Most Sorrowful...

Glory be to the Father, and to the Son, and to the Holy Spirit. As it was in the beginning, is now, and ever shall be, world without end. Amen.

O my Jesus, forgive us our sins. Save us from the fires of hell. Lead all souls to heaven, especially those in most need of thy mercy.

Eternal Father, I offer You the most Precious Blood of Your Divine Son, Jesus, in union with the Masses said throughout the world today, for all the Holy Souls in Purgatory, for sinners everywhere, for sinners in the Universal Church, those in my own home and within my family. Amen.

The Fourth Luminous Mystery – The Transfiguration

I offer you, Lord Jesus, this ninth decade in honour of the miracle on the mountain; through this mystery and the intercession of your holy Mother I ask for the grace to always proclaim your glory. Amen.

By thy Holy and Immaculate Conception, O Mary, purify my body and sanctify my soul.

Our Father

Hail Mary...blessed is the fruit of thy womb, Jesus shown to us in all His glory.

...Holy Mary, Mother of God, Most Pure...

...Holy Mary, Mother of God, Most Prudent...

...Holy Mary, Mother of God, Most Humble...

...Holy Mary, Mother of God, Most Faithful...

...Holy Mary, Mother of God, Most Devout...

...Holy Mary, Mother of God, Most Obedient...

...Holy Mary, Mother of God, Most Poor...

...Holy Mary, Mother of God, Most Patient...

...Holy Mary, Mother of God, Most Merciful...

...Holy Mary, Mother of God, Most Sorrowful...

Glory be to the Father, and to the Son, and to the Holy Spirit. As it was in the beginning, is now, and ever shall be, world without end. Amen.

O my Jesus, forgive us our sins. Save us from the fires of hell. Lead all souls to heaven, especially those in most need of thy mercy.

Eternal Father, I offer You the most Precious Blood of Your Divine Son, Jesus, in union with the Masses said throughout the world today, for all the Holy Souls in Purgatory, for sinners everywhere, for sinners in the Universal Church, those in my own home and within my family. Amen.

The Fifth Luminous Mystery – The Institution of the Eucharist

I offer you, Lord Jesus, this tenth decade in honour of the institution of the Eucharist; through this mystery and the intercession of your holy Mother I ask for the grace of eternal life through your Body and Blood. Amen.

By thy Holy and Immaculate Conception, O Mary, purify my body and sanctify my soul.

Our Father

Hail Mary...blessed is the fruit of thy womb, Jesus truly present in the most Holy Eucharist.

> ...Holy Mary, Mother of God, Most Pure...
> ...Holy Mary, Mother of God, Most Prudent...
> ...Holy Mary, Mother of God, Most Humble...
> ...Holy Mary, Mother of God, Most Faithful...
> ...Holy Mary, Mother of God, Most Devout...
> ...Holy Mary, Mother of God, Most Obedient...
> ...Holy Mary, Mother of God, Most Poor...
> ...Holy Mary, Mother of God, Most Patient...
> ...Holy Mary, Mother of God, Most Merciful...
> ...Holy Mary, Mother of God, Most Sorrowful...

Glory be to the Father, and to the Son, and to the Holy Spirit. As it was in the beginning, is now, and ever shall be, world without end. Amen.

O my Jesus, forgive us our sins. Save us from the fires of hell. Lead all souls to heaven, especially those in most need of thy mercy.

Eternal Father, I offer You the most Precious Blood of Your Divine Son, Jesus, in union with the Masses said throughout the world today, for all the Holy Souls in Purgatory, for sinners everywhere, for sinners in the Universal Church, those in my own home and within my family. Amen.

The Five Sorrowful Mysteries

The First Sorrowful Mystery - The Agony in the Garden

I offer you, Lord Jesus, this eleventh decade in honour of your Agony in the Garden of Olives; through this mystery and the intercession of your holy Mother I ask for a deep sorrow for all my sins. Amen.
By thy Holy and Immaculate Conception, O Mary, purify my body and sanctify my soul.

Our Father

Hail Mary...blessed is the fruit of thy womb, Jesus in agony.

> ...Holy Mary, Mother of God, Most Pure...
> ...Holy Mary, Mother of God, Most Prudent...
> ...Holy Mary, Mother of God, Most Humble...
> ...Holy Mary, Mother of God, Most Faithful...
> ...Holy Mary, Mother of God, Most Devout...
> ...Holy Mary, Mother of God, Most Obedient...
> ...Holy Mary, Mother of God, Most Poor...
> ...Holy Mary, Mother of God, Most Patient...
> ...Holy Mary, Mother of God, Most Merciful...
> ...Holy Mary, Mother of God, Most Sorrowful...

Glory be to the Father, and to the Son, and to the Holy Spirit. As it was in the beginning, is now, and ever shall be, world without end. Amen.

O my Jesus, forgive us our sins. Save us from the fires of hell. Lead all souls to heaven, especially those in most need of thy mercy.

Eternal Father, I offer You the most Precious Blood of Your Divine Son, Jesus, in union with the Masses said throughout the world today, for all the Holy Souls in Purgatory, for sinners everywhere, for sinners in the Universal Church, those in my own home and within my family. Amen.

The Second Sorrowful Mystery - The Scourging at the Pillar

I offer you, Lord Jesus, this twelfth decade in honour of your cruel Scourging; through this mystery and the intercession of your holy Mother I ask for the grace of holy purity and to mortify my senses. Amen.

By thy Holy and Immaculate Conception, O Mary, purify my body and sanctify my soul.

Our Father

Hail Mary...blessed is the fruit of thy womb, Jesus being scourged.

> ...Holy Mary, Mother of God, Most Pure...
> ...Holy Mary, Mother of God, Most Prudent...
> ...Holy Mary, Mother of God, Most Humble...
> ...Holy Mary, Mother of God, Most Faithful...
> ...Holy Mary, Mother of God, Most Devout...
> ...Holy Mary, Mother of God, Most Obedient...
> ...Holy Mary, Mother of God, Most Poor...
> ...Holy Mary, Mother of God, Most Patient...
> ...Holy Mary, Mother of God, Most Merciful...
> ...Holy Mary, Mother of God, Most Sorrowful...

Glory be to the Father, and to the Son, and to the Holy Spirit. As it was in the beginning, is now, and ever shall be, world without end. Amen.

O my Jesus, forgive us our sins. Save us from the fires of hell. Lead all souls to heaven, especially those in most need of thy mercy.

Eternal Father, I offer You the most Precious Blood of Your Divine Son, Jesus, in union with the Masses said throughout the world today, for all the Holy Souls in Purgatory, for sinners everywhere, for sinners in the Universal Church, those in my own home and within my family. Amen.

The Third Sorrowful Mystery - The Crowning with Thorns

I offer you, Lord Jesus, this thirteenth decade in honour of your being Crowned with Thorns; through this mystery and the intercession of your holy Mother I ask for contempt of the world. Amen.

By thy Holy and Immaculate Conception, O Mary, purify my body and sanctify my soul.

Our Father

Hail Mary...blessed is the fruit of thy womb, Jesus crowned with thorns.

> ...Holy Mary, Mother of God, Most Pure...
> ...Holy Mary, Mother of God, Most Prudent...
> ...Holy Mary, Mother of God, Most Humble...

...Holy Mary, Mother of God, Most Faithful...
...Holy Mary, Mother of God, Most Devout...
...Holy Mary, Mother of God, Most Obedient...
...Holy Mary, Mother of God, Most Poor...
...Holy Mary, Mother of God, Most Patient...
...Holy Mary, Mother of God, Most Merciful...
...Holy Mary, Mother of God, Most Sorrowful...

Glory be to the Father, and to the Son, and to the Holy Spirit. As it was in the beginning, is now, and ever shall be, world without end. Amen.

O my Jesus, forgive us our sins. Save us from the fires of hell. Lead all souls to heaven, especially those in most need of thy mercy.

Eternal Father, I offer You the most Precious Blood of Your Divine Son, Jesus, in union with the Masses said throughout the world today, for all the Holy Souls in Purgatory, for sinners everywhere, for sinners in the Universal Church, those in my own home and within my family. Amen.

The Fourth Sorrowful Mystery - The Carrying of the Cross

I offer you, Lord Jesus, this fourteenth decade in honour of your carrying the Cross; through this mystery and the intercession of your holy Mother I ask for the grace to embrace my own cross. Amen.

By thy Holy and Immaculate Conception, O Mary, purify my body and sanctify my soul.

Our Father

Hail Mary...blessed is the fruit of thy womb, Jesus carrying His cross.

...Holy Mary, Mother of God, Most Pure...
...Holy Mary, Mother of God, Most Prudent...
...Holy Mary, Mother of God, Most Humble...
...Holy Mary, Mother of God, Most Faithful...
...Holy Mary, Mother of God, Most Devout...
...Holy Mary, Mother of God, Most Obedient...
...Holy Mary, Mother of God, Most Poor...
...Holy Mary, Mother of God, Most Patient...
...Holy Mary, Mother of God, Most Merciful...
...Holy Mary, Mother of God, Most Sorrowful...

Glory be to the Father, and to the Son, and to the Holy Spirit. As it was in the beginning, is now, and ever shall be, world without end. Amen.

O my Jesus, forgive us our sins. Save us from the fires of hell. Lead all souls to heaven, especially those in most need of thy mercy.

Eternal Father, I offer You the most Precious Blood of Your Divine Son, Jesus, in union with the Masses said throughout the world today, for all the Holy Souls in Purgatory, for sinners everywhere, for sinners in the Universal Church, those in my own home and within my family. Amen.

The Fifth Sorrowful Mystery - The Crucifixion

I offer you, Lord Jesus, this fifteenth decade in honour of your Crucifixion and shameful Death on

Calvary; through this mystery and the intercession of your holy Mother I ask for the conversion of sinners, perseverance for the just and relief for the souls in Purgatory. Amen.

By thy Holy and Immaculate Conception, O Mary, purify my body and sanctify my soul.

Our Father

Hail Mary...blessed is the fruit of thy womb, Jesus crucified.

> ...Holy Mary, Mother of God, Most Pure...
> ...Holy Mary, Mother of God, Most Prudent...
> ...Holy Mary, Mother of God, Most Humble...
> ...Holy Mary, Mother of God, Most Faithful...
> ...Holy Mary, Mother of God, Most Devout...
> ...Holy Mary, Mother of God, Most Obedient...
> ...Holy Mary, Mother of God, Most Poor...
> ...Holy Mary, Mother of God, Most Patient...
> ...Holy Mary, Mother of God, Most Merciful...
> ...Holy Mary, Mother of God, Most Sorrowful...

Glory be to the Father, and to the Son, and to the Holy Spirit. As it was in the beginning, is now, and ever shall be, world without end. Amen.

O my Jesus, forgive us our sins. Save us from the fires of hell. Lead all souls to heaven, especially those in most need of thy mercy.

Eternal Father, I offer You the most Precious Blood of Your Divine Son, Jesus, in union with the Masses said throughout the world today, for all the Holy Souls in Purgatory, for sinners everywhere, for sinners in the Universal Church, those in my own home and within my family. Amen.

The Five Glorious Mysteries
The First Glorious Mystery - The Resurrection

I offer you, Lord Jesus, this sixteenth decade in honour of your glorious Resurrection; through this mystery and the intercession of your holy Mother, I ask for love of God and fervor in your service in the hope of my own resurrection. Amen.

By thy Holy and Immaculate Conception, O Mary, purify my body and sanctify my soul.

Our Father

Hail Mary...blessed is the fruit of thy womb, Jesus risen from the dead.

> ...Holy Mary, Mother of God, Most Pure...
> ...Holy Mary, Mother of God, Most Prudent...
> ...Holy Mary, Mother of God, Most Humble...
> ...Holy Mary, Mother of God, Most Faithful...
> ...Holy Mary, Mother of God, Most Devout...
> ...Holy Mary, Mother of God, Most Obedient...
> ...Holy Mary, Mother of God, Most Poor...
> ...Holy Mary, Mother of God, Most Patient...

...Holy Mary, Mother of God, Most Merciful...

...Holy Mary, Mother of God, Most Sorrowful...

Glory be to the Father, and to the Son, and to the Holy Spirit. As it was in the beginning, is now, and ever shall be, world without end. Amen.

O my Jesus, forgive us our sins. Save us from the fires of hell. Lead all souls to heaven, especially those in most need of thy mercy.

Eternal Father, I offer You the most Precious Blood of Your Divine Son, Jesus, in union with the Masses said throughout the world today, for all the Holy Souls in Purgatory, for sinners everywhere, for sinners in the Universal Church, those in my own home and within my family. Amen.

The Second Glorious Mystery - The Ascension

I offer you, Lord Jesus, this seventeenth decade in honour of your triumphant Ascension; through this mystery and the intercession of your holy Mother I ask for an ardent desire for heaven, our true home. Amen. By thy Holy and Immaculate Conception, O Mary, purify my body and sanctify my soul.

Our Father

Hail Mary...blessed is the fruit of thy womb, Jesus ascending to heaven.

...Holy Mary, Mother of God, Most Pure...

...Holy Mary, Mother of God, Most Prudent...

...Holy Mary, Mother of God, Most Humble...

...Holy Mary, Mother of God, Most Faithful...

...Holy Mary, Mother of God, Most Devout...

...Holy Mary, Mother of God, Most Obedient...

...Holy Mary, Mother of God, Most Poor...

...Holy Mary, Mother of God, Most Patient...

...Holy Mary, Mother of God, Most Merciful...

...Holy Mary, Mother of God, Most Sorrowful...

Glory be to the Father, and to the Son, and to the Holy Spirit. As it was in the beginning, is now, and ever shall be, world without end. Amen.

O my Jesus, forgive us our sins. Save us from the fires of hell. Lead all souls to heaven, especially those in most need of thy mercy.

Eternal Father, I offer You the most Precious Blood of Your Divine Son, Jesus, in union with the Masses said throughout the world today, for all the Holy Souls in Purgatory, for sinners everywhere, for sinners in the Universal Church, those in my own home and within my family. Amen.

The Third Glorious Mystery - The Descent of the Holy Spirit

I offer you, Lord Jesus, this eighteenth decade in honour of the mystery of Pentecost; through this mystery and the intercession of your holy Mother I ask that the Holy Spirit may come into our souls. Amen.

By thy Holy and Immaculate Conception, O Mary, purify my body and sanctify my soul.

Our Father

Hail Mary...blessed is the fruit of thy womb, Jesus filling us with the Holy Spirit.

>...Holy Mary, Mother of God, Most Pure...
>...Holy Mary, Mother of God, Most Prudent...
>...Holy Mary, Mother of God, Most Humble...
>...Holy Mary, Mother of God, Most Faithful...
>...Holy Mary, Mother of God, Most Devout...
>...Holy Mary, Mother of God, Most Obedient...
>...Holy Mary, Mother of God, Most Poor...
>...Holy Mary, Mother of God, Most Patient...
>...Holy Mary, Mother of God, Most Merciful...
>...Holy Mary, Mother of God, Most Sorrowful...

Glory be to the Father, and to the Son, and to the Holy Spirit. As it was in the beginning, is now, and ever shall be, world without end. Amen.

O my Jesus, forgive us our sins. Save us from the fires of hell. Lead all souls to heaven, especially those in most need of thy mercy.

Eternal Father, I offer You the most Precious Blood of Your Divine Son, Jesus, in union with the Masses said throughout the world today, for all the Holy Souls in Purgatory, for sinners everywhere, for sinners in the Universal Church, those in my own home and within my family. Amen.

The Fourth Glorious Mystery - The Assumption

I offer you, Lord Jesus, this nineteenth decade in honour of the Resurrection and triumphant Assumption of your holy Mother into heaven; through this mystery and her intercession I ask for a tender devotion to so good a Mother. Amen.

By thy Holy and Immaculate Conception, O Mary, purify my body and sanctify my soul.

Our Father

Hail Mary...blessed is the fruit of thy womb, Jesus raising thee up.

>...Holy Mary, Mother of God, Most Pure...
>...Holy Mary, Mother of God, Most Prudent...
>...Holy Mary, Mother of God, Most Humble...
>...Holy Mary, Mother of God, Most Faithful...
>...Holy Mary, Mother of God, Most Devout...
>...Holy Mary, Mother of God, Most Obedient...
>...Holy Mary, Mother of God, Most Poor...
>...Holy Mary, Mother of God, Most Patient...
>...Holy Mary, Mother of God, Most Merciful...
>...Holy Mary, Mother of God, Most Sorrowful...

Glory be to the Father, and to the Son, and to the Holy Spirit. As it was in the beginning, is now, and ever shall be, world without end. Amen.

O my Jesus, forgive us our sins. Save us from the fires of hell. Lead all souls to heaven, especially those in most need of thy mercy.

Eternal Father, I offer You the most Precious Blood of Your Divine Son, Jesus, in union with the Masses said throughout the world today, for all the Holy Souls in Purgatory, for sinners everywhere, for sinners in the Universal Church, those in my own home and within my family. Amen.

The Fifth Glorious Mystery - The Coronation

I offer you, Lord Jesus, this twentieth and last decade in honour of the Coronation of your holy Mother; through this mystery and her intercession I ask for perseverance in grace and the crown of glory. Amen.

By thy Holy and Immaculate Conception, O Mary, purify my body and sanctify my soul.

Our Father

Hail Mary...blessed is the fruit of thy womb, Jesus crowning thee.

> ...Holy Mary, Mother of God, Most Pure...
> ...Holy Mary, Mother of God, Most Prudent...
> ...Holy Mary, Mother of God, Most Humble...
> ...Holy Mary, Mother of God, Most Faithful...
> ...Holy Mary, Mother of God, Most Devout...
> ...Holy Mary, Mother of God, Most Obedient...
> ...Holy Mary, Mother of God, Most Poor...
> ...Holy Mary, Mother of God, Most Patient...
> ...Holy Mary, Mother of God, Most Merciful...
> ...Holy Mary, Mother of God, Most Sorrowful...

Glory be to the Father, and to the Son, and to the Holy Spirit. As it was in the beginning, is now, and ever shall be, world without end. Amen.

O my Jesus, forgive us our sins. Save us from the fires of hell. Lead all souls to heaven, especially those in most need of thy mercy.

Eternal Father, I offer You the most Precious Blood of Your Divine Son, Jesus, in union with the Masses said throughout the world today, for all the Holy Souls in Purgatory, for sinners everywhere, for sinners in the Universal Church, those in my own home and within my family. Amen.

Concluding Prayer

Hail, Holy Queen, Mother of Mercy, our life, our sweetness, and our hope! To you we cry, poor banished children of Eve; to you we send up our sighs, mourning and weeping in this valley of tears. Turn then, most gracious advocate, your eyes of mercy toward us; and after this our exile, show to us the blessed fruit of your womb, Jesus. O clement, O loving, O sweet Virgin Mary:

V. Pray for us, O holy Mother of God.

R. That we may be made worthy of the promises of Christ.

In the name of the Father, and of the Son, and of the Holy Spirit. Amen.

Appendix xv

The True Knights Novena for Chastity and Purity

OPENING PRAYER

Veni, Creator

Come Holy Ghost, Creator Blest,

And in our hearts take up Thy rest;

Come with Thy grace and heav'nly aid

To fill the hearts which Thou hast made,

To fill the hearts which Thou hast made.

O Comfort Blest to Thee we cry,

Thou heav'nly Gift of God most high;

Thou fount of life and fire of love,

And sweet anointing from above,

And sweet anointing from above.

Praise be to Thee Father and Son,

And Holy Spirit Three in one;

And may the Son on us bestow

The gifts that from the Spirit flow,

The gifts that from the Spirit flow.

Prayer for Purity *(St. Thomas Aquinas)*

Dearest Jesus! I know well that every perfect gift, and above all others that of chastity, depends upon the most powerful assistance of Thy Providence, and that without Thee a creature can do nothing. Therefore, I pray Thee to defend, with Thy grace, chastity and purity in my soul as well as in my body. And if I have ever received through my senses any impression that could stain my chastity and purity, do Thou, Who art the Supreme Lord of all my powers, take it from me, that I may with an immaculate heart advance in Thy love and service, offering myself chaste all the days of my life on the most pure altar of Thy Divinity. Amen.

Jesus, Fortress of mankind,

You are Immaculate as God and Man!

That I may remain in a state of purity.

Strengthen my body, spirit and soul

To continually reflect Your chastity.

Protect my soul in its daily struggles,

Guiding it to ponder on Your Godliness.

Defend me from the forces of evil,

Those that seek to acquire my soul:

I am truly Yours forever and ever.

Holy is my King, the Conqueror of sin!

Day 1 - Scripture Reading - Exodus 20:1-17

And the Lord spoke all these words: I am the Lord thy God, who brought thee out of the land of Egypt, out of the house of bondage. Thou shalt not have strange gods before me. Thou shalt not make to thyself a graven thing, nor the likeness of any thing that is in heaven above, or in the earth beneath, nor of those things that are in the waters under the earth. Thou shalt not adore them, nor serve them: I am the Lord thy God, mighty, jealous, visiting the iniquity of the fathers upon the children, unto the third and fourth generation of them that hate me: And shewing mercy unto thousands to them that love me, and keep my commandments. Thou shalt not take the name of the Lord thy God in vain: for the Lord will not hold him guiltless that shall take the name of the Lord his God in vain. Remember that thou keep holy the sabbath day. Six days shalt thou labour, and shalt do all thy works. But on the seventh day is the sabbath of the Lord thy God: thou shalt do no work on it, thou nor thy son, nor thy daughter, nor thy manservant, nor thy maidservant, nor thy beast, nor the stranger that is within thy gates. For in six days the Lord made heaven and earth, and the sea, and all things that are in them, and rested on the seventh day: therefore the Lord blessed the seventh day, and sanctified it. Honour thy father and thy mother, that thou mayst be longlived upon the land which the Lord thy God will give thee. Thou shalt not kill. Thou shalt not commit adultery. Thou shalt not steal. Thou shalt not bear false witness against thy neighbour. Thou shalt not covet thy neighbour's house; neither shalt thou desire his wife, nor his servant, nor his handmaid, nor his ox, nor his ass, nor any thing that is his.

Pray Psalm 51 and Closing Prayer.

Day 2 - Scripture Reading - Job 31:1-6

I made a covenant with my eyes, that I would not so much as think upon a virgin. For what part should God from above have in me, and what inheritance the Almighty from on high? Is not destruction to the wicked, and aversion to them that work iniquity? Doth not he consider my ways, and number all my steps? If I have walked in vanity, and my foot hath made haste to deceit: Let him weigh me in a just balance, and let God know my simplicity.

Pray Psalm 51 and Closing Prayer.

Day 3 - Scripture Reading - Proverbs 6:20-32

My son, keep the commandments of thy father, and forsake not the law of thy mother. Bind them in thy heart continually, and put them about thy neck. When thou walkest, let them go with thee: when thou sleepest, let them keep thee, and when thou awakest, talk with them. Because the commandment is a lamp, and the law a light, and reproofs of instruction are the way of life: That they may keep thee from the evil woman, and from the flattering tongue of the stranger. Let not thy heart covet her beauty, be not caught with her winks: For the price of a harlot is scarce one loaf: but the woman catcheth the precious soul of a man. Can a man hide fire in his bosom, and his garments not burn? Or can he walk upon hot coals, and his feet not be burnt? So he that goeth in to his neighbour's wife, shall not be clean when he shall touch her. The fault is not so great when a man hath stolen: for he stealeth to fill his hungry soul: And if he be taken, he shall restore sevenfold, and shall give up all the substance of his house. But he that is an adulterer, for the folly of his heart shall destroy his own soul.

Pray Psalm 51 and Closing Prayer.

Day 4 - Scripture Reading - Matthew 5:27-28

Jesus said to his disciples: "You have heard that it was said, You shall not commit adultery. But I say to you, everyone who looks at a woman with lust has already committed adultery with her in his heart. If your right eye causes you to sin, tear it out and throw it away. It is better for you to lose one of your members than to have your whole body thrown into Gehenna. And if your right hand causes you to sin, cut it off and throw it away. It is better for you to lose one of your members than to have your whole body go into Gehenna. "It was also said, Whoever divorces his wife must give her a bill of divorce. But I say to you, whoever divorces his wife (unless the marriage is unlawful) causes her to commit adultery, and whoever marries a divorced woman commits adultery."

Pray Psalm 51 and Closing Prayer.

Day 5 - Scripture Reading – 1 Corinthians 6:9-20

Know you not that the unjust shall not possess the kingdom of God? Do not err: Neither fornicators nor idolaters nor adulterers: Nor the effeminate nor liers with mankind nor thieves nor covetous nor drunkards nor railers nor extortioners shall possess the kingdom of God. And such some of you were. But you are washed: but you are sanctified: but you are justified: in the name of our Lord Jesus Christ and the Spirit of our God. All things are lawful to me: but all things are not expedient. All things are lawful to me: but I will not be brought under the power of any. Meat for the belly and the belly for the meats: but God shall destroy both it and them. But the body is not for fornication, but for the Lord: and the Lord for the body. Now God hath raised up the Lord and will raise us up also by his power. Know you not that your bodies are the members of Christ? Shall I then take the members of Christ and make them the members of an harlot? God forbid! Or know you not that he who is joined to a harlot is made one body? For they shall be, saith he, two in one flesh. But he who is joined to the Lord is one spirit. Fly fornication. Every sin that a man doth is without the body: but he that committeth fornication sinneth against his own body. Or know you not that your members are the temple of the Holy Ghost, who is in you, whom you have from God: and you are not your own? For you are bought with a great price. Glorify and bear God in your body.

Pray Psalm 51 and Closing Prayer.

Day 6 - Scripture Reading – Ephesians 5:1-17

Be ye therefore followers of God, as most dear children: And walk in love, as Christ also hath loved us and hath delivered himself for us, an oblation and a sacrifice to God for an odour of sweetness. But fornication and all uncleanness or covetousness, let it not so much as be named among you, as becometh saints: Or obscenity or foolish talking or scurrility, which is to no purpose: but rather giving of thanks. For know you this and understand: That no fornicator or unclean or covetous person (which is a serving of idols) hath inheritance in the kingdom of Christ and of God. Let no man deceive you with vain words. For because of these things cometh the anger of God upon the children of unbelief. Be ye not therefore partakers with them. For you were heretofore darkness, but now light in the Lord. Walk then as children of the light. For the fruit of the light is in all goodness and justice and truth: Proving what is well pleasing to God. And have no fellowship with the unfruitful works of darkness: but rather reprove them. For the things that are done by them in secret, it is a shame even to speak of. But all things that are reproved are made manifest by the light: for all that is made manifest is light. Wherefore he saith: Rise, thou that sleepest, and arise from the dead: and Christ shall enlighten thee. See therefore, brethren, how you walk circumspectly: not as unwise, But as wise: redeeming the time, because the days are evil. Wherefore, become not unwise: but understanding what is the will of God.

Pray Psalm 51 and Closing Prayer.

Day 7 - Scripture Reading – Colossians 3:1-15

Therefore if you be risen with Christ, seek the things that are above, where Christ is sitting at the right hand of God. Mind the things that are above, not the things that are upon the earth. For you are dead: and your life is hid with Christ in God. When Christ shall appear, who is your life, then you also shall appear with him in glory. Mortify therefore your members which are upon the earth: fornication, uncleanness, lust, evil concupiscence and covetousness, which is the service of idols. For which things the wrath of God cometh upon the children of unbelief. In which you also walked some time, when you lived in them. But now put you also all away: anger, indignation, malice, blasphemy, filthy speech out of your mouth. Lie not one to another: stripping yourselves of the old man with his deeds, And putting on the new, him who is renewed unto knowledge, according to the image of him that created him. Where there is neither Gentile nor Jew, circumcision nor uncircumcision, Barbarian nor Scythian, bond nor free. But Christ is all and in all. Put ye on therefore, as the elect of God, holy and beloved, the bowels of mercy, benignity, humility, modesty, patience: Bearing with one another and forgiving one another, if any have a complaint against another. Even as the Lord hath forgiven you, so do you also. But above all these things have charity, which is the bond of perfection. And let the peace of Christ rejoice in your hearts, wherein also you are called in one body: and be ye thankful.

Pray Psalm 51 and Closing Prayer.

Day 8 - Scripture Reading – 1 Thessalonians 4:1-9

For the rest therefore, brethren, pray and beseech you in the Lord Jesus that, as you have received from us, how you ought to walk and to please God, so also you would walk, that you may abound the more. For you know what precepts I have given to you by the Lord Jesus. For this is the will of God, your sanctification: That you should abstain from fornication: That every one of you should know how to possess his vessel in sanctification and honour, Not in the passion of lust, like the Gentiles that know not God: And that no man overreach nor circumvent his brother in business: because the Lord is the avenger of all these things, as we have told you before and have testified. For God hath not called us unto uncleanness, but unto sanctification. Therefore, he that despiseth these things, despiseth not man, but God, who also hath given his holy Spirit in us. But as touching the charity of brotherhood, we have no need to write to you: for yourselves have learned of God to love one another.

Pray Psalm 51 and Closing Prayer.

Day 9 - Scripture Reading – Revelations 14:4-12

These are they who were not defiled with women: for they are virgins. These follow the Lamb whithersoever he goeth. These were purchased from among men, the firstfruits to God and to the Lamb. And in their mouth there was found no lie: for they are without spot before the throne of God. And I saw another angel flying through the midst of heaven, having the eternal gospel, to preach unto them that sit upon the earth and over every nation and tribe and tongue and people: Saying with a loud voice: Fear the Lord and give him honour, because the hour of his judgment is come. And adore ye him that made heaven and earth, the sea and the fountains of waters. And another angel followed, saying: That great Babylon is fallen, is fallen; which made all nations to drink of the wine of the wrath of her fornication. And the third angel followed them, saying with a loud voice: If any man shall adore the beast and his image and receive his character in his forehead or in his hand, He also shall drink of the wine of the wrath of God, which is mingled with pure wine in the cup of his wrath: and shall be tormented with fire and brimstone in the sight of the holy angels and in the sight of the Lamb. And the smoke of their torments, shall ascend up for ever and ever: neither have they rest day nor night, who have adored the beast and his image and whoever receiveth the character of his name. Here is the patience of the saints, who keep the commandments of God and the faith of Jesus.

Pray Psalm 51 and Closing Prayer.

Closing for Each Day of the Novena

Psalm 51

Have mercy on me, O God, according to thy great mercy. And according to the multitude of thy tender mercies blot out my iniquity. Wash me yet more from my iniquity, and cleanse me from my sin. For I know my iniquity, and my sin is always before me. To thee only have I sinned, and have done evil before thee: that thou mayst be justified in thy words, and mayst overcome when thou art judged. For behold I was conceived in iniquities; and in sins did my mother conceive me. For behold thou hast loved truth: the uncertain and hidden things of thy wisdom thou hast made manifest to me. Thou shalt sprinkle me with hyssop, and I shall be cleansed: thou shalt wash me, and I shall be made whiter than snow. To my hearing thou shalt give joy and gladness: and the bones that have been humbled shall rejoice. Turn away thy face from my sins, and blot out all my iniquities. Create a clean heart in me, O God: and renew a right spirit within my bowels. Cast me not away from thy face; and take not thy holy spirit from me. Restore unto me the joy of thy salvation, and strengthen me with a perfect spirit. I will teach the unjust thy ways: and the wicked shall be converted to thee. Deliver me from blood, O God, thou God of my salvation: and my tongue shall extol thy justice. O Lord, thou wilt open my lips: and my mouth shall declare thy praise. For if thou hadst desired sacrifice, I would indeed have given it: with burnt offerings thou wilt not be delighted. A sacrifice to God is an afflicted spirit: a contrite and humbled heart, O God, thou wilt not despise. Deal favourably, O Lord, in thy good will with Sion; that the walls of Jerusalem may be built up. Then shalt thou accept the sacrifice of justice, oblations and whole burnt offerings: then shall they lay calves upon thy altar.

Spend 15 minutes in Contemplative Prayer

Pray One Our Father, Hail Mary, Glory Be to the Father or The Rosary for Purity

Closing Prayer

Lord God, through your prophet Ezekiel you promised your people,

"I shall our clean water over you and you will be cleansed;

I shall cleanse you of all your filth and of all your foul idols.

I shall give you a new heart, and put a new spirit in you;

I shall remove the heart of stone from your bodies and

give you a heart of flesh instead.

I shall put my spirit in you, and make you keep my laws."

Therefore, I beg You, O Lord Most High,

through the Immaculate Heart of Mary,

create in me a pure heart and a steadfast spirit.

Make me pure in mind, heart, and soul; thought, word, deed, desire, and attire.

[Add your personal request for purity, chastity, celibacy, and/or virginity here.]

May this be solely for Your praise, honor, and glory and not for recognition or approval from mankind.

Let us pray. Lord Jesus Christ, Son of the Living God, lover and guardian of purity, I implore your great mercy, that as you preserved your mother from the stain of body and soul that you may deign to bless me in the sanctification of my body and soul, so that I may be purified from all uncleanness of mind and body and may merit to be presented worthily to you by the hands of the Angels in the passing of this life. Amen.

Information About
True Knights & Combat Training

The True Knights Mission Statement

True Knights is a formal confraternity of Christian men, under the patronage of Our Lady of the Immaculate Heart, St. Joseph, St. Michael the Archangel and several others. We are dedicated to strengthening the family through the teachings of Christ through His Church, the One, Holy, Catholic and Apostolic Church. The primary mission of True Knights is to men who are fathers of children still living at home. However, we warmly welcome Christian men of all ages, callings, and states in life: grandfathers wanting to strengthen their children and grandchildren; single men preparing for the vocation of marriage or priesthood and consecrated celibacy; and especially pastors serving as indispensable spiritual fathers in the family of God. Participation is open to all men who agree with, and who are willing to promote, the commitments of The True Knights Code of Chivalry. As True Knights, we are not just concerned with our own families but strive for a Christlike concern for the spiritual and material welfare of other families in our community, in our parish, and in other localities throughout the world. As True Knights we also have a special call to fight against the evil of Pornography and the swath of destruction to souls it leaves in it's wake. True Knights has been recognized as a authentic lay Confraternity by the Most Reverend Bishop Edward Slattery of the Diocese of Tulsa.

What is True Knights Combat Training?

Personal Coaching to Achieve and Maintain Sexual Purity!

Combat Training is personal one-on-one purity coaching to help you break-free of impurity and stay pure. This is all done in an informal manner. Your coach will be your friend, your accountability partner and always, your brother in Christ. Your coach will be someone who will share personal successes and suggest strategies to overcome your own struggles. Combat Training is 100% Biblical because the Catholic Church and her teachings are 100% Biblical. (Visit www.TrueKnights.org for more on the 100% Biblical Teaching of the Catholic Church.) Combat Training draws upon the Truths of the Catholic Faith and utilizes the great treasure of graces that God has given all of us to live a life free from the clutches of the enemy's hold on our lives through lust. True freedom is the goal of True Knights Combat Training and true freedom can only be found in Jesus Christ and His Church.

In True Knights Combat Training we will cover the True Knights 7 Steps to Freedom and Purity (found on page 52 of this book.)

No matter what your problem may be with your struggle with impurity, your coach understands and will not judge you. He has been there, he knows and when joined with the Grace of Almighty God, nothing is beyond the help of Jesus Christ and His mercy.

IT'S TRUE...YOU CAN LIVE A PURE AND HOLY LIFE! THIS WORKS!

For More Information on True Knights Combat Training

If you struggle with impurity and want to finally break free and win the war of addiction and impurity in your life, join True Knights in the battle and together, with Christ, we can do it. This is war and it won't be easy but, all things are possible with God! So put on the Armor of God and join in the fight.

Visit www.TrueKnights.org and inquire about Combat Training.

About the Founder of True Knights and the Combat Training Coach

Kenneth Henderson, MI

"My object is...to have the Truth made known to all who are astray and to have it revealed by God's help through my ministry, commending itself so well that they may embrace and follow it."

-- St. Augustine of Hippo

After 13 years of marriage, Kenneth Henderson was given an ultimatum by his wife, get help for his self centered irresponsible ways or she was getting a divorce, and she meant it. Kenneth had a severe problem with pornography addiction and was living a self-centered life based on the twisted ideals that our modern "enlightened" society says are important. All this would ultimately bring Ken literally to his knees. After many attempts of trying to solve the problems on his own, and with secular means (marriage therapists, psychologist and self-help books), Ken made a heartfelt cry out to a God that he didn't even know if he believed in. Weeks later, in a profound and miraculous way, God made Himself known to Ken, not by an apparition or locution, but with an interior understanding. The Holy Spirit had set his heart in fire and set Ken on a path that guided him back to the Truths of the Church and as he began to learn those Truths and incorporate them into his life; he was able to break free of his addiction and restore the love that was once present in his marriage. After a miraculous conversion, Ken's marriage was saved from ending up among the many failed marriages in our society. Very soon after his return to the faith, Ken began working on what is now known as True Knights, a non-profit apostolate dedicated to helping marriage and family life by calling husbands and fathers to be True Husbands and True Fathers for their families; and break free from the stranglehold that pornography addiction and sexual impurity has on many, many men. His True Knights Combat Training is a process of one-on-one phone purity coaching and is consistent with Roman Catholic Church teachings, traditional family values and virtues.

Ken has given talks, seminars and classes to many men, women and teens across the nation and the ministry is growing. He has also appeared on EWTN's "Life on the Rock" and the "Journey Home" and is a frequent guest on talk radio programs on various Catholic Radio stations. His conversion story has been published in a book by Ascension Press called, *Amazing Grace for Married Couples*, the latest in a series of books about Catholic conversions and stories of hope. He is quite adept in the teachings of the Church concerning life, human dignity and sexuality and Catholic Apologetics. His witness and dedication to helping men seek God and fight the attacks of sexual impurity in their lives have inspired many and have provided individuals and couples with tremendous hope and encouragement that purity is possible and marriages can be saved.

Though Ken has no formal training in theology or therapy he does have many years of experience of suffering with sexual impurity and the grace and wisdom of God that set him free from addiction in his own life. Ken brings a passion for helping individuals and couples to be the best they can be. As a speaker Ken brings a culmination of church teaching coupled with his own marriage and family experience and presents it in a practical and energizing way that is sure to inspire. On June 21, 2006 True Knights received the Blessing and enthusiastic Approval from Bishop Edward Slattery of the Diocese of Tulsa and has been given the go ahead to move to establish a public Confraternity for men who wish to grow closer in their walk with Christ and achieve holy purity.

He has been married for 17 years and has three beautiful children: Connor born February 12, 1999, Fiona born November 13, 2001 and the newest addition to the Henderson Clan, Patrick Joseph born on April 29, 2005.

You can read Ken Henderson's conversion story at www.TrueKnights.org or in
Amazing Grace for Married Couples from Ascension Press

About Kenneth Henderson's Speaking Ministry

For more information about Kenneth Henderson's speaking ministry contact:

Kenneth Henderson
Founder of True Knights • Catholic Apologist & Chastity Speaker

P.O. Box 3113
Broken Arrow, Oklahoma 74013-3113
VoiceMail 1-800-950-2008
Info@TrueKnights.org
www.TrueKnights.org

Feel free to contact True Knights and let Ken know what topic you would like him to tackle for your group and he will put together a memorable presentation. Here are just some of his recent talks and topics that have inspired many to live a life renewed in their faith:

Ken's Talk Topics include...

The Biblical Roles of Husbands and Fathers:
Our Call to be Servants. Priests and Warrior Kings!

In today's society, many men are falling short of the true calling of what men should be. Ken will reveal to your group what it means to be a True Knight for the Family. He covers the things that have led to the current problems in our world and how men, husbands and fathers hold the keys to deliver their families out of the bondage of the secular world and into the salvation of God's saving mercy.
(A 4CD Recording of this talk can be purchased from Saint Joseph Radio. Call 1-800-500-4556)

My Journey from Darkness into Light

Ken will tell you about his conversion and how that by the grace of God the Truth of the Catholic Church was revealed to him. (Read his story online - www.TrueKnights.org)

7 Steps to Purity and Freedom

Learn how to break free of the slavery of Pornography addiction. Ken will tell how to do this with his 7 Steps to Freedom and Purity. (See the 7 Steps to Freedom and Purity on page 52.)

Humility-The Key to Truth

Ken will discuss how Pride is the number one reason why people reject Truth. Learn how to destroy the effects of Pride in your own life with the greatest weapon against Pride...Humility. It is only by Humility that we can truly know Truth...not by human understanding or reason, but Humble submission to God!

The Loss of All that is Sacred

The current problems in our world are a result of embracing the profane and discard anything that is True. Hear how the world could be changed if only we would embrace the greatest gift God gave to the world...the Body, Blood, Soul and Divinity of His Son Jesus in the Holy Eucharist. (Based on his paper "The Loss of All that is Sacred." Available online at www.TrueKnights.org)

More on next page...

The One True Church
Ken will show you from the Bible and the writings of the Early Church Fathers proof that Christ founded "ONE" Church and how our world would be a much different place if ALL Christians were to embrace the One True Church...secularism and relativism could be destroyed.

Of Course You Realize, this Means War
The world we live in is not a very friendly place. There is suffering, sorrow and danger everywhere. But the real danger we face is not physical...but spiritual! Learn how to fight the good fight and stay strong through prayer, the sacraments and devotion to the Holy Angels and Saints.

Why Must I Suffer?
A discussion on the reason for suffering in the world and how we should unite our suffering with the Passion of Christ and His Crucifixion on the Cross. (An ideal talk for Lent.)

Understanding Mary, Why is she so important?
Mary is the shortest and surest way to her son Jesus. By loving our mother we love her son even more. Mary is the sure way to a happy marriage, and leading our spouses, children and ourselves to heaven.

The Domestic Church
The Church's Liturgical Year is so rich...how can you bring it into the life of your home? Ken shares the traditions behind what the Church has done since the early Christian era, and provides you with simple methods, to bring the Faith alive in your home! (An ideal talk for Advent or Lent.)

Handing the Faith Down to Your Children
In this talk, Ken offers ideas and suggestions on how parents can help their children grow in the faith. He discusses how the child--at different ages--can grow in prayer, virtue, and understanding of the faith.

The Family - A Sacrament to the World
Ken shows how the family is not our idea, but God's, and how the family is what will bring us to heaven. Dealing with family members that are not Catholic...and don't like that we are!

Parents can be Saints Too!
How can we become holy, not despite but through our parenting?

Apologetics Talks
The Church, The Sacraments, Mary, Communion of Saints, Last Things,etc... Learn how to talk to and answer attacks by non-Catholics, and explain your faith from the Bible and the writings of the Early Church Fathers.

The Wonder of the Saints
Ken has a series of talks that discuss the wonders, miracles and holy lives of many different Saints, including: Joseph, Michael the Archangel, Benedict, Thomas More, Louis Mary de Montfort, John Bosco, Patrick of Ireland, Augustine of Hippo, Francis de Sales, Therese of Lisieux, and many others.

True Knights is a non-profit organization.
If you would like to help the True Knights International Apostolate, Inc., its programs and website, please send your tax deductible donation to:

True Knights
P.O. Box 1331

Broken Arrow, Oklahoma 74013-3113

or visit us online at www.TrueKnights.org

Jesse Romero
Catholic Lay Evangelist

Jesse Romero is a full-time bilingual Catholic Lay Evangelist, who is nationally acclaimed for his dynamic, upbeat Christ centered preaching. A resident of southern California and a retired Los Angeles Deputy Sheriff, he is a devoted husband to Anita and father of their children; Paul, Annmarie and Joshua. He was a three time World Police boxing champion and a two time U. S. A. Kickboxing champion.

During his nearly 20 years as a Los Angeles Deputy Sheriff, Jesse experienced the dark side of society everyday; yet he also saw the evidence of God's work in some of the most unexpected places. What made the difference? His faith in JESUS!

Today, Jesse is committed to keeping the Faith alive by speaking at parishes and Catholic events throughout the United States. As a speaker, Jesse has the ability to make the sometimes-complex teachings of the Faith understandable with his straight talk approach. His messages are simple, orthodox and delivered with energy and conviction that has become a Jesse Romero trademark. The audience is left with an indelible impression that our Catholic Faith is something to be worn visibly and proudly, not kept hidden away. He is a five-alarm wakeup call; the phrase "use it or lose it" takes on a whole new meaning in the hands of Jesse Romero.

Jesse is a cradle Catholic who experienced an interior conversion thru the reading of the Gospels. His conversion has launched him into a preaching ministry wherein he is lighting fires in the hearts of Catholics across the country. Jesse speaks with a sense of urgency on Christ centered Catholicism at Conferences and in the media. He is a much-sought out lay speaker in the Catholic Church, having preached in well over 1,000 Catholic Church pulpits in the last couple of years.

"I am a straight shooter, I shoot straight for the heart, I have conviction, passion and I give straight talking, no nonsense, no spin, bible centered, Holy Spirit fire brand Catholicism."

Jesse Romero M.A. (Franciscan University of Steubenville)
The Latin Lover of Jesus & Mary
Catholic Lay Evangelist ⋄×

www.jesseromero.com

About: Jesse Romero   *141*

Prayer Requests

_____ _____ _____
_____ _____ _____
_____ _____ _____
_____ _____ _____
_____ _____ _____
_____ _____ _____
_____ _____ _____
_____ _____ _____
_____ _____ _____
_____ _____ _____
_____ _____ _____
_____ _____ _____
_____ _____ _____
_____ _____ _____
_____ _____ _____
_____ _____ _____
_____ _____ _____
_____ _____ _____
_____ _____ _____
_____ _____ _____
_____ _____ _____
_____ _____ _____
_____ _____ _____
_____ _____ _____
_____ _____ _____

Prayer Requests

Answered Prayers

_____   _____   _____
_____   _____   _____
_____   _____   _____
_____   _____   _____
_____   _____   _____
_____   _____   _____
_____   _____   _____
_____   _____   _____
_____   _____   _____
_____   _____   _____
_____   _____   _____
_____   _____   _____
_____   _____   _____
_____   _____   _____
_____   _____   _____
_____   _____   _____
_____   _____   _____
_____   _____   _____
_____   _____   _____
_____   _____   _____
_____   _____   _____
_____   _____   _____
_____   _____   _____
_____   _____   _____
_____   _____   _____
_____   _____   _____
_____   _____   _____

Answered Prayers

_____   _____   _____
_____   _____   _____
_____   _____   _____
_____   _____   _____
_____   _____   _____
_____   _____   _____
_____   _____   _____
_____   _____   _____
_____   _____   _____
_____   _____   _____
_____   _____   _____
_____   _____   _____
_____   _____   _____
_____   _____   _____
_____   _____   _____
_____   _____   _____
_____   _____   _____
_____   _____   _____
_____   _____   _____
_____   _____   _____
_____   _____   _____
_____   _____   _____
_____   _____   _____
_____   _____   _____
_____   _____   _____
_____   _____   _____

CPSIA information can be obtained at www.ICGtesting.com
Printed in the USA
BVOW042342040112

279762BV00003B/137/A